CW01507561

White Male Stand-Up

White Male Stand-Up

Alan Davies

monoray

First published in Great Britain in 2025 by monoray, an imprint of
Octopus Publishing Group Ltd
Carmelite House
50 Victoria Embankment
London EC4Y 0DZ
www.octopusbooks.co.uk

An Hachette UK Company
www.hachette.co.uk

The authorized representative in the EEA is Hachette Ireland,
8 Castlecourt Centre, Dublin 15, D15 XTP3, Ireland (email: info@hbgi.ie)

Text Copyright © Alan Davies 2025

Distributed in the US by Hachette Book Group
1290 Avenue of the Americas, 4th and 5th Floors
New York, NY 10104

Distributed in Canada by Canadian Manda Group
664 Annette St., Toronto, Ontario, Canada M6S 2C8

All rights reserved. No part of this work may be reproduced or utilized in any form or by any means, electronic or mechanical, including photocopying, recording or by any information storage and retrieval system, without the prior written permission of the publisher.

Alan Davies asserts the moral right to be identified as the author of this work.

Hardback ISBN: 978-1-80096-257-6
Trade paperback ISBN: 978-1-80096-258-3
eISBN: 978-1-80096-260-6

A CIP catalogue record for this book is available from the British Library.

Typeset in 10.25/14.5pt Farnham Text by Six Red Marbles UK, Thetford, Norfolk.

Printed and bound in Great Britain

10 9 8 7 6 5 4 3 2 1

This FSC® label means that materials used for the product have been responsibly sourced.

Your talent is employable
so make your life enjoyable.

–Lionel Bart, *Oliver!*

Author's Note

Some names have been changed and past conversations re-created or combined, since memory is incomplete at best and no two people, when asked to write down gossip they'd shared only last week, would be likely to reproduce the same dialogue.

Contents

CONTENTS

PART TWO

CONTENTS

PART THREE

Introduction
or
Your Nearest Exit
May Be Behind You

Before we start on this volume of memoir, I should provide some context by mentioning the goings-on in my two previous books, both about my early life.

The first, from 2009, was *My Favourite People and Me 1978–1988* (the publisher added the *And Me* to an already off-putting title). It featured chapters on forty-four people who influenced me growing up. Comedians like John Belushi, musicians like John Lennon, some sports stars and political figures, as well as my Granny Price and my college drama teacher Piers Gladhill, who helped me start in stand-up comedy.

Fighting for light beneath the canopy of my views on so many people were some of my childhood stories, including a search for my mum's grave when I was sixteen. She'd died from leukaemia ten years previously having not been told she was terminally ill, which meant she'd been unable to say goodbye to her three children.

By the age of fifteen, I was in a state of perennial conflict with my father, older brother and younger sister. Mum was almost never spoken of. I didn't have any pictures of her. On my sixteenth birthday, in 1982, I inherited a 50cc Yamaha. Now I had the freedom to explore.

I understood that my mother was buried in Harlow, Essex, where my friend Ernie lived. In *My Favourite People* I wrote about us riding our noisy motorbikes out to Parndon Wood Cemetery, at the end of his road, and searching in silence through the rows of white headstones, before learning that Mum had been cremated and her ashes consigned to an unmarked grave.

When my father held that first book in his hands he'd said, 'I'm a bit worried about how I might come across in here.'

But he needn't have been concerned, since I'd left out so much, including the most significant thing that happened to me, after Mum died, which was being sexually abused by Dad between the ages of roughly eight and thirteen.

Even when the book became the basis for a three-part television series on Channel 4 called *Teenage Revolution*, and despite being made aware that the producers were going to interview Dad about my early life, I still didn't mention that he was a child molester. So, they learned what he thought of my aptitude for cricket (not much) and little else, while he remained hidden in plain sight.

Dad had agreed to be interviewed for television about my childhood; that's how brazenly secure he felt.

The same year I'd gone to look for Mum's grave, 1982, Dad remarried and we moved house, to next door. That summer, my Bancroft's School report stated: 'He is wasting his time.'

My dad had been a pupil at Bancroft's in the forties, and revered the whole institution, but I dropped out of the sixth form to work in a greengrocer's owned by a friend of my new stepmother.

After I'd offered my services to our local paper, the *Gazette*, hoping to become a football reporter, and been abruptly turned away, my stepmother suggested Loughton College of Further Education, where I enrolled in media studies while also trying a theatre course.

I was desperate to move out of home and left, in 1984, to take drama at the University of Kent, though this meant leaving behind my first love, Justine, and eventually breaking both our hearts.

I already knew when I arrived in Canterbury that I wanted to write and perform comedy, but in time understood I'd be better off as a stand-up. I wasn't a natural collaborator, but I was funny and had no ambition to find a job, having developed an aversion to authority figures (blame my dad) that made most workplaces untenable.

What happened next is, in part, what this book is about. Stand-up went well for me. In case you weren't there, these are quotes from reviews of my live shows in the nineties:

'Brilliantly funny' –*The Times*
'Incredibly funny' – *Daily Record*
'Cryingly funny' – *The Telegraph*
'Belly-achingly funny' – *The Daily Mirror*
'Seat-rockingly funny' – *The Guardian*
'Effortlessly funny' – *The Evening Standard*
'Screamingly funny' – *Scotland on Sunday*
'He can't help being funny' – *The Daily Mirror*

There followed a big TV break as Jonathan Creek, after which I was recognisable almost everywhere and became a rich and famous celebrity, so that's cool, right?

But the past can never simply be a closed chapter; it travels with us. And despite moving away from home, and finding a lucrative path to tread, I remained complicit in keeping my abuse hidden for decades, staying out of sight as a 'survivor' and developing coping strategies, among them alcohol, marijuana and for many years a workaholic devotion to success as a stand-up comedian.

A psychotherapist later told me that my teenage delinquency (shoplifting, graffiti on buses, etc.) might have been a good sign to anyone who knew I'd been bereaved and abused in childhood, since it was evidence I was trying to make space for myself in the world. I wasn't going under, as many victims do, through self-harm or even suicide.

By my late forties, however, despite having found a funny, talented and beautiful wife, Katie, and with three children we cherish, and even after a happy fiftieth birthday party, I was still struggling with my secret pain.

In September 2016, I took the decision, having been looking at courses as far back as 2001, to apply for a two-year creative-writing MA at Goldsmiths.

A choice that became more significant than I could ever have expected, given what came next.

In June 2017, my stepmother revealed to my sister that our father had accumulated huge amounts of pornography featuring exclusively boys. She'd known for years but claimed to have said nothing in order to protect me – a famous person subject to press intrusion – when in reality she was shielding her husband, of thirty-five years at that point, and their respectable life together at the bowls club.

The revelation transformed my understanding of my abuse.

I considered having my father arrested for historic sexual offences. His porn collection remains stored with a lawyer. The Crown Prosecution Service said a conviction would lead to a custodial sentence but that Dad was unlikely to face trial, since, by the time my stepmother revealed the truth, he was eighty-four and suffering from Alzheimer's.

I'd just begun to write about my father, in the safely anonymous space of my writing course, but now had the impetus to publish that story and in 2020 my second book came out, taking its title from the phrase my dad used to my siblings if I was ever acting up: *Just Ignore Him*.

The response to the book has often been moving. Some survivors have told me they were encouraged, by my writing, to share their own childhood traumas with family, and even spouses, for the first time.

Several people I've known for years have told me their abuse stories, having never said anything before. I'm grateful to all of them.

Since *Just Ignore Him* is concerned with my life in the seventies and eighties, this follow-up, *White Male Stand-Up*, continues from there. I imagined setting down some funny anecdotes and name-dropping the greats of comedy and television in Britain over nearly four decades, and there is some of that, but soon realised that wasn't the whole story; and after a worrying visit to the doctor's surgery, I began to look back in depth. What I saw was a man bouncing around as if inside a showbiz pinball machine, searching for the love of an audience and the sanctity of some replica of family life.

It had been obvious for years, not least to Katie, that fired in the heated kiln of my childhood, and coexisting with the survivor made there, was an angry boy. His story is prominent in these pages.

If my last book was written on behalf of a damaged child, this one is a record of what happens when baked-in rage is unmanaged. I've created and performed comedy for decades, while repressing and suppressing so much. Becoming a comedian, or having any sort of public life, is often about building an edifice. This book is about taking one down, a story of working and living in the presence of a terrible secret and the possibility that everything could be lost in a moment.

Includes jokes.

Part One

Home Testing Kit

19th September 2024. Morning.

Sometimes, first thing in the morning, you can release quite a dark fluid into the clear waters of your toilet bowl, or something bright green if you've taken too many vitamin pills, or a radioactive yellow after overdoing the glucose drink during a hangover. Ideally, your flow should be clear from time to time, indicating good hydration. All of these are to be expected, but pinky-red water is a bad sign.

Fortunately, I had some home testing kits, purchased while in the grip of an imaginary health scare brought on by print advertising. They were on offer: buy five, get one free.

The kit was sleekly packaged, with stylish graphic design and a slide-out box as if it were an expensive pen or a new phone. It was like Christmas morning, opening it up, though any test that shows up negative seems like money wasted and all those materials going to landfill is regrettable.

The tester is a scarlet-coloured piece of plastic about a foot long and an inch and a half across. It's bent into a flexible hook to grip the rim of the toilet bowl, with a surface held just above the water onto which you attach a yellow adhesive strip and that's what you wee onto.

If the colour is unchanged you bin the lot, feeling like you made a mistake similar to putting a few quid in a pub fruit machine and getting nothing back.

My mate Gary once took me to the Eagle in Wanstead, close to where he lived with his mum. He and I were in the same year at Bancroft's. One afternoon someone came to take him from the classroom to the headmaster's office. I waited outside for him and when he finally emerged he said he had to go home because his dad had died.

My mum went to heaven during the school summer holiday, so in year one (as it's called now) I had a mother and in year two I did not. This became part of the reason Gary and I were friends, though mainly it was because at break we'd go to Chiltern Way, across the road from the science block, and smoke cigarettes together, and up to the Shell petrol station for more smoking behind the garage shop at lunchtime. He and his mum smoked Dunhill. I tried every brand available, and collected the various nicely designed boxes, but settled on Marlboro when they started doing a pack of ten for 50p.

So, we're in the Eagle smoking fags, Gary seventeen, me sixteen, and he's on the fruit machine, a serious business indicative of maturity. After a couple of spins, a flashing light told us he'd earned 'nudges', meaning the three reels had stopped and you could move them, one symbol at a time, to form a winning line (three lemons paid well).

Gary pulled out a scrap of paper on which he'd written the order of the symbols on each of the reels, information he'd accrued from many similar sessions. The handwriting was tiny and he squinted furtively as he consulted his crib sheet, not wanting the bar staff, landlord or anyone else see him defraud the machine. One nudge up on the left reel, two nudges down on the right and we heard the satisfying sound of his money coming back, and several other people's too. A few faces turned towards us as the clunking alerted them to a payout. No one smiled when someone else won.

There were enough coins to go to the adjacent fag machine and buy a new pack of Dunhill, which rested in a sturdy pullout drawer. There would be sixteen or eighteen fags in it, never twenty, since the vending machine had a fixed price.

I positioned the testing kit in the bowl of my bathroom toilet.

Katie and the kids were out of the house. It was just me upstairs with the dog downstairs. Instinctively it's a private, solo operation.

I took aim and the yellow adhesive patch turned a rich, dark colour, not unlike Farrow & Ball's gorgeous Hague Blue, which we once considered for our front door.

I consulted the urine-test user guide from the box and the new colour, now drying into a blend of Hague Blue and Vardo Green, was indicating blood is present. I could take the test strip to Leyland Paints on Finchley Road and they'd colour match it. Be worth considering as an option in the porch.

Sinking to the bottom of the bowl were two reddy-brown bits of something. I must have passed them too, but didn't feel anything.

Investigating further online, the outcome of my first search (blood in urine) was unequivocal: visible haematuria = phone your doctor.

No remedies or over-the-counter medication are mentioned, ring your GP immediately.

I called the doctor's surgery, from whom it's tricky to get an appointment without at least one full moon passing. They asked me for my name and I said: Alan Roger Davies.

My middle name is possibly in honour of a great uncle who lost a leg in World War One and subsequently joined the Royal Canadian Mounted Police. The Alan is after Alan Ladd, my mum's favourite movie star, which makes it feasible that Roger is nothing to do with the one-legged Mountie and is instead after Roger Moore, who was gorgeous on television as *The Saint* in 1965, the year of my conception. I know Mum adored Richard Burton but my dad already had a nephew called Richard so perhaps that wasn't an option.

Once I'd been identified by name and date of birth (6th March 1966) they asked why I'd called.

'Little bit of blood in my wee this morning,' I said.

The person on the other end disappeared for a few seconds and then said: 'The doctor will ring you this morning. Is 10.30 OK?'

'Yes, that's fine, thank you.'

For the next two hours, I was acutely attuned to the sound of my phone ringing, checking it wasn't on silent half a dozen times and remembering the Irish comic Sean Hughes doing a show about living alone and picking up his landline to check for a dial tone as the phone never rang.

The doctor called at 10.35 and asked me for my full name, my date of birth, and about the colour of my urine and whether there were any small red-brown clots in the water. I decided to forgo my fledgling Farrow & Ball colour-chart stand-up routine and said: 'Yes, there were a couple, actually.'

'Can you come in at 3.30?' she said.

'Tomorrow?' I said.

'No, this afternoon.'

'Oh,' I said. 'Yes.'

'Arrive at 3.10 and ask for a couple of sample bottles from reception.'

'OK, thanks.'

During the second Covid lockdown, we rehomed a Springer Spaniel/ Husky cross in the hope she would be good for our children's mental health. After I put the phone down, I sat at the kitchen table for so long the dog came over to look up at me and nudge my hands in my lap. I've never stroked her so gently.

Semi-Detached Suburban Boys

John Lennon had been voted, by the public, as one of the top-ten Greatest Britons ever. There was to be a televised debate among a panel of well-known advocates who'd made a documentary each (since all the greats were dead) and a winner would be declared. That was to come, for now I was in Liverpool making a film about the Beatle's extraordinary life.

Although I'd started out as a stand-up comic, I was known by 2002 as a mainstream television actor, not a maverick outsider like Lennon. I'd recently completed a four-year contract as the face of a High Street bank in a TV ad campaign, hardly the choice of a counter-culturalist, so I wasn't sure I was the right person to present this documentary, but said yes mainly because some of the filming was to be in New York.

As a teenager I'd supported the Campaign for Nuclear Disarmament, so a tick from John for that perhaps. Had he not been murdered in 1980 he might have been on the huge CND march to Hyde Park that I joined in October 1981 when my favourite band, the Jam (led by Paul Weller, a brilliant songwriter influenced by Lennon), played on the back of a flatbed truck en route.

Long before settling in Manhattan, Lennon grew up with his Aunt Mimi in a semi-detached house called Mendips on Menlove Avenue in suburban Liverpool. One evening in the summer of 1958, John's mother, Julia, had been to visit her sister, and was going back to her own house, where her seventeen-year-old son was waiting. She was hit by a car and died.

So that was how I came to be standing in the garden at Mendips, imagining

13

Mimi seeing off Julia for what would be the last time and empathising with John, unable to say his own goodbye to his beloved mum.

As I looked up at the house, it increasingly seemed to resemble the one where I was born, in Balgonie Road, Chingford, a town on the border of East London and Essex.

Both suburban homes were semi-detached, with access to the garden down the same side, the front door on the left as you look from the street and windows with small ventilators above that had a stained-glass feature. It was that detail that took me back.

But what memory was being triggered? I lived briefly in Chingford but we moved in 1968, when I was two and my mum was pregnant with my sister, to Loughton. As I write this I can't picture the rear of my first childhood home; but, whatever was happening, I looked at the little stained-glass windows and began to cry, for lost mothers, and damaged childhoods.

I was weeping in John Lennon's back garden.

This was unlike me. My preferred option is to secrete tears in private, ideally behind a locked door in a room no one knows I'm in; but on this day I was with people 'from work', who I liked but had only recently met.

I hadn't expected to be upset, and was now worried that Kate, our director, might want to include my personal pain in her documentary. I don't suppose she would have done, the film was not about me, but that was my irrational fear. Habitually I hid my inner sadness, but my eyes sometimes let me down with inopportune leaking. I had to dry them straightaway; there was a piece to camera coming up. Work before feelings.

I've previously imagined that our past, our memories, lie at the bottom of our personal river bed, like silt, and may be disturbed when new events splash into our individual current and disrupt the fragile environment, mixing emotions past and present and influencing our reactions to events. This is partly why people have different responses to, for example, a dead stranger's childhood home. Their waters are clouded and unclear.

But this image of clouds of sediment, drifting in the currents of life before

14

settling back down peacefully and never breaking the surface, now seems inadequate.

Some events trigger an emotional response to something buried that is reactivated instantly, like a light switch. As if a synapse long unused or repurposed has been shocked into life, an electrical charge occurs in the brain as some door is opened, as if Lara Croft has found access to a lost chamber in *Tomb Raider*. These memories leap into view above the surface of your personal waters like flying fish. And the sight of them becomes a strong memory in itself.

A flying fish offers a glimpse of something silver, fast, racingly alive but quickly gone again. Activity was triggered in my brain that day, through some combination of circumstances.

As I looked at Lennon's house and recalled my own family home from my first two years, I was unable to add to the memory. I'd been too young. No images linger of us as a family there; Mummy, Daddy, my older brother and me. No mealtimes, Sunday roasts, first ice cream, hearing *Yellow Submarine*, no toasted teacakes or baked jam tarts. Dad coming home from work, the smell of Mum's sweet peas; or being tucked in at night, in my bedroom – or was it ours? Did I share with my brother? Were there bedtime stories? What were my favourites? Did I sometimes sleep with Mummy in her bed? Where are the cousins, the snow, the rain, the grass in the garden, the bouncing balls and the toy cars?

I know we were referred to as 'the boys', as in: 'The boys like the boats in the harbour.' My mother wrote that on a postcard in the late sixties, handed to me not long ago by an older cousin who knew how few mementoes of Mum I had.

Everything changed after she'd gone to heaven. In time, I became convinced that my dad never wanted a second boy; they'd have preferred a girl.

'No, we wanted another boy,' he said, before adding that they'd hoped for a second son so my brother had someone to play with.

Despite the absence of any tangible memory, as I stood in the back garden of a house vaguely similar to ours, like so many built between the wars (but outside which a boy's mother was knocked a hundred feet down the road by an off-duty policeman, a learner driver), an interior fault line widened and tears slipped out. *Please don't spill down my cheeks . . . Do I have a tissue?* I imagine Mum would have insisted I had a hankie, when I was a boy; I know her mum always had one up her sleeve. My mum would wet hers with a bit of spit and clean my face. Or was that Granny? Who can really remember anything?

That Way Madness Lies

To write this book, I started by piecing together where I'd been when. I have some diaries, but they're not journals, mainly just dates and appointments, so some gigs, TV and radio jobs can be placed in chronological order. Plus, I have archive, boxes of audio and video cassettes, newspaper cuttings, programmes, flyers, photographs.

Looking through old tapes, trying resuscitate my memory, I came across one labelled *Work in Progress*, with a TX (transmission) date of 15th May 2000.

It turned out to be a Radio 4 play that I was in with Frances Barber.

I listened to the whole forty-five minutes and, even though I wasn't suffering having to see myself, I still thought I was rubbish – what was that voice?

Much of olden-days *Me* I now find embarrassing. Why was I pulling that face, or waving my arms around? Shame looms up, but then the same is true if I'm walking along and see myself reflected in a car window. Frances Barber's voice is rich and smooth like strong coffee for the ears; recordings could be marketed as a natural alternative to sildenafil.

I sounded like a rabbit trapped under a kicked-over e-bike.

The only reason I mention this play is I have no recollection of doing it at all and not a single line or scene brought anything back. I met Frances Barber again recently, when recording *Love Your Weekend with Alan Titchmarsh*. She was wearing a stylish jacket with a picture of Lennon and McCartney on the back and 'The Beatles' written on the front, which she was asked to cover with a scarf as it was considered a brand logo. I asked her about our radio play and she'd also forgotten it.

Next I watched a VHS from around 1994 (I could date it by the shirt I wore) of me reviewing a Peter Cook video on *The Little Picture Show*, fronted by the husky and constantly amused Mariella Frostrup, whose style was to relax in an armchair, legs crossed in a mini-skirt and boots, addressing the viewer as if she was waiting for them to come round to hers. Sadly, my piece to camera was recorded in her absence.

In his video, Peter Cook was rambling to camera in various guises. It wasn't funny and I was rude about it. Now I can see it was shameless to take a fee and chalk up another TV appearance while slagging off a great comedian, whose albums recorded with Dudley Moore were among the most played in my bedroom throughout my adolescence.

Only now does it occur to me that the PR team who'd secured a review on Mariella's show would be in contact with Peter Cook, so someone might have told him about my comments or, worse still, had he tuned in, he'd have found his enjoyment of the show's witty and pretty host ruined by some upstart so-called comedian who deserved a bunch of fives.

The thought of Peter Cook seeing me slag him off makes me go red with shame, not least because, having looked him up, I now know he died a few weeks later.

Another tape, I'm a couple of years older now and hired as a team captain, along with Fred MacAuley, on a BBC1 panel show hosted by Tony Hawks (three white men, obvs) called – as Stephen Fry would say, 'quite wrongly' – *The Best Show in the World, Probably*.

One of our guests was the great broadcaster Terry Wogan. After the recording, some internal doubt prompted me to ask him: 'Do you ever watch yourself back?'

'God, no,' he said, 'that way madness lies.'

And yet here I am, looking back at myself and flirting with insanity. What's more, I'm considering 'digitising my archive' to create a record of use only as a reliable source of embarrassment to me.

It's what Narcissus would have done had he been an analogue-era television personality.

If you've seen any of my television work, you may regard my shame as inevitable and consider it a failing that it's taken this long to register; but the point is, I used to take pride in my public persona and its bankability, my ticket-selling power and the bookable vibe I gave off for TV talk shows. Whoever was hosting didn't matter, I gave 'good guest'.

Clive James, whose show was a joy to take part in, said to me, with characteristic perspicacity: 'It's a kind of tyranny, what you do, isn't it? You take over and make the show run at your speed.'

He was smiling as usual and I took it as a compliment, but I can see now that my approach could tip into bullying (a popular pastime on nineties panel shows, as evidenced by the treatment of Paula Yates on *Have I Got News for You*).

In that same Terry Wogan episode of *The Best Show in the World, Probably*, Dominic Holland was on my team. I knew him well from the comedy circuit. He was a good comic but not assertive, just mild and thoughtful.

The recording was idling and it was quiet in the darkness beyond the cameras. I suspected the studio audience was bored. My rising fear caused my TV persona to probe Dominic for weakness. I began to mock and deride him, fake-laughing at his size and his boyish features, behaviour which I would've defended as trying to 'get a laugh'.

Nowadays Dominic writes novels while the eldest of his four sons, Tom, a year old at the time, is playing Spider-Man in Hollywood. Perhaps he could use that time-travelling device from *Avengers: Endgame* and swoop back to the nineties to seal my stupid mouth with web.

That my persona was identifiably fraudulent can be summed up in a quote from *Closer* magazine published not long after that panel show was broadcast. Its tone was matter-of-fact: 'People either love or hate mop-haired comedian Alan Davies.'

I sought out Katie to read that line out loud to her and she added: 'Or are indifferent to.'

'Yes,' I said, silently considering whether that was better or worse.

When I started in stand-up, I'd felt I was motoring into the future and soon my independence would ensure the past wouldn't exert any hold over me. I loved being alone onstage, at first for the adrenaline rush and later for the confidence and cash that it gave me. For my first gig, at the Whitstable Labour Club in March 1988, aged twenty-two and still a student, I had short hair and a smooth but worried face, as if someone had attached googly eyes to a skinned chicken breast. My hands shook as I went through my act at terrific speed.

Afterwards, I stood at the back of the room with a drink, as bewildered as a first-time parachutist who has landed unscathed having expected to die, only to find no one gives a shit.

First rule of parachuting: no one cares unless you die.

One of my fellow fourth-year drama students came over. 'Nice set,' he said, in a lower register than I'd heard him use when singing along to *The Rocky Horror Show* soundtrack at a drama party.

How dare he say 'set' to me? How did he know a stand-up act was called a set? I didn't.

'Thanks,' I said, in a discouraging tone, as if the laughs I'd generated ranting about the lack of a cashpoint in the town were no more than I expected.

Three years earlier, when we were teenage freshers, the same chap had tried to persuade me not to drive back to campus after a house party in Whitstable. I'd been gulping a quarter of Co-Op own-brand whisky and – with the angry boy inside me threatening to make an appearance – I was dismissive of him and another concerned young man from our course. I drove the six miles back to campus pissed, navigating through the village of Blean by staring at the white lines in the middle of the road. I imagine he thought me a fool from that day on and it was nice of him to come and congratulate me now. Incapable of accepting his compliment, I took it to mean he was after a little of my action and grimaced as if to say: 'Yeah, I'm aware it was a *good set.*'

After a moment he walked away, leaving me with no one to talk to. I just stood there watching my friend's band through the cigarette smoke.

I'd had a similar experience after getting big laughs alongside fellow student Jackie Clune in a production of Steven Berkoff's *Decadence* the year before, going down to the bar after the show and experiencing the drop-off in adrenaline and euphoria as the audience dissipated and the praise dried up.

Now here I was in the Labour Club surreptitiously trying to keep the thrill alive, again on my own, drink in hand. Only this time it wasn't the end of a production; it was the beginning of something. All I needed was another place to try my 'set'. I thought about little else for the next five years.

The smallest club on London's alternative comedy circuit was The Mousetrap, a basement room with a painted-white brick interior. I'd phoned for an open spot and one day in the autumn of 1988 I opened the Cabaret pages in *Time Out* and saw, for the first time ever, my name in the listings:

Alan Davies

A flush of excitement rushed through me, as if I was in a car passing over a humped-back bridge. The gig was four days later – an eternity – and on the night I was early.

Someone on the door held a list of names, with people gathered round them peering at it. It seemed they didn't completely tally with those mentioned in *Time Out*. I was invited to come back in a couple of weeks. It seemed a long way back to Loughton, having been anxious about performing since four o'clock in the afternoon.

Eventually my open spot came around and I did well enough to be booked in for a twenty soon afterwards. This was how things usually went for me. I never did more than one open spot in any club. As soon as they saw me, they booked me; my ego was already ballooning even at this most moderate of successes at the novice end of showbiz. And I'd accept every gig, even though going from five minutes to ten and then the standard twenty were big steps each time.

Going into comedy had given me an audience and a place where appreciation and praise could follow. It also set me on a path I didn't identify as risky, fame and wealth were nowhere in sight and, in any case, I saw no flipside to either. I possibly thought that I was unusually robust and that the worst things that were going to happen in my life had already passed.

I had no way of knowing that I was looking for something else.

Stone Him

Claire and Roland Muldoon were forthright lefties who shared an enthusiasm for the eccentric performers on the Alternative Cabaret circuit. They had succeeded in restoring the Hackney Empire as London's leading New Variety venue, providing the persuasive energy that culminated in the reopening of a grand but neglected theatre – once threatened with demolition – on 9th December 1986.

By 1989, the *City Limits* 'New Act of the Year Show' was staged at the Empire and I was a runner-up behind twenty-nine-year-old Keith Dover, also from Essex, who I'd met at Ian Chapman-Pilchard's 'Hackney Cabaret' the previous month. He'd been the closing act, and had offered a kind word about my set as the open spot.

Keith's day job was at Ford's in Dagenham and his high-octane description of an East End wedding brought a huge reaction from the Empire crowd.

As the camp and hilarious host, Julian Clary, read out the runners-up in reverse order, we each went up onstage. When it was my turn he said: 'He's got a lovely complexion when you see him close up.'

Keith was already edging forwards down the centre aisle and he bounced onto the stage, throwing an arm round Julian before grabbing his trophy and waving it in the air like the FA Cup.

'I think we can assume Keith is a heterosexual,' said Julian.

That gig brought my first five-minute TV spot on LWT's *1st Exposure*, alongside Keith, Eddie Izzard, Simon Munnery, James Macabre and many others.

Claire Muldoon gave me plenty of work at the various gigs she ran (even after I did a set to complete silence at the Old White Horse in Brixton). Most of the performers shared the Muldoons' politics: opposition to Thatcher's government and Apartheid in South Africa; support for CND and the Anti-Nazi League, with a 'Coal Not Dole' badge from the recent Miners' Strike in a drawer somewhere. We were non-racist and non-sexist and in most clubs that was appreciated.

There was one club, though, where no one gave a fuck about that shit.

Malcolm Hardee (aged about forty, shabby suit, cigarette, thick-rimmed glasses and 'oi oi' instead of 'hello') ran the notorious Sunday Night at the Tunnel Palladium, a gig renowned for its lawless atmosphere and hecklers who could be funnier than the acts.

Despite all this, I went there for an open spot in February 1989 wearing my stand-up attire – jeans and a T-shirt that had a mass of bright colours across the front depicting some sort of garish face.

The pub was massive and located on the left immediately after the Blackwall Tunnel. Inside I met Malcolm for the first time.

'I'm here for an open spot, Alan Davies.'

'Oi, oi,' he said, 'very good, have you come far?'

'Essex,' I said.

'Oh yeah?' he said. 'Not too bad then.'

'No, it's easy to here.'

'You're not wearing that shirt, are you?'

'Yes, I thought I would,' I said, under the misapprehension that my T-shirt suggested madcap comedy.

'They'll have a go at that.'

'It'll be OK.'

'They'll have a go at it,' he said. 'Have you got something else you can put on?'

'No.'

'What's your opening line?'

'Sorry?'

'Your opening line, what do you open with?'

'I don't know, I don't really have an opening line,' I said.

He lit a cigarette.

'You'll be on after the interval,' he said, and moved off.

In the first half, an act went down badly and the audience began to hum. This collective 'mmm' grew louder, eventually becoming a cry for 'mmmmmmMALCOLM!' to return from the bar and rescue the beleaguered comic.

When my time came, the heckling started before Malcolm had introduced me.

'Now it's time for the open spot,' he said.

'STONE him!' someone cried out.

'Cruuuccciifffyyy 'im!' shouted someone else, to huge laughter.

Malcolm was saying something about giving them a chance and then said my name. I had to walk from the back of the room through the crowd and up a few steps to the stage, which was quite wide and deep. Despite barely looking old enough to get served, I was holding a pint of beer. The room went quiet.

'What are you drinking?' said a voice from the darkness.

'Directors,' I said.

'Nice shirt,' said someone else I couldn't see.

'It's the new Millwall goalkeeper's shirt,' I said, 'designed to confuse the opposition, they're going to wear it against West Ham.'

Millwall Football Club was nearby, and their fans – presumably sprinkled through the audience – hate West Ham United.

There was a ripple of non-committal noise, which seemed to settle down to: 'Go on then, son, you've got five minutes.'

Putting my pint down on the stage next to me, I launched into my 'animal activists and the dolphin' routine in which I suggested (with accompanying mime) that a US Navy-trained mine-laying bottlenose would have done a better job than the fanatics who blew up an admin block at Bristol university and not the vivisection labs they were targeting.

At the end of my set, I picked up my glass and raised it to acknowledge the audience. There was rapturous applause and cheering. As I stepped down from the stage many of them were on their feet. I walked back through a guard of honour and heard: 'Well done, son,' several times, receiving a couple of firm pats on the back.

Malcolm was up onstage: 'There you are,' he said, 'open spot, very good, gets nothing; fella on before, shit, hundred quid, that's showbiz.'

It had all been tongue in cheek, the audience enjoying the theatre of giving some new kid a standing ovation after five minutes, but in there was an acknowledgement that I'd survived something, and they loved that. Malcolm rewarded me with a paid twenty-minute booking only four weeks later.

'By the way,' he said, 'that's not Directors you're drinking.'

'Isn't it?' I said, looking at my beer. 'I asked for Directors.'

'The landlord's done a deal with Whitbread: none of the pumps have the beer they say they do.'

I went back the next month and did my twenty but it was my last set at the Tunnel. The pub closed down following a raid by the drugs squad involving four hundred officers and a helicopter – at least that's what Malcolm told me.

Some time later, Malcolm booked me for a gig in Bungay, Suffolk, and asked me to drive him up there via Brick Lane so he could pick up a curry. He didn't realise which bit of Essex I lived in and apologised for making me take such a detour.

'I thought you'd come in on the A13.'

'No, I'm more Epping Forest.'

'M11?'

'Yes.'

'We'll pass your house going to Suffolk, will we?'

'I don't mind.'

'Sorry,' he said, 'do you want to get any curry?'

'No, I'm all right.'

'Sure?' he said. 'Couple of samosas maybe? Bit of naan for the road?'

'No, I'm OK.'

He lowered himself into the passenger seat wielding bags of food.

'Do you mind me eating this in here?'

'No, I don't mind, try not to get it on the seats.'

'I won't, don't worry.'

Normally I'd have my *A–Z of London* on the passenger seat but instead it was Malcolm, pulling his heavy coat out as wide as it would go before opening up three or four foil cartons and eating a full meal off his lap. There was a fair bit of curry down his front but that wasn't the sort of thing that would bother him.

Malcolm passed all his contacts onto his much younger brother Alex, who booked shows for colleges, and soon I was offered my first proper gigs 'out of town' at Liverpool Polytechnic and Manchester University.

'Steve Murray's driving,' said Alex, 'you'll be on with Ian Cognito and Sean Lock.'

Steve looked a bit like Mr Incredible, squashed into the driver's seat of his Vauxhall Astra. He could sound like Tommy Cooper and he played on that in his act, during which he tortured teddy bears. For the finale, he'd turn a portable record player on its side, attach a bear to the turntable and throw darts at it. The crowd would erupt when he hit the teddy and again when he switched from 33 to 45rpm. He'd appeared on *The Last Resort with Jonathan Ross* on Channel 4, which had been popular when I was a student in Whitstable. We'd all leave the Neptune early to go home and watch.

Ian Cognito's real name was Paul Barbieri, though everyone called him Coggers. Some acts had odd stage names, a post-punk throwback with echoes of Sid Vicious and Johnny Rotten (James Macabre was really Jim Miller). This marked them out as not motivated by conventional registers of success. Few of them owned (as I did) a red leather Filofax with green lining.

Since I knew the people who owned the company (David Collischon lived opposite us in Loughton; his wife, Lesley, was a surrogate mum to my sister), my Filofax had been complimentary, but it was also big and difficult to conceal. If I took it a to a gig in the hope I might book in some future dates, I looked like a yuppie on the make. The comedian Paul Ramone (real name Roger) asked me, in reference to my practical loose-leaf organiser with its informative inserts: 'Is that serious or for a joke?'

'It's my diary,' I said.

He gave me a withering look. I left the Filofax at home after that.

Some on the circuit held the view that we weren't in comedy to earn cash and improve but to be mavericks, sneering at the rat race and living as outliers, in the margins, with our difficult upbringings or undiagnosed neurological conditions.

Sean Lock and I had started out in 1988 within a few weeks of each other. At the beginning, it felt like certain people were in your year and older comics were like kids higher up the school. I once went into the old Comedy Store dressing room to find Paul Merton and Arthur Smith busy with some cigarette papers and sharing a joke. Like a first year who'd wandered into the sixth-form common room, I turned around and went straight back out again.

The first gig on our comedy road trip was to be at Liverpool Poly on 2nd May 1989, just two weeks after the Hillsborough disaster had devastated the city. There was a notice in the corridor offering support for people affected. It was a sombre time but the show wasn't cancelled and we were all pleased to go down well in front of an enthusiastic young audience.

The next morning, Steve took us to a National Trust-run former cotton mill at Styal in Cheshire, where we saw the schoolroom provided for children of the workers and some of the toys the kids had, among which were pig knuckles.

The game was to bounce a ball, pick up as many knuckles as you could, and catch it again. Sean and I pulled our sleeves down over our hands and pretended to be pigs who'd had their trotters taken off.

'I hope you're enjoying that game?'

'Was it worth it?'

'I've no hands now, so thanks for that.'

Sean had a knack for keeping a joke going like a plate-spinning act, and we batted lines back and forth about embittered pigs until we couldn't laugh any longer. The day was like a school trip without teachers. Arriving for the show at Manchester University that evening, we were spent from hours of giggling. Fortunately, Steve's teddy bears saved the night.

In my family, after Mum died, there were also four of us on car journeys and I had to sit in the front because, in keeping with the prevailing family narrative, my brother and sister each found it impossible to share the back seat with me in peace. In Steve's Astra, travelling up and down motorways, in and out of service stations, it was as if I'd found three older brothers who'd chosen to never have a cross word with one another.

Contents Insurance

In October 1989, after touring Canadian Fringe festivals for three months, I had enough dollars saved to rent a room in London.

The Canada show had consisted of my fledgling stand-up set, a monologue from my girlfriend Wendy and a couple of sketches, all under the name The Furrowed Brows. A friend from university, Jason Blake, had been around the Fringe circuit and told me you keep all your box-office takings, so, if you lived cheaply, you could make money, which I did, first in Winnipeg in July and then in Edmonton in August, Vancouver in September and Victoria in October.

Wendy had initially stayed behind to attend her graduation ceremony, so in Manitoba I'd had to do a solo hour. It took me a week of gigs to shake off the uptight, stood-behind-the-microphone-in-navy-slacks look I'd deployed on *1st Exposure* earlier that year.

By the last show, I'd ditched the microphone altogether and, since it was thirty-five degrees, was cavorting about in shorts with 'CANADA' printed on them. I'd worked out that the audience were more likely to enjoy themselves if I was.

I met the Edmonton comedy troupe Three Dead Trolls in Baggie in Winnipeg and opened for them in their holdover shows, which were packed out and riotous. I went to Yuk Yuk's comedy club and managed to get myself a weekend working as MC for Steve Shuster and Ronnie Edwards.

I also met a woman I liked, with spiky bleached hair and cool cutoff shorts; but, as we lay sweltering under a ceiling fan, I regretfully told her I was chastely waiting for my girlfriend.

In Edmonton, The Furrowed Brows took to the stage for the first time in *The Seed of Doubt*. We filled our time slot, just, though it was patchy at best. But we befriended the Three Dead Trolls (there were four of them, Wes, Joe, Neil and Cathleen) and later stayed in a log cabin in the foothills of the Rockies, with them and two street performers, Danny and Rick, from SAK Theatre in Florida.

We went 'horseback riding' and the cowboy helping me on to my horse, named Highwood, said: 'If you like rodeo, this is the one for you.'

Danny and Rick took the lead but Highwood surged in front at Kentucky Derby pace as I lost both reins and stirrups. There was hysterical laughter behind me as I threatened to 'sue them all' before they caught up and saved me. The next day, I couldn't stand with my legs together and none of my new friends could look at me without laughing, which I took as a positive.

After a couple of shows at the next Fringe there was a big picture of The Furrowed Brows on the arts page in *The Vancouver Sun*. The caption read: 'These British comics did not go over well.'

I felt inflated at first and then immediately deflated like a balloon that hasn't been tied off.

Despite our mediocre act, I learned (particularly from a noon show in Victoria for five people) that the audience have chosen you and they want to enjoy themselves, so gigs always start with everyone willing to pull the same way. If it doesn't go well, it's not the punters' fault (unless you're at the Tunnel Palladium).

Victoria is the most English of Canadian cities, it even had red buses, so served as a halfway house before the long flight home. I'd made some friends for life at the Fringes and when I returned to the London circuit found I'd improved and more bookings started coming in.

By December, helped by my Canadian dollars, I had enough to find somewhere to rent. Wendy didn't want to look together so I advertised as a tenant in *City Limits* magazine, mentioning that I was a stand-up comedian to make me appealing.

There were no enquiries. Wouldn't anyone want to share with a comedian? Unbelievable!

Fortunately, *Loot*, London's weekly advertiser, was full of places. I called about a room in a Hackney tower block. The stench of urine in the lift seemed recent and I turned around before I'd even hit the button for the tenth floor.

The room I eventually found was in a terraced house on a quiet crescent in Stoke Newington, not far from Arsenal's then home ground in Highbury. There was a big hedge at the front and a blue front door. The youngish landlord, Mr Cooper, was small and neat, with creases in his trousers and combed brown hair. One of his eyes drifted, which took some getting used to, but he was friendly and told me he worked in the theatre, so I played my comedian card and that did not deter him from showing me a large ground-floor room with a wooden double bed, high ceilings, shelving in the alcoves either side of a fireplace and French windows opening out to a garden that backed onto Abney Park Cemetery. A scrawny little cat greeted me to seal my approval.

Mr Cooper had space for three tenants, and the two lads in the upstairs rooms weren't his soulmates.

'They work in the City,' he said, as if broaching an embarrassing medical condition. Pinching his face in, he added: 'There's often a lot of rugby kit in the washing machine.'

Early it became apparent that one of those lads had a bowel issue and an aversion to toilet brushes. The other one left me an astonishingly unpleasant note after I'd switched on the shared answerphone when I went out, even though he'd been 'fucking in' at the time, waiting for his girlfriend to call. Open your bedroom door and listen out for calls, you prick, I didn't say.

Abney Park Cemetery was overgrown and home to foxes that sometimes strayed into our garden. Equally furtive were the local gays who cruised the graveyard whenever it was open, as if on a rota. I was twenty-three with a bottom like a small pumpkin, and evidently emitted clouds of olfactory stimulant wherever I roamed. I avoided eye contact but might as well have left a trail of condoms behind me. Men would bob up from behind headstones, noiselessly enquiring.

I was out gigging in comedy clubs five or six nights a week, so would get home late and watch episodes of *Cheers* on video. That was up until the first burglary, when my rented VCR disappeared.

'The insurance doesn't cover you, I'm afraid,' said the landlord.

I didn't know what contents insurance was and lost a second VCR in the next burglary, even though I'd wired the plug through a hole in the shelf. They smashed it. After that I locked my bedroom door when I went out.

After a few months, the blokes upstairs were replaced by a graphic designer and a young woman who was emphatically not a City type. Both were good fun around the kitchen table, especially when discussing the landlord's new Spanish boyfriend, who tossed his mane of black hair as if taking part in a twenty-four-hour photoshoot seven days a week.

The lovers would occupy the bathroom for hours, steam clouding the opaque window as in the scene in *Titanic* where Winslet and DiCaprio hide in a car on the cargo deck and the windows mist up, leaving only a suggestive handprint on the glass.

The rest of the time, the boyfriend baked cakes with the oven on constantly and the gas fire roaring in the kitchen. Various sponges were presented as acts of generosity to the tenants, who were more concerned with the increasing gas bill and decreasing bathroom access. Then, unexpectedly, he picked a fight with me.

'Why do you lock your bedroom door when you go out?' he said.

'Because we've been burgled twice.'

'It's antisocial,' he said.

'It's an empty room. I don't lock it when I'm here.'

'You shouldn't ever lock it.'

What?

'Why do you want to go in my room?' I said.

'Why *don't* you want me to go in there?' he said, believing he'd found the upper hand.

'You don't even live here!' I said.

He gasped and put his palm against his chest, the fingers splayed straight out.

'I got down on that toilet floor on my hands and knees and scrubbed!' he said.

I liked living in Stoke Newington but I left without a goodbye. Instead, after I'd struggled to get my belongings past the boyfriend's bicycle in the hall, the angry boy in me took a drawing pin from the corkboard by the phone and punctured as many holes as I could into his tyres.

I was tempted not to mention that in case you developed a low opinion of me. I should have baked them a cake – not that I knew how; all I ate was cheese on toast.

Fancy a Toot?

The stage was made up of two platforms, with the mic stand balanced over an uneven gap down the middle. I was looking down the long upstairs room at Balham's Banana Cabaret with some trepidation; it was one of the bigger rooms on the circuit and it was packed.

I needed to assert myself, but the microphone was vibrating and a nasty noise came out over the PA. I moved the stand left and right but couldn't improve things. People in the front row were frowning, then someone suggested I take the mic out of its stand.

'Just take the poxy thing out and hold it.'

Or that might have been a voice in my head.

I was recently back from Canada and had returned to lurking behind the stand, feet together, shoulders hunched, eyebrows raised to look as unthreatening as possible. Short hair, clean-shaven, shirt tucked in, delivering a high-pitched lispy monologue with no reference to the room, or anyone in it.

I took hold of the mic and pulled it from its stand, generating some ironic cheering.

'Hello!' I said and trod on the cable, pulling it out of the microphone. The metal connector hit the floor. Now no one could hear me. I'd never plugged a cable into a mic before, and my hands were shaking more than ever as I picked it up. I managed to plug it in, causing another loud and unpleasant sound, and then looped the cable over my little finger at the base of the mic so it wouldn't come out again, a habit I still have to this day.

Like an infant who has learned to walk, as soon as I used the whole stage,

I never went back, discovering the way I moved my limbs could generate laughter, just being on one leg, or striking a daft pose. From then on I was rarely still.

I don't know where I took my first steps as an infant, but I know exactly where I was when I learned to walk as a comedian. Balham, made famous by Peter Sellers as the Gateway to the South.

'I'm doing a telly show at Balham Banana, wanna be in it?' said Ian Cognito over the phone.

'What would I be doing?' I said.

'I've got you down for Morris dancing.'

'What?'

'Some fucking stand-up obviously, you daft pillock, what do you think?'

'OK,' I said.

There was good turnout of unknown comedians who all wanted to be on telly. Coggers had built an extension on his flat in Walthamstow and was now taking a similar DIY approach to his career. I didn't know who'd be doing the editing or pitching to broadcasters, or who was financing it. No one asked those questions, or ever saw the finished product.

Everything took ages, which I later discovered is the norm with filming. Coggers came in at one point looking agitated and asked a table of bored comedians if any of us fancied 'a toot'.

I'd never heard the phrase but gleaned somehow that it meant doing a line of coke and declined. I told Sean Lock I was wary of drugs after someone I went to school with died from an overdose.

'Sorry to hear that, what did he OD on?' said Sean.

'I don't actually know,' I said.

'You don't know?' said Sean.

'No,' I said.

'When did he die, your mate?'

'When he was twenty-one, two or three years ago, he was about the same age as me. Supposedly he'd nearly overdosed once before so it looked like suicide the second time.'

Sean tapped the end of his rollup into a big brewery ashtray.

'No reason for you not to do a bit of Charlie,' he said, with a grin.

'I don't fancy it,' I said.

'Make up your own mind,' he said. 'You should try everything once.'

Though I don't suppose he meant overdosing.

Costakis

Cabaret nights at the Red Rose were held every Friday and Saturday in a large function room on the back of the Labour Club in Finsbury Park. There was a low stage at the side of the room, with tables around it and rows of seats behind with posters on the walls about Cuba and Nicaragua.

My first chance to play there came on 3rd March 1989, three days before my twenty-third birthday, in a competition held as part of a London Comedy Festival. My second gig was the following week's final, when my dolphin routine paid off again and I won, my prize a paid spot at . . . the Red Rose.

One of the judges was Jo Brand, who I'd seen perform there six months earlier. She stood still, holding the mic just under her chin, all in black with lace-up boots and her hair spiked up, then she'd move the mic stand, 'So you can see me.' Every line was a big laugh, one after another; no meandering stories, just grownup jokes for grownups.

After her set, she'd stepped off the stage to join her friends and had a cigarette lit before the applause had died down. The group she'd joined brought to mind the punky/gothy kids in the year above when I was doing media studies at Loughton College, one of whom had supposedly been gonged off at the old Comedy Store after appearing as Cass the Cunt.

Many comedians who lived in North or East London would gather at the Rose after their own gigs elsewhere. The bar was cheap and open until midnight.

Jo was always with Jim Miller (aka James Macabre), although I was oblivious to their actual relationship until one night I was at Jim's flat at the

Elephant and Castle and he offered me the sofa to sleep on. I realised later that he and Jo were together in the next room.

There was also a new-material night, Every Other Monday, at the Camden Head in Islington. This doubled as a social event in the Pizza Express afterwards and became so popular there wasn't enough space for all the comics; so in 1990, me and Jenny Lecoat, one of the best female comics around, set up the Fortnight Club on the alternate Mondays, using a poster created by my graphic-designer housemate.

We were joined by the Rubber Bishops. Bill Bailey and Martin Stubbs wore red cassocks and did spoof versions of pop songs.

Martin was tall and deadpan and Bill was seemingly able to play anything on the guitar while maintaining a wild-eyed look and swinging his long hair. I'd first seen them at the Comedy Store, where they finished their set with a rousing version of the Clash's 'Should I Stay or Should I Go' changed into 'Should I Suck or Should I Blow'. As soon as the song ended they'd shout: 'Thank-you-very-much-good-night!' and exit sharply to loud demands for 'MOOORRRREEE!!'

They encored three times that night, which was unheard of. In the dressing room I asked them where their costumes came from.

'Are you really monks?' I said.

'Yes, that's right,' said Bill.

'We're on day release,' said Martin.

'No, we're not, actually,' said Bill.

'No,' said Martin.

'Well, you're very funny,' I said.

'Thanks,' they said.

A social group formed at the Red Rose, with Jo and Jim, Andy Linden, Keith Dover, the Crisis Twins (John Gordillo and Simon Clayton), Jeff Green, Mark Lamarr and Hattie Hayridge.

After the Rose, we'd cross Seven Sisters Road to eat at Costakis, where the gregarious proprietor served Keo Cypriot lager and Irish coffee until two in the morning, with people scooping up taramasalata in pitta bread with one hand while holding a cigarette in the other.

The restaurant's full name, Costakis Anamnesis – I've since learned online – suggests a place where (according to Plato) all knowledge could be recalled. Our favourite game was to recall sitcom theme tunes and see who could identify them.

There was constant laughter around that table. Everyone loved situation comedies and Silk Cut, in that order. There were a few Arsenal fans too and soon Keith Dover, Simon Clayton and I, along with Patrick Marber, had season tickets together at Highbury.

There was also much talk of unusual acts who had stopped gigging by the time I'd started. I wish I'd seen Andy Linden and Cliff Parisi being two Argentinian soldiers in the Falklands who had joined the Port Stanley Amateur Dramatic Society. Apparently, they threw a fair bit of corned beef around, which caused a stir when they performed at the Earth Exchange vegetarian café in Highgate.

I also never saw the Iceman, who would bring on a block of ice and spend twenty minutes breaking it up or melting it by various means. Nostalgia for the eccentric early days of the circuit was growing. Some were lamenting how the clubs were now full of 'white male stand-ups'.

There's a line in Truman Capote's *Grass Harp* where a character wishes he could have called upon a wizard to bottle up the voices and laughter from his childhood kitchen so he could always hear them again. Those nights at Costakis left a similar impression on me. We'd come together via many different routes, but had coalesced, largely around Jo, into a kind of family.

Come the end of December 1991, virtually the whole group from the Red Rose set off for Wells-next-the-Sea to spend New Year in a rented cottage, though some of us would have to go back to London for double-pay New Years's Eve gigs.

I offered to drive back afterwards. Jo, Jim and Mark Lamarr, in his usual fifties suit, Zippo lighter to hand, were my passengers. As we navigated the pitch-black Norfolk roads, they realised they were running out of cigarettes and no shops would be open until well into 1992. Things became quite tense until we found a twenty-four-hour Shell garage near Fakenham. They bought sixty fags each.

At the cottage we drank and played games. Janet Street-Porter had said that comedy was 'the new rock and roll' but our favourite pastime was the 'name game', where you pick names out of a hat and describe them to a partner.

Andy Linden, who referred to himself as 'your uncle' and became known as such to us all, once put in only people called Cooper. The penny slowly dropped during the game as Gary, Henry, Terry, Tommy and finally Mini Cooper all came out.

The rest of the time we went to a pub where we played darts, though what we'd hoped for was a trivia machine. Jo and Jim were formidable in a pub quiz, backed up by their friend Jez Feeney, an affable character in contrast to the argumentative Jim, who'd frequently express his greatest fear: that we'd run out of booze.

'You don't understand. I'm Scottish, I need my liquor,' he'd say.

Jim was Oxford educated and seemingly determined not to benefit from the privilege. He'd loved the attitude of punk, but aside from that held an eclectic range of interests, including the Native peoples of North America. He'd created a map showing the lands occupied by the various tribes. He'd also studied Classics and was the first person I knew to create a website. His was about Roman architecture. He explained to me that the idea, on this new thing called the internet, was to find an area of interest that no one else had yet touched upon and then people would find you.

In Cornwall, at the end of 1992, we rented two houses, one big, one small. I was in the latter with Jez, Uncle and my new girlfriend, Angela, who I'd met a few weeks before. We named our place Tranquillity Cottage by way of comparison to the big house, where ten people seemed to be constantly arguing

One night, Jim was at the centre of a dispute over a game of Risk. I found the rules and, unfortunately, it turned out that he was in the wrong. There was a silence.

'Those are the old rules,' he said, and the uproar continued.

*

Around this time, Jim wrote a script for a comedy Western, featuring roles for each of the peer group we'd formed, with everyone's character revealing some truth about them.

Jim had me down as a cowboy who'd traded his 'gun for a badge' and was now on the side of The Man against the unruly outlaws he'd once hung out with. They actually shot some scenes on video but nothing came of it, except a lot of fun on the day, I imagine. I wasn't there and perhaps Jim had foretold something about me that I missed at the time.

The Caff

In 1990 the Comedy Café opened on Rivington Street, in the dilapidated East London district of Shoreditch, round the corner from a lonely old gay pub, the London Apprentice.

The owner, Noel Faulkner, was a mix of patter, opinions and Tourette's-style tics, and these traits allowed him to engage harmoniously with the myriad comics who washed up at his club over the years to come, whatever addiction, mental-health crisis or disorder of the ego might have befallen them.

Noel's popularity increased still further when he opened up a large upstairs space at the Caff, as we called it, like a cross between a green room and a squat.

'I'm thinking of buying some old sofas for this place,' said Jo Brand one day, surveying the inadequate furnishings in our new den.

'Let us chip in,' I said.

'No, no, no,' she said, 'I've got a few quid spare.'

During the Italia 90 World Cup, increasing numbers of comedians gathered to watch England and Ireland's progress on a TV Noel had brought in.

There was a huge crowd for England's semi-final against West Germany, but everyone found a vantage point and an epic evening climaxed with Keith Dover, his face painted with the cross of St George, battering the door to the room, yelling: 'Why, why, why? It's never us!'

The Germans had won on penalties. I suspect the Irish and Scottish cohort went downstairs to toast Chris Waddle, whose final kick was possibly in orbit.

Later, a pool table appeared. The master of the baize was Ricky Grover, a big man with boxing, hairdressing and now stand-up on his CV. In his hands a regular cue resembled a chopstick. We'd pass convivial remarks; if either of us missed, the other would say: 'Appreciate it.'

At the end of each game, Ricky's favourite rule came into play, and he'd call: 'One-'anded on the black.'

Only once did I succeed with that shot and Ricky seemed happier than when he won. Hanging round the pool table upstairs at the Caff, smoking joints, was my recreation of choice for most of the early nineties. It became a treasured hangout, with a downmarket feel, and it was private, which was handy, because by now people were appearing on TV.

Hattie Hayridge had a part in *Red Dwarf*, Mark Lamarr was hosting Channel 4's *The Word* and Jo had her own series, *Through the Cakehole*, for which she hired as many of her friends as she could as performers or writers. I appeared in a sketch.

It quickly became a downside of Jo's TV success that she was now recognisable. After closing at the Caff, we'd head round the corner to the twenty-four-hour bagel shop on Brick Lane, where Jo had previously gone in and chatted to the staff, cracking jokes while ordering. Now she often stayed in her car.

'Are you coming in, Jo?' I said one night.

'Nah,' she said. 'It looks busy. There's bound to be a pissed bloke who wants to know if I'm a lesbian.'

One of us would take her order while someone else sat with her in the car, smoking fags.

Thank You, Doctor

19th September 2024. Afternoon.

Having picked up two sample bottles from the receptionist at the surgery, I squeezed sideways into a disabled toilet with a confusing split door that took me a minute to work out.

Holding the tiny sample bottle over my urinary meatus, I realised I'd have to pause mid-flow, a recommended prostate exercise (or so I was told long ago, by my mate Darren). I took it as a sign of good health that I passed that test once for each sample. I was called in for my appointment soon afterwards.

The GP was young, tall, fair-haired and smiling, with an empathetic manner. After checking my name and birth date he crossed the room, still seated as his chair had casters, and dipped a urine-testing strip into one of my samples. Then he watched while I waited. It didn't take long.

'Showing strongly for blood,' he said. 'Are you experiencing any pain when you pee?'

'No,' I said.

'No pain?' he said, still looking at the strip.

'No,' I said, starting to wonder if it would be better if I was.

'It's not showing any sign of infection,' he said. 'Blood can mean a UTI, a urinary tract infection, but we'd expect some pain if that were the case.'

As he said that, he propelled himself away from his little testing station, rolling his chair up to his desk, alongside which I sat wearing an expression like a dog who thought he was going for a walk and finds himself at the vet.

The doctor began an extensive list of questions about my general lifestyle, working environment, diet, alcohol consumption, and whether I'd ever smoked, all the while typing my answers into his computer.

'I used to smoke, until the ban came in, whenever that was, 2007? Before that I smoked for about twenty-five years.'

At sixteen I'd hold a cigarette in the corner of my mouth but pointing straight forward, copying a picture of James Dean (all because a girl I fancied told me Dean was the most beautiful man who'd ever lived). I'd seen Paul Weller onstage with the Jam, lighting a cigarette and then sticking the filter in the end of his Rickenbacker's fret board so the smoking tip pointed up. The cigarette burned slowly during the three-minute masterpiece he then played before taking a drag as we cheered in our thousands. Weller smoked Rothmans; I knew that because there was a pack on the inner sleeve of *All Mod Cons* (arguably the greatest album ever recorded). I bought a pack but they were disgusting compared to Silk Cut.

'OK,' said the doctor, finishing up his notes and looking at me with concern. 'I'm going to put you on a two-week cancer pathway.'

'Right,' I said.

'Blood in the urine is a common symptom of bladder cancer. This doesn't mean I think you have bladder cancer, but we need to check that.'

'Yes,' I said.

'So, I'm going to send your second urine sample away to the lab and you also need to go to the Royal Free for some blood tests. You can book an appointment online, it's quite easy.'

I began to look at my phone with the intention of beginning that process.

'Or, actually, I can just print you off a referral here and if I write "urgent" on it they'll see you this afternoon without an appointment.'

'What do they do for bladder cancer?' I said.

'A cystoscopy is the first thing. Have you had one before?'

'No, is it a camera up the penis?'

'Yes, it's not very nice but it's not as bad as it sounds,' he said.

I didn't ask if he'd had one himself. He'd turned away to take something from his printer.

'If they find something,' he said, 'then surgery is the first thing, and after that you may have a BCG treatment, which is a vaccine solution in the bladder to stimulate your own immune system to fight cancerous cells. But, as I say, first things first: I'll just write "urgent" on here and then you give this' – he handed me a sheet of paper – 'to the blood-test reception at the Royal Free.'

'OK. Thank you, doctor.'

'Do you have anything else going on, any blood in your stools?'

'I have some haemorrhoids, have had for years, so there's sometimes blood.'

'Do you want me to examine your rectum?'

I didn't really fancy that, afflicted as I am by wanting new people to like me. Hoping for an opportunity to crack a joke, I was relieved when he said: 'Actually, a rectal examination can agitate the area and potentially affect the results of the PSA test, prostate-specific antigen, that will be included when they send your blood away, so it's better if I don't examine you today. Even cycling can have the same effect.' I'd be walking there anyway.

'OK, that's fine,' I said, 'I do have one other thing.'

'What's that?'

'An itchy nipple.'

'Itchy nipple?'

'Yes,' I said, resisting making a joke about Itchy Nipple being a fine Kentish brew and the recipient of three awards from the Campaign for Real Ale.

And so the nice doctor examined my right nipple, which had been itchy enough weeks ago for me to have a telephone appointment and be told to try antihistamines.

'There are no lumps or anything there,' he said. 'It's probably just dermatological so I'd suggest hydrocortisone cream.'

'OK. Thanks, doctor. I'll go straight to the Royal Free now,' I said.

The hospital is five minutes' walk from the surgery.

A Saxophone

It was about half one in the morning and I'd opened my set at the old Comedy Store with something I'd just come up with in the dressing room, joking around with Jack Dee. I forget the line, because I only said it once, when it disappeared into the thick silence of an audience who'd found no humour in it.

The quiet unnerved me. I was slow to follow up, having no link from this new bit of rubbish, so the next thing I said drew silence too. I wasn't winding them up; it was more as if I wasn't there. I dared not look to my right, where the audience disappeared into blackness and a heckle could come at you like a rock. The sound booth was against the wall to my left and in the back corner was the dressing room. I wondered when the door might open as the other comics came out to watch a death.

If you were on late at the Store it wasn't unheard of to have an audience member asleep in the front row. That wasn't happening now, though. There were two young women sitting there and one whispered: 'He's lost it.'

Shamefully, I abandoned my post.

Kim Kinnie decided who appeared on that stage. He was well-liked by the comics, Scottish, diminutive and camp; he used to choreograph the strippers at the Raymond Revue bar where the Comedy Store had begun. Now he booked the acts and ran the shows.

Kim had given me this chance of a ten-minute spot and I'd failed him. At the beginning of my career, I performed like a car that's low on petrol: if I didn't catch something in the room early on, I might conk out. At those moments, you need to apply mental jump leads.

I'd had a similar experience at the Bearcat in Twickenham, a big room that always seemed to be full. Some lads at the back started baaing like sheep. I tried to make light of it, but it got louder. I was baaed off.

The other comics didn't look at me, as if I might be contagious. I sat outside at a picnic table. Only Eddie Izzard – with a neat side parting, and his hands in front of him as if he was always ready to juggle – came to offer a supportive word.

After I'd died at the Store, Kim Kinnie thought I should keep gigging for six more months and then I'd be ready. It reminded me of failing my driving test at seventeen; I'd gone to pull away, having reversed round a corner, and instead continued to go backwards.

In January 1990, Kim offered me a paid twenty and it went well. He was delighted for me and I was booked in for more dates, the last of which was Saturday 31st March.

I went to Kennington Park that morning to join a protest against Margaret Thatcher's Poll Tax. It was a huge march, with the usual discrepancy between the official figures of 70,000 and estimates of up to 200,000. There were one or two comics there, including Jim Miller. As we set off, the anarchists at the front were becoming feisty under their black or red flags. There was to be a rally in Trafalgar Square at 2.30pm but I ducked out before that to go to see Arsenal play Everton.

Around 7pm I headed into town on the tube for my gigs at the Store. At Goodge Street on the Northern Line, there was an announcement that Tottenham Court Road and Leicester Square stations were closed so I had to walk; it's less than a mile, though.

At Charing Cross Road there was a barrier of riot police, recognisable by their circular shields like dustbin lids. Bits of debris and broken glass lay everywhere you looked. Off to the left was Denmark Street, famous for its music shops with displays of all kinds of instruments. There seemed to be no window left intact.

The police let me through without a word; there weren't many people about by now. There was further carnage in Cranbourn Street, where the Renault showroom was wrecked.

Before mobile phones and the internet, it was impossible to know what was going on. The march had become a riot after the rally, with people penned in at Whitehall and Trafalgar Square. Trouble supposedly began after the arrest of a man in a wheelchair but fighting broke out everywhere and then the police drove vans into the crowd to break it up, which didn't end well. The rioting was the worst seen in London for a hundred years. Within months, Margaret Thatcher was gone; a sad day for comedians across the circuit, as she'd been a reliable punchline for years.

Arriving at the Comedy Store in Leicester Square, I expected both shows (at 8pm and midnight) to be cancelled, but when I went down the steps into the room, it was packed.

Onstage I praised the audience for making the effort and then asked them what instruments they'd managed to pick up on Denmark Street. The atmosphere was buoyant and excitable, which is why one of my biggest-ever laughs at the Store came when someone shouted: 'What did you get?'

'A saxophone,' I said.

The joke never drew such a big laugh again so I soon dropped it. We'd all found each other in Leicester Square that night, in the midst of something a bit frightening and without being sure whether everyone would make it home again. Some kind of Blitz spirit meant the evening couldn't fail.

Duck Soup

The XXXX cabaret clubs in Birmingham were sponsored by Castlemaine, the Australian brewery named after the town in which it was established during the gold rush in Victoria in the 1850s.

That particular area had previously been known for hard volcanic tachylyte, a material used for tools or weapons, but there was now an influx of tens of thousands of people looking for a precious metal too soft for much practical use.

The effect of the gold rush on the indigenous population, the Dja Dja Wurrung, was catastrophic, with huge loss of life due to conflict, starvation, disease and the contamination of the water supply.

The *National Indigenous Times* reported in 2024 that, after years of hearings and negotiations, the Dja Dja Wurrung had struck a profit-sharing deal with the operators of Victoria's largest gold mine, having been historically excluded from the benefits of the wealth generated on their land. It's estimated that the state has received almost A$300 billion in revenue.

In the 1850s, however, the new brewery was thriving. After a hard day's panning for gold, prospectors didn't give a XXXX for anything else.

The XXXX brand itself – denoting the relative strength of the alcohol – was founded in the twenties and by the nineties was being heavily promoted in the UK where *Neighbours*, Kylie Minogue and *Crocodile Dundee* had helped create a positive image for all things Australian.

This was good news for comedy in the West Midlands. In most towns outside London, the lack of a successful club prevented local acts from improving.

Birmingham had two XXXX clubs and one local perfecting his craft in those rooms was the resident compere, Frank Skinner, whose longtime friend and manager, Malcolm Bailey, ran the clubs. He booked me for the first time in 1990.

The Bear Tavern in Bearwood had a high-ceilinged function room upstairs that could seat two hundred. Behind the stage was a curved back wall concealed by brown curtains that had to have been there since the seventies at least. Behind the audience was a bar and a backroom from where Malcolm, his mate Keith and the acts could watch the show. This might be what you'd come up with if you were to design a comedy room; and it had a lived-in quality like a secondhand car, which is what most of the acts drove and probably most of the punters too.

Most importantly, it was packed; the sponsorship enabled Malcolm to bring the best acts up from London, for welcome midweek gigs. The clubs were thriving and soon he offered to be my first manager.

Not long after I became part of the stable at Duck Soup Entertainment, Malcolm asked me about compering the XXXX gigs when Frank was unavailable, not only in Birmingham but also Cheltenham and Bristol. That would be four nights a week out of town and then weekends in London at Jongleurs and the Comedy Store. I could make as much as a grand some weeks.

The first time I went on as compere, a Brummie voice called out: 'You're not Frank.'

'Where's Frank?' said another.

Having fended off these gentle enquiries, I wandered over to the curtain at the back of the stage and pulled it back, revealing a window overlooking the street. Perhaps it looked like I was going to jump. There was a shop across the road called City Fruits that never seemed to close and I began to describe the goings-on there, to near silence. I came back to the front of the stage and it felt like a tightrope walk. Things warmed up a bit after I dropped in some material; and fortunately all the acts I introduced that night were great. Over the next few weeks, Frank's fans adjusted their expectations and new people filled any spaces in the crowd. After a while, if I just went over to check on City Fruits they'd start to laugh, and I began to love it in Birmingham.

Not all the acts were from London. Some, like Stu Who, came down from Glasgow and others, like Caroline Aherne, from Manchester.

Caroline donned a nun's habit, as Sister Mary Immaculate, picking off punters left and right with timing that lived up to her stage name. There was something husky and down to earth about her voice that made her easy to listen to, and a playfulness in the eyes as she stood virtually still taking the tone of a disappointed woman of God addressing the lost and destitute. She was charming and funny offstage too; all the boys hung around laughing at her wisecracks. Malcolm wanted her to join Duck Soup and we both tried to persuade her to work on an act as herself, but she was not keen, as if the nun character gave a layer of protection.

The Bearwood gigs were on Wednesdays and the last XXXX was in King's Heath on Thursdays, after which I'd often drive back to London with a carload of comedians.

On one occasion I had Harry Hill next to me. He'd gone down a storm with his unusual style of breaking off and unexpectedly resuming stories; these daft callbacks delighted audiences and combined with his suit, thick-soled shoes and high-collared shirt to create a wonky, other-dimensional feel. Like Caroline, Harry was funny offstage too, quick to laugh and undercut whatever was going on. There were a couple of other comics in the back and the M6 was deserted as we set off. Soon, though, a pair of large black Bentleys, travelling nose to tail, appeared in the middle lane. Moving gradually alongside the first car, we all looked across to see a chauffeur with a peaked cap and no passengers. Curious. We moved up level with the lead vehicle. Again, there was just a driver, only this one wasn't wearing a cap and instead had a mane of blond hair and an unmistakeable profile.

Harry recognised him first. 'It's Barry Manilow!' he said.

We all laughed.

'No, it is, look.'

'It is, that's Barry Manilow,' said a voice from the back.

Harry began to sing, in that hilarious style familiar to all of us from his act, which he peppered with snatches of pop songs.

'You write the songs that make the whole world sing!'

We all joined in: 'You write the songs, you write the songs!'

We repeated the mantra, pointing at the music legend on every 'you'.

To us it was hilarious, but when Barry Manilow glanced across to see four twenty-something lads in an old Vauxhall yelling at him, he immediately floored it and disappeared down the road, the second car racing to catch up. There's no way he could have heard that we were paying tribute: in a Bentley, no one can hear you scream.

On another Thursday, Lee Evans was driving back to London. I was next to him in the front and there were three other comics in the back. As we headed out of Birmingham, someone piped up to say they fancied chips. Lee had a high-energy, cartoonish style of comedy that could take any gig to a different speed entirely, and his driving was similar. He turned the car around without warning, through some junction where it felt like a U-turn was frowned upon. A chip shop was spotted and he threw the car towards it, finding a spot to let us scramble out like catering forces in a rapid deployment.

Minutes later we were all eating piping hot chips and Lee set off again, but the detour had taken us off my usual route.

'Which way, which way?' said Lee.

'That turn, I think.'

'What? That one.'

Lurch. Wheelspin. Surge.

'No, not that one.'

'Tell me, tell me.'

'I'm looking for signs,' I said.

'M6 that way,' said a voice from the back seat.

'Where? Where?' said Lee.

'Wasn't that a red light?' said someone else.

It was, quickly followed by a blue one.

A West Midlands Police Rover pulled over in front of us as Lee slowed to a stop. A policeman emerged and wandered up.

Lee was asked to, 'Step out of the vehicle, please.' Then the copper walked him back to their car and they both got in.

We all sat in Lee's car wondering what was going on in the Rover. Maybe they'd just drive off with him?

After a moment, the officer was out of the Rover again and strolling back towards us. He opened the driver's door and looked at four wide-eyed faces, eating chips, as if he'd discovered a den of defenceless cubs.

'So, youse are all comedians are youse?'

We all paused our eating and nodded simultaneously. A minute or two later, Lee was walking back towards us, his gait unmistakeable and somehow funny even though he wasn't trying to be. He jumped in and closed the door.

'What happened?' I said.

'They said I committed seven offences.'

We all laughed.

'And they've let you off?'

'Yeah.'

'What were the seven?'

'Speeding, driving with no lights on, not indicating, going through a red light, doing a U-turn where you can't, turning right on a no-right-turn and stopping in a no-waiting zone.'

It didn't look like it at the time, but maybe Lee always knew exactly what he was doing.

There was only one night at Bearwood when things really went wrong. We had an act on called Sham the Uncoordinated Juggler. He would ride a unicycle and juggle flaming clubs. On this occasion, as he leaned against the curtains at the back of the stage, he unknowingly set light to the pelmet. In a proper theatre everything would be flame retardant but this was a boozer. The curtains caught next.

Sham looked down at me in panic. Still high up on his unicycle near the ceiling, he'd extinguished his clubs and was holding them out to me. I went onstage and took them, the audience laughing even louder at my involvement, which seemed to confirm this was a setup, just part of the act. Sham leaped off the unicycle and yanked the curtains down from their rail to stamp out the now considerable blaze. When we had finally put the fire out, Sham, who always went down well, received possibly the biggest ovation of his life and then went off to recover while I returned the mic stand to the front of the stage and resumed compering as the smoke cleared.

'Did you think that wasn't a real fire?' I said.

Laughter.

'You all could have died!'

More laughter.

'In the event of a fire, stay in your seats and laugh like a drain, is that the drill in Birmingham?'

Louder laughter.

'No one wants be the one to pick up a fire extinguisher in case it's a false alarm and then everyone else takes the piss, is that it?'

Hysteria.

'The landlord's downstairs, he's thinking, "Bloody hell, the comedy's going well tonight." He has no idea how close he was to losing the whole pub.'

And then I had to stop talking because it was too much for the audience. A PhD student could spend years researching the subject of crowds and comedy and still not work out why it was all so hysterical to them, but I've never forgotten it – and wherever Sham is now, I bet he hasn't either.

All those acts at the XXXX, and my rapport with the crowd, as well as a few late nights on Wednesdays and hilarious journeys home on the Thursdays, made the whole experience up in Birmingham fantastic for me. I found a huge family there, about two hundred of them in Bearwood, and our relationship flourished especially during the joke competition every week when loads of them entered on scraps of paper.

My favourite entry came after the question I set up was:

'What's the difference between Ted Heath and a sieve?'

And the winning answer:

'You can't fence with Ted Heath on your face.'

In the summer of 1991, the XXXX clubs took a break and I was at the Edmonton Fringe when the news arrived from Edinburgh that Frank

Skinner had unexpectedly won the Perrier Award, ahead of Eddie Izzard and Jack Dee. I took a stack of quarters to a Canadian payphone and rang Malcolm.

'I hear Frank's won the Perrier, congratulations!' I said.

'I no longer represent Mr Skinner,' he said.

'What?'

Referring to the company that had promoted the show, he said: 'Frank's now managed exclusively by Avalon.'

While energetic, young comics scuttled from club to club, delighted to avoid having 'proper jobs', there were some more business-minded people around who had spotted the earning potential of the circuit. A comedy industry gold rush was beginning, and over the next few years a handful of new agents and promoters were going to stake some lucrative claims. The universally well-liked Malcolm, meanwhile, would have to endure being congratulated by everybody in Edinburgh while repeatedly breaking the news that he'd been dropped.

Climbing the Ladder

Eighteen months after the Poll Tax riots, where I'd lined up behind the anarchists as they attempted to smash the system, I was in the Halifax Building Society securing a mortgage.

I was looking at a loan of forty-two thousand, enough for a studio flat in Bow, when my father revealed he'd set money aside to help his children in buying their first homes and gave me fifteen thousand pounds. I could now afford a two-bed flat with a garden on Evering Road, halfway between Stoke Newington and Clapton. It didn't occur to me, until writing these words, that this was part of maintaining my silence about his earlier misdemeanours.

I asked Wendy to move in with me, but she came round with a housewarming present of a yellow teapot and declined. I don't like tea, though I still have the pot. That was it for us really, though we limped on for a bit longer.

I spent most of my twenties on secondhand furniture. The first items in my new flat included Ian Cognito's old armchair, Keith Dover's old bed and a wicker seat that Kristin Brunt (Bill Bailey's girlfriend and the queen of repurposing) had found in a skip and painted gold.

I later found a table and chairs in an inexpensive but stylish new shop on the North Circular called IKEA. But Kris's chair served me well and was still in use right up until 1st May 1997, when I had friends round to watch the General Election and the wicker disintegrated under the Bunterish bulk of a certain loudmouth comic from South London. Suffice to say, it was the funniest thing that happened all night – and that includes Michael Portillo losing his seat during a euphoric Labour landslide.

Most of my income in the early nineties was from playing London's big comedy clubs, Jongleurs and the Comedy Store.

The original *jongleurs* were not just French jugglers but itinerant minstrels, troubadours, acrobats – medieval outliers with an appetite for life beyond their village.

Jongleurs was now the name given to the largest comedy room in London, over a pub in Battersea, that could seat three hundred people at tables, eating and quaffing lager from pitchers.

Their shows finished with modern *jongleurs*, by then known as 'spesh acts'. The room's high ceiling and wide stage were ideal for jugglers. Steve Rawlings balanced furniture on his face, the Two Marks did slapstick on stilts and Paul Morocco launched ping-pong balls from his mouth through a hole in the ceiling and caught them again, causing the place to erupt.

Paul had a chaotic reputation. One Edinburgh Fringe, I bumped into Jack Dee, who said: 'I've just seen Paul Morocco in the bank.'

'Oh yeah,' I said. 'How is he?'

'He was trying to cash a cheque but he had no ID so he pulled out one of his flyers and was pointing at it and then at his face.'

'Did they believe him?'

Jack said he'd gone over to Paul at the counter and said, with the clerk looking on: 'All right, Dave? How's the court case coming on?'

Kim Kinnie came into the dressing room at the Store one night to say that Jongleurs had been on the phone:

'One of the Two Marks has fallen off his fucking stilts in the early show.'

'Which Mark?' I said, meaning was it Mark Heap or Mark Saban.

'Fuck should I know? He's fallen and he can't get up, lying there like a tortoise, I imagine. Does anyone want to fill their gap?'

I was the only one who could make it, which would mean an extra hundred quid. The Store paid only seventy a set.

My father was extremely serious about money throughout my childhood, keeping a daily cashbook to account for every penny ('*Evening News*, 10p' etc.). Cash became a deciding factor in most of my decision-making.

There was no stage door at Battersea Jongleurs so you'd have to squeeze past the audience queuing up the stairs, not all of whom believed you were one of the acts. This night, the way was clear and I went up two at a time to the corridor at the top.

There was an old set list in my back pocket, but it was only there out of superstition. The gig flew by, the laughs were loud and I had a stormer, a chicken korma, as Jo Brand used to say.

From then on, I regularly closed at Jongleurs, including at the opening night of their Camden club in 1991 (which had a low ceiling so was no good for jugglers).

One night at Camden, I mentioned I'd been to see Arsenal that day. Usually, half the crowd hate football and the rest hate Arsenal. So, inevitably, a Spurs fan in the crowd yelled out an insult.

I wish I'd thought of something wittier but instead I lazily humiliated the heckler by having the whole audience shout 'Fuck off, you wanker!' at him.

After the show, I was in the dressing room with Mickey Hutton and Simon Munnery. A small man in his thirties appeared in the doorway.

'Where's that fucking last bloke?' he said.

I'd been wearing a red shirt onstage and had since pulled a jumper over it.

'He went that-a-way,' said Mickey, pointing out of the dressing room just as a doorman appeared. Now it was the intruder's turn to say 'He went that way,' before running off, leaving the bouncer looking down the corridor.

It's hard to say whether the other comics would have helped me or relished spreading the news that I'd had my head kicked in at Jongleurs by a tiny Spurs fan. As a Geordie, Mickey was familiar with drunks on the Bigg Market in Newcastle, and Simon, despite his skeletal frame, vast intellect and thick glasses, was a dark horse. He was a good footballer, and in one friendly game in the park we kicked opposite sides of the ball simultaneously, leaving me with a mystery leg sprain that lingered on for weeks.

If ever I see Simon, even now, he murmurs in my ear: 'I broke your leg.'

In fact, only last week I had someone doing repairs to my roof and he said: 'I know Simon Munnery, he sends his regards and says he's sorry for breaking your leg.' Within days, an old friend emailed out of the blue saying she's a neighbour of Simon Munnery: 'He sends his regards and says he's sorry for breaking your leg.'

This gag has been running for over thirty years.

There was a period when my stepmother's Alsatian, Sasha, was staying at my flat. She'd bitten next door's dog, which had previously attacked our Yorkshire Terrier. It was an act of revenge that ended badly when the neighbour didn't take her dog to the vet and it needlessly died from a puncture wound, all terribly sad and avoidable. The neighbour called the police and my brother, who'd been walking the Alsatian at the time, was charged under the new Dangerous Dogs Act.

While we awaited Sasha's trial, I'd sometimes have to take her to gigs. One night in Battersea Jongleurs I tied her up in the dressing room and went down to do my set. She dragged two chairs down the stairs to a landing and turned 180 degrees before taking the next flight into the corridor among the punters. Regrettably, both she and the furniture were intercepted before she could join me onstage.

The next week, I was in that same dressing room with Bob Mills, Frank Skinner and Steve Coogan.

'Whassa matter with you?' said Bob.

I told them about Sasha's appointment with the magistrates. The three of them improvised a mock trial with a judge and barristers. Frank did his uncanny Kim Kinnie impression and Coogan brought out several voices. They cheered me up and made each other laugh.

And the dog was granted a reprieve, in both their mock trial and the real one.

*

In July 1992, Jongleurs booked a corporate event at Beverley Racecourse. The highly capable and popular young club manager at Battersea, Lisa White, was to drive a minibus up to Yorkshire. Arthur Smith would compere, with me, Steve Coogan and the Tracy Brothers doing sets. The headliner was veteran Norman Collier, he of the birdlike walk and cutting-out microphone jokes.

Coogan arrived from Manchester in an imported Mazda MX5. Our dressing room had scales to weigh the jockeys and primary-school-height coat hooks. Mark Billingham from the Tracy Brothers towered over the furniture like an NBA player.

The client was an electrical retailer and nearly all the guests were men, so fifty young women from Leeds had been hired to fill out the marquee. Despite this, the gig went well and there was bonhomie on the little benches afterwards when Steve Coogan burst in.

'Somebody come!' he said. 'There are two of them!'

'What?' said Mark.

'Two. Two girls,' said Steve. 'I need someone to come and talk to the other one.'

None of us wanted to go out there. Steve darted back to the marquee only to return almost immediately.

'They've gone,' he said.

'Who's gone?' said Mark.

'The girls!' he said, his voice rising in pitch. 'All the girls! Gone, all gone!'

'Gone where?' said Mark.

'Leeds!' said Steve. 'The lot of them, on a coach at midnight.'

By the time Lisa was ready to drive us to our hotel, Steve had recovered. Indicating his shiny two-seater, he said: 'Who'd like a ride in the fanny-magnet?'

'I would,' I said.

No sooner had I shut the passenger door than we were surging away, with the minibus stationary behind us.

At one point we were going round a roundabout at over a hundred. It took me a moment to realise the imported speedo was marked out in kilometres per hour. While I was working out how fast that was, Steve unclipped the soft top, which flew back. Now, there was an array of stars above, with barely any light pollution, as Steve might have mentioned had he been doing his new character Alan Partridge at the time. He pushed the accelerator again and I began to feel his seduction technique working on me. I was the fanny. Looking at him, I asked why he had a reputation for having lots of money even though we all did the same gigs. He turned to me, dropped his voice an octave and said: 'The new Talbot Solara,' with the throaty purr he used in the voiceover studio. With a lopsided grin, he looked back at the road just in time to see our hotel, a low building set back from the road. Having swung us through the gated entrance, he pointed the Mazda at the distant building and accelerated as if he wanted to drive straight through to the breakfast area in the conservatory.

Unseen in the darkness, the driveway didn't go straight but twisted and turned all the way to the forecourt. Steve threw the wheel right and left but couldn't stay on the tarmac and we were soon pitching around on a grassy area with paddock fencing ahead. The pretty MX5, popular with hairdressers in the nineties, is no off-roader. As we slid about I had time to picture the nearest A&E, where they take jockeys after a fall, imagining all the tiny gurneys in a row.

We stopped just before the fence and the engine pinged and hissed in the night. By now the minibus was pulling up like a large tortoise to comfort a frightened Japanese hare. The other comedians were doubled over in laughter. Steve styled it out with an expert Murray Walker impression and went to bed.

I played Jongleurs over a three-year period until the end of 1993, when I stopped taking gigs there having done thirty Christmas parties in twenty days, back and forth between Battersea and Camden as fast as my Cavalier would take me.

A furious driver appeared alongside me one night on Waterloo Bridge. He nosed his car in front so I was up against the barrier and began to knock a socket wrench against my passenger window. I'd no idea what I'd done.

'We're not fuck-ing play-ing,' he said.

We were both on our own.

He repeated himself with a sing-song lilt in his voice: 'We're not *fuck-ing play-ing*!' as if to emphasise his psychotic potential. Nowadays too many people, especially kids, are medicated to manage moods, but thirty years ago I'd say that was not sufficiently the case.

Later, onstage, I said: 'Is there some agreement that once you cross the Thames into South London it's game on and everyone's racing?'

Roars of laughter.

'I didn't even know what I'd done.'

A crescendo of noise.

'If you're late for work, you should be able to display a flashing green light so that lunatics might think: "Leave him, he's working."'

Applause.

This became a 'banker' routine, especially in South London, where anything that emphasised the locals' lawlessness was appreciated. Jim Miller saw me at a gig in East Dulwich, disarming the crowd with flattery.

'That was clever,' he said afterwards. 'They love to be told they're outlaws in South London.'

As ever, Jim could see something about me that I wasn't aware of myself.

Two Minutes Live

Ushered into my spot on the studio floor, I gripped the weight of the largest handheld radio mic I'd ever seen, like a dormant light sabre, and waited for Jonathan Ross to introduce me, live on Channel 4.

I was slim, barely needed to shave in the morning and I'd had my haircut specially, short as usual, not quite a flat-top but with a number four on the clippers round the sides and back. The barber, whose shop was a few doors up from Stoke Newington station, had said: 'Are you working today?'

'Tonight,' I said. 'I work evenings.'

'Oh yes, what time you finish?'

'About two.'

'In the morning?'

'Yes, I've got four gigs tonight, I'm a comedian.'

He looked at me in the mirror with an expression that combined frowning and smiling, as if I'd told him I was a stripper.

'Yes, my first gig is on TV actually.'

'Is it? What show you on?'

'*Tonight with Jonathan Ross.*'

'What's that?'

'Jonathan Ross? He's on every night at six thirty, on Channel 4.'

'No, I don't know that one; I'm always in the shop at that time.'

'He used to do *The Last Resort* on Fridays.'

We didn't chat any more. He charged £4.

I'd started to wear stretchy long-sleeve tops with two or three buttons at the top, always done up. A couple of months earlier, an exasperated photographer tasked with capturing a good image of me for *The Face* magazine ended up lending me his own shirt to wear over a T-shirt. I began to button it up.

'No, no,' he said, 'leave it unbuttoned!'

It was a good picture, black and white, the shirt flapping in the breeze, me looking away as if the attention was unwanted, and the copy was flattering. *The Face* had a reputation for finding the next big thing; they'd put unknown model Kate Moss, aged sixteen, on the cover the previous year, and now they'd be featuring *me* (on half of page eighteen).

The Face article, alongside my status as respected comedy writer Malcolm Hay's *Time Out* Young Comedian of the Year 1991, told me I was being noticed. My ego was growing accordingly, which was why I'd insisted on being interviewed by Jonathan Ross, not just do two minutes of stand-up as requested.

Jonathan introduced me with a broad smile and I raced through my set like I was all four members of a sprint-relay team, handing the baton from joke to joke, there were laughs, I was done, take a bow, it's over, oh no, here he comes, I forgot the interview bit. I was flooded with adrenaline and in awe. I'd watched Jonathan so much over the years.

Feigning incredulity, Jonathan asked me if it could possibly be true that I'd 'achieved so much' and yet had never played the Edinburgh Festival? (he didn't list my non-existent achievements).

My stage persona evaporated and I became a damaged boy struggling to keep my nerves in check with a display of smile-free mumbling masquerading as self-deprecation while complaining that the Edinburgh Fringe was a rip-off for the performers (it still is).

'I go to Canada every summer,' I said, 'to do Fringes there' – as if I'd unlocked a secret that everyone at the Biggest Arts Festival in the World had missed. But then Jonathan, the practised interviewer who Madonna chose for an exclusive that year, tripped me up with this curveball:

'Where can we see you play next?'

'I'm doing the pub next door to the Hackney Empire.'

He laughed, but stopped when he noticed that I was being serious.

'That's a bit sad, isn't it?' he said. 'The pub next door to the Hackney Empire.'

'We're competing with the 291 Club, which is a huge success,' I said, establishing my knowledge of the comedy scene while asserting that circumstances beyond my control were keeping me next door for the moment.

'Oh, of course, that's a huge show, isn't it?' he said.

'Yes,' I said.

Had he heard of the Empire's Black comedy night that played to an almost entirely non-white crowd? On those Fridays the circuit I knew convened for a tiny gig in the Samuel Pepys, literally next door.

'I'm also on at the Comedy Store tonight,' I said.

'Oh yes,' said Jonathan, 'the Comedy Store.'

That commanded respect.

And it was over.

It didn't occur to me that the gear change between my stand-up persona and the regular me was so marked. Looking back, I can imagine viewers thinking: 'He was quite funny but a bit of a surly twat.'

When I was applying for universities eight years previously, my tutor at Loughton College told me that he'd put in my reference: 'May come across as diffident in interview.'

Back home in the small hours, after all my other gigs, I watched the show on video, and when Jonathan came to shake my hand I paused the picture and chuckled to myself at the sight of me with the man we used to watch on TV as students, as if I'd been temporarily admitted to a shiny world of fame.

Four weeks later, I was rebooked for another two minutes on Jonathan's show and they wanted topical material, which I managed to come up with. No chat this time, which was for the best, since, after I'd announced on television that I eschewed the Edinburgh Festival, Malcolm Bailey was making plans to take me up there.

Blue-Haired Blood-Taker

19th September 2024. Late afternoon.

'This is no good,' said the man at the Royal Free Hospital blood-test reception, indicating the handwritten word 'urgent' at the top of my referral note. 'This needs to be printed on here.'

'The doctor said if he wrote "urgent" I could have blood tests without making an appointment.'

'No, no, no, you need to have an appointment; you could have written this on here yourself.'

'I didn't, though, the doctor did.'

'There are no more appointments today. Come back tomorrow with it printed out.'

'There must be a reason he wrote "urgent",' I said.

'You need to go back to the doctor and have him print it out again.'

'I can't go back there now; that's silly and it's probably too late. I'm only doing what he said.'

The blood-test department is easy to find because the signs to it have a royal-blue background, different from all the others. Two people sit behind glass dealing with a line of patients, usually numbering four or five at least. Once you're checked in there are rows of seats in a waiting area with no windows, just screens on the wall where your name will appear with a number for the bay you need to go to. The nurses with their needles are along a corridor leading away from the front row of seats.

Half a minute or more ticked by with me just standing in front of the glass.

'You could come back at four fifty-five,' said the receptionist.

'I can?'

'Yes. Don't wait here, but come back at that time and you can have your blood tests then.'

'OK, thank you so much.'

Now I wished I'd taken a notepad or even my laptop so I could do some work on this book. The hospital has a W H Smith near the entrance but they didn't sell any paper or pens so I went to a newsagent to find something. I thought I'd sit with a coffee in the Gail's bakery across the road. It occupies the former site of Booklovers' Corner, the secondhand bookshop that George Orwell worked in, and lived upstairs from, when he was writing *Keep the Aspidistra Flying* in the thirties.

There must have been twenty people queuing up in Gail's. The first branch opened nearby on Hampstead High Street two decades ago and the locals seem to love it. I didn't want to wait so I went two doors down to the much bigger Starbucks. There was no line at all in there. The locals hate it.

At 4.55pm, back at the blood-test department, a nurse with blue hair took six vials of blood and didn't stop smiling throughout, making the whole experience go by quickly. He said he was 'a fan' and that he hoped everything worked out for me with the tests.

'Thank you,' I said, trying to return his smile. 'Thank you.'

She May Be Trying to Die

In the summer of 1991, while visiting my relatives in Australia, I did some stand-up spots in Melbourne, sharing the bill with a young Irish comic, Jimeoin. We agreed to do a show at the following year's Adelaide Fringe, as a double bill, fifty-fifty split.

Not long before the festival, Jimeoin appeared on *Tonight Live with Steve Vizard* and his agent called me.

'Jimeoin's been mobbed in the street,' she said.

'Shit, is he OK?'

'Ever since he did *Vizard* it's gone gangbusters.'

'Oh right, I thought you meant attacked.'

'No, mobbed.'

'I see.'

'It's happened in two different cities,' she said.

'Right,' I said. 'Is Adelaide off or on?'

'Including *Perth.*'

'Does he want more of the money?' I said.

'He's huge now, he's literally just exploded.'

'So he'll be headlining and I'll support?'

'Is 35 per cent OK?' she said.

Not really.

'That's fine,' I said. 'I'm really coming to see my grandmother.'

'That's so nice,' she said. 'And I've arranged for an MC too. You'll love her, her name's Judith Lucy.'

*

68

My mum's mum had emigrated in 1979 to be with her surviving daughter, Hazel, in Adelaide. A little flat was built for her on the side of my aunt and uncle's house. But Granny wasn't home when I landed on 29th February 1992. She'd descended into a silent sadness in Glenside Hospital.

Glenside was originally the Public Colonial Lunatic Asylum of South Australia. Various name changes ensued during more than a century of psychiatric care on the site. Scenes from the film *Shine* about the Australian pianist David Helfgott were shot there.

Helfgott, portrayed by Geoffrey Rush in an Oscar-winning performance, was given electric-shock treatment after he suffered a serious breakdown.

When I first visited, Granny was in a chair next to her bed, staring through floor-to-ceiling windows at the gardens behind the hospital. I spoke to her and she didn't flicker.

'She's not eating,' said a nurse. 'She may be trying to die.'

That evening, Auntie Hazel told me they were planning on electric-shock treatment to snap Granny out of it.

'She's had it before,' said Hazel and we sat quietly, contemplating the horror.

Hazel had suggested I occupy Granny's annex, so I could come and go late at night without waking them up. I perched on the edge of Granny's bed, filled with thoughts of her and my mum. What if I didn't get to talk to her? What if she did make herself die?

Then I went down to the Fringe site for my first show.

The Star Club was warehouse-sized and could hold several hundred. Like most Fringe spaces, it had been repurposed for entertainment. Access to the stage was on one side with the dressing room on the other; so, before the audience came in, Judith Lucy and I went and sat in a windowless hotbox together.

Judith is a couple of years younger than me but started doing stand-up (in Melbourne) around the same time. She had a shock of black hair, pale skin and a wry smile and seemed to fit in with the way I managed stress at the time: crack jokes, laugh, do show, go to bar.

Jimeoin would usually arrive at the interval but Judith and I sweltered in that dressing room each night, bonding over using clear-plastic beer cups to catch the rodent-sized brown cockroaches all around us. Once confined, they'd skitter about as if creating sound effects that Ridley Scott might have used in *Alien*.

After a couple of shows, it was my twenty-sixth birthday. I went to see Granny in hospital but she still wasn't responding. Then I heard that our show had been reviewed in the *The Advertiser*. I sought out the paper, hoping for a quote I could use to help sell tickets at other festivals.

The reviewer hadn't enjoyed himself, you'd have thought we'd trapped him under a plastic beer cup. After some unenthusiastic lines about TV's Jimeoin, he wrote: 'His accomplices were simply awful.'

Judith and I called each other Simply and Awful all week.

The following night, with the gig sold out, Judith went on and stormed it. She was still laidback but there was an edge to her delivery. She introduced me and we grinned in passing, the usual tag-team camaraderie of the comics' union in place. I followed her lead, louder, on the front foot, and all the routines linked together seamlessly.

At the end of my set, I headed back to the hotbox to the sound of a gratifying ovation. Judith called me back and I reappeared, with freshly lit cigarette (so cool), only for her to lead the audience in singing 'Happy Birthday'. She knew my gran was in hospital, and something I might normally have found embarrassing became a memorable gesture.

A couple of days and several thousand volts later, Granny Price was eating with plastic cutlery, probably because she was at risk of hurting herself rather than others. She hadn't had her belt and laces removed, but then she'd never worn either in all the years I'd known her. I remember her fur-lined ankle boots with the zip along the top of her foot from the seventies. She was, however, a flight risk; always had been, always would be.

'They zapped me, Alan,' she said. 'I don't like it.'

We looked at each other as if some current of love could pass between us again. A lifetime with no power, or what might be called 'agency' today, lay behind and in front of her. But the lesson imposed on her and many other women with mental-health issues was: 'You won't get far, so take these tablets and sit down.'

Anniversaries

I was at the Comedy Café in Shoreditch as usual, chatting to a woman leaning on the bar who wore orange Lycra shorts and had spectacular hair, shaved at the sides with a mane of curls tumbling down from the top of her head, making her look about six feet tall.

'I'm Den,' she said.

I started spending time with her at lock-ins at the London Tavern, near my flat, or in her squat by Clissold Park, where her housemates would forage for leaves to make (undrinkable) tea.

The 22nd of August 1992 was the twentieth anniversary of Mum's death. It fell in the three-day window I had between a truncated run at the Edmonton Fringe and my solo debut in Edinburgh.

I wanted to visit Mum's place of rest and Den came with me.

From the car park we took the short walk up the hill to the woods where Mum's ashes are buried. The silence of the place causes you to quieten your voice and then stop speaking altogether. We found a place to sit on the grass in the sunshine.

Within a few minutes, great sobs pulsed out of me like bubbles of gas surfacing from the seabed. I'd never cried about Mum in front of anyone except my father, when he came to tell me she'd gone to heaven and I had to be brave.

Den comforted me until I'd recovered. She was a spiritual soul, inclined to the laying-on of crystals (during which I fell asleep, so couldn't deny that I felt better afterwards – because I did).

The memory of losing myself in grief that day is all the stronger given the absence of those feelings in the past. Over the previous three summers in Edmonton, I'd had shows on 22nd August and had not remembered my mum at all. Perhaps by going to the grave – wherever it was – I was facing up to two decades of denial.

I knew Den for only three months. One night we argued over something and I left. When I realised she was coming after me, in tears, I ran away. Regrettably, I lost touch with her for good. She'll have no idea how important that August afternoon was to me and how grateful I am.

The Love Child of Alan Ladd

RADIO DJ: Welcome to Edinburgh, Alan Davies! Now, this is your
first Fringe, is that right?

ALAN: Thank you! No, actually, I did a show as a student, in 1986.

DJ: So, you've done some flyering on the Royal Mile?

A: Oh yes, we sang songs, in fact. We were doing a musical version of
Lysistrata! – with an exclamation mark, like *Oklahoma!*

DJ: Were you? My goodness, can you sing?

A: I stood behind people who could.

DJ: And so, six years on, you're here with your first solo show at the
Fringe, *The Love Child of Alan Ladd*.

A: Yes, at the Assembly Rooms.

DJ: How's it been going?

A: Pretty good. I'm on quite late so you can hear the gunfire from the
Tattoo during my show.

DJ: Can you? Is it gunfire or fireworks?

A: I don't know, I've not been.

DJ: So, the show is built on the idea that you're the love child of fifties
Hollywood star Alan Ladd?

A: Kind of.

DJ: Well, that's the name of it.

A: It's a stand-up show in which I speculate that my dad might not be
my dad since we don't get on, but there's lots of other material.

DJ: Why don't you get on?

A: I was a bit badly behaved as a teen, after my mum died.

DJ: I'm sorry to hear that, about your mum.

A: Oh, don't worry, it was a long time ago.

DJ: You don't look like a delinquent on the flyer I'm looking at here, with your little cowboy hat and toy gun. Positively angelic.

A: I kind of went along with the designer on that.

DJ: You're influenced by the Village People?

A: Ha, no. It's fair to say I'm no cowboy.

DJ: Now, speaking of cowboys, you may know that Alan Ladd's family have got wind of your show and they're none too pleased.

A: Yes, I know there have been complaints – well, *a* complaint.

DJ: We have on the line now Wilma Ladd, who is in Philadelphia. Wilma, can you hear me?

WILMA: Yes, hello.

DJ: Welcome to the show! I've got the young English comedian Alan Davies with me.

A: Hello.

DJ: So, Wilma, you're actually related to Alan Ladd?

W: Yes, he was a cousin of my grandfather, and this suggestion that he had a love child in England is completely untrue. It's a fabrication.

DJ: We understand that you want Alan here to stop doing the show.

W: We want him to change the name of the show and to cease making this suggestion, we want him to state publicly that it's not true and to, you know, desist.

DJ: Alan, did you think how upsetting this would be for people in the Ladd family?

A: No, I must admit that hadn't occurred to me. I can only apologise, I don't think anyone from the Alan Ladd family has seen the show, it's meant to be comedy, and in fact Alan Ladd died in 1964, two years before I was born, so it's not a real assertion.

W: Then it won't trouble you to stop?

A: No one believes for a second that it's real. The show pays great tribute to Alan Ladd, I was named after him, my mother adored him.

W: But she did not have an affair with him and a child by him.

DJ: It sounds clear that Alan isn't seriously suggesting that?

W: Well then why say it at all? Use a fictional name? Denigrating the dead is not funny, it's slander and we're considering taking this further.

DJ: You're going to sue Alan Davies?

A: —

DJ: Are you an Alan Ladd fan, Alan?

A: I've watched several of his films recently, looking for material. *Shane* is the best, but I admit I prefer Cheryl Ladd. I had a picture of her on my bedroom wall, from *Look-In* magazine.

W: What are you saying about Cheryl?

A: I loved her in *Charlie's Angels*.

DJ: Wilma, is there anything you'd like to add today?

W: Just that this episode has been greatly upsetting for all of us here and we cannot understand what has prompted it. What has become of so-called comedy?

DJ: Alan?

A: I can only apologise for any hurt caused. Come and see the show, eleven forty-five every night in the Edinburgh Suite at the Assembly Rooms, and you'll see no one is denigrated at all.

DJ: Thank you both for joining us. We'll be back after the news, with more stories from our great festival.
[OFF AIR]

A: Thanks for the plug.

DJ: That's OK. She was lively, couldn't believe we managed to get her on the phone.

There had been no complaints from the Ladd family. It was all an old-fashioned publicity stunt with an actress on the end of the phone. Waiting outside the studio was Anna, the PR who'd cooked it up.

She was working for Simon Fanshawe and Lucy Barry, the promoters arranged for me by Malcolm Bailey. They also had shows by Louise Rennison and *The Golden Girls*' Bea Arthur on that year.

'Thanks, Anna,' I said.

'I enjoyed that,' she said. 'One of my better ideas.'

'It was a good one.'

'How's your show going?' she said.

'Simon told me that people are saying I'll be good in five years.'

That evening, outside a newsagent, I noticed a headline poster for the *Evening News* that read:

FILM STAR
LOVE CHILD
ANGER

I took it home with me.

That Cannot Stay There

10th October 2024.

Once you're on a cancer pathway, with examinations planned and test results pending, you begin to receive text messages, emails and alerts from the NHS app on your phone.

I was initially given a flexible cystoscopy appointment for early November, but then a text came asking me if I'd like to have it earlier and I was booked in for 10th October.

On the day, I went to the Royal Free's urology department, where they had no record of my appointment. I struggled to find the relevant message on my NHS app, as I had no phone signal in the hospital. The receptionist in urology took my full name and date of birth and soon found where I needed to go, which was two floors down. I remembered the number of the clinic as soon as he said it, but nonetheless took the wrong lift on my way down.

Katie had wanted to come with me but she'd be walking our youngest to school at that time, so I went to all the wrong places by myself.

I sat in a waiting area for a while, reading *Infinite Jest* by David Foster Wallace. It's eleven hundred pages long and it occurred to me that, if I did have cancer, I might not make it to the end.

On the upside, the NHS app told me that my blood tests had come back fine, the only blip being a high HbA1c level of 42 (yes, *Level 42*) classing me as prediabetic. I was told I should lose 10 per cent of my body weight to reach an acceptable body-mass index, and that that ought to bring my number down.

I dropped 5 per cent by putting down *Infinite Jest*.

A nurse collected me and showed me into a room with a single bed in front of a big TV. He told me to change into a back-to-front gown, the type that exposes your bare bottom if not fastened. I was surprised as I was sure they wanted to access my penis. Dutifully, I lay on the bed while he asked me what my full name was and my date of birth and whether I was on medication, the usual.

'The doctor will be here soon,' he said and disappeared through the door behind me. I waited for a while before deciding to retrieve my glasses from the chair where my clothes lay. I always wear them for watching TV.

The doctor bustled into the stillness of the room. He was Italian, maybe about thirty, and wiry. I could feel all the bones in his hand as he gripped mine tightly by way of greeting. He spoke with an unmistakeable Italian rhythm, in contrast to the nurse's African accent, and his manner was matter-of-fact but not unfriendly.

'You are 'ere for a ceest-oscopy,' he said. 'This is correct?'

'Yes,' I said.

'OK, could you lift your gown please?'

I could sense a couple of other people behind me, to whom I was not introduced. As I reached down to lift my gown, the two strangers began to hum 'The Stripper', made famous in a sketch by Morecambe and Wise.

If only – they were silent throughout.

I lifted the thin fabric to reveal no underwear and bare legs with socks on. There was no sound, neither a gasp nor a groan. While I've long been aware that penile magnitude is not my strong suit, that it should cross my mind at that moment shows the depth of my paranoia.

The silence in the room at the unveiling of my genitals was similar, I imagine, to a cricket changing room when the captain returns from the middle having been out first ball.

The doctor broke the ice by reaching over and lightly pushing my penis from side to side as if it were a playful kitten lying on its back, all the time murmuring instructions to the nurse who was to help him with the camera.

'Thees eez local-anaesthetic gel,' said the doctor and it was as if I'd dipped my cock into an icy gin and tonic (not that I know what that feels like). Then he started to push something down into my urethra. There are two sphincters down there, to aid with pushing out fluid, and these offer some resistance to a camera with a torch attached passing through. I wished I known how to relax this gag reflex. Instead, I gripped both sides of the bed and tried not to make any noise.

'Sorry,' I said, 'I've not had one of these before.'

'Eez OK,' he said. 'Zat eez zee worse part.'

And it was, as the GP had said, not very nice but not as bad as you think. I looked up at the TV and was glad of my glasses because now I could see inside myself.

The bladder wall is criss-crossed with what I presume are veins but also ridges, not unlike the pattern on the roof over the Great Court at the British Museum. Everything is a sandy colour and unlike anything I'd seen before, as if created to represent something alien in a sci-fi.

'I am filling you with water,' said the doctor. At no point did I look down to see the tubes going into me. I couldn't take my eyes off the TV and recalled a line written by David Renwick for Adrian Edmondson in *Jonathan Creek*. His character was TV executive Brendan Baxter, who'd just had a colonoscopy that was so impressive he was considering 'putting it forward for a BAFTA'.

The camera in my bladder was roving around scanning for abnormalities, with its accompanying light illuminating the walls as if we were watching *The X-Files* and Mulder and Scully were searching for clues by torchlight. The interior glistened and shone. No one was speaking now; we all watched the TV as the camera cable came into view, disappearing down a hole that led to the urethra. As the search continued, I was just beginning to think we'd seen the whole thing when a small growth appeared. Lighter in colour than the bladder wall, it looked like a coral you might see growing on a reef, an impression created by the water flooding the bladder. Its upper parts moved in the current.

'That should not be there,' said the doctor.

'No?' I said, though it was apparent that it was out of place.

'No, this 'as to go. It eez a malignant tumour and it cannot stay there. I'm going to send you to the OR.'

For a moment I thought I'd be going to for an operation right then.

'It must be taken out of there. I will recommend urgently, within two weeks, I 'ope, but within a month certainly. I'm sorry but it cannot stay there.'

The Karma bakery round the corner from the Royal Free has an image of a sheaf of wheat on its window that really resembles the thing inside me, in the same off-white colour. The doctor made one last sweep of the bladder with the camera and then took it out. Water ran between my legs. He said he would have a chat with me in a minute, before I left.

It took a few minutes to get dressed. Coming out of the clinic, I looked for the doctor and saw only the two men who had been observing, sitting in a little side room. One of them called for me to go in and there, in the corner, was the doctor.

'OK,' he said, 'I'm sorry to say that you have a tumour in your bladder, but it is small; it is one that we can take out.'

'Will I lose the use of my bladder for a while after the operation?' I said, imagining coping with a bag outside my body.

'No, no, no,' he said, 'nothing like that. We will perform a trans-urethral resection of the bladder tumour, a TURBT, this is by accessing the tumour and removing it through the urethra.'

'Will I have a general anaesthetic?' I said.

'Yes, definitely,' he said.

'Why did it bleed,' I said, 'and then stop?'

'As the tumour grows, it can push against blood cells. These may rupture and so you see quite a lot of blood but then this can heal again, so the blood stops.'

He finished up the notes he was typing, reassuring me again that he would say this was urgent and it should be done within two weeks and that it was small and they could get it out.

'Thank you, doctor,' I said.

He turned to look at me, reached across to shake hands, and said:

'All the best.'

And then I realised there was a chance I might not get better.

A nurse stopped me as I was leaving and handed me a clipboard, with a lengthy form to fill in for preassessment.

It occurred to me, as I went through ticking boxes, that this thing inside me originated and grew in total darkness, noiselessly multiplying its cells without triggering any reaction from my immune system. I began to imagine it hating being found, like a mouse suddenly revealed when you lift a sofa. Except this was a growth, stuck fast, perhaps regretting that it had ruptured some blood cells, causing evidence of its existence to leak out. Within three or four days, a new blood-testing kit came up clear, so if I'd ignored that first lot of blood, or not noticed it, perhaps because I was using a urinal, the tumour would have carried on. But because I rang the doctor, because I confirmed it with a testing kit, because I searched 'blood in urine' online and then did not run a mile when a cystoscopy was suggested, I'd discovered that I had this tumour inside me.

It doesn't mean it's cancer; no one has used that word yet. There'll be a biopsy of tissue removed from the site of the tumour, and a histology report to follow.

I was sent to the preassessment department, where there must have been sixty or seventy people waiting to go through the process before surgery. I texted Katie:

> Still here, got to have an op in a
> couple of weeks. They have to
> remove a thing. Try not to worry.
> Should be OK as it's small, found
> it early and all that. I'm in a queue
> at preassessment x

While Katie was on her way to come and meet me, a cheerful Italian nurse took blood from my arm for various tests. Her whole approach brought to mind a holiday rep, as if I was about to enjoy two weeks in Rimini and she was going to tell me when the karaoke night was and book me on an all-you-can-drink boat trip.

Another needle went in: 'Don't look at it!' she said. 'I don't want to 'ave a celebrity faint on me!'

Katie arrived and we ambled around looking at the cafés near our house before deciding to eat at home. In the kitchen, I went online and looked at tumours. Since the doctor hadn't said 'cancer', Katie was still hopeful that maybe it was a harmless lump of gristle.

When we'd first met, in 2005, she'd been with her friend from work, Suzanne Milligan. They were on barstools, side by side, and Suzanne, Katie has since told me, was my champion throughout, from that first day. She was ever present, at our wedding, at landmark birthdays, always available for a funny text exchange or a dim sum lunch in town as if they still worked in the same office. Suzanne had died from breast cancer the previous Christmas Eve. Her husband, Andy, asked Katie to read a Seamus Heaney poem at the funeral, which she did, despite holding back tears and being conscious of the Irish contingent watching on. The only person she wanted to listen to her read was Suzanne; and afterwards she cried long and deeply, sitting in the car park, as the next set of mourners began to arrive.

Katie was nowhere near past that loss and now here I was with cancer in a light pencil awaiting confirmation. No, thank you, not just yet.

But the urologist, who'd seen these things before, had said 'malignant tumour' and although there are round, flat tumours that are commonly benign, ones like mine, which grow erratically, looking like a cross between a cauliflower and a sea anemone, they have to go.

Skunk

Louise Rennison was in her early forties but looked about ten years younger. She was the least boring person I ever met: unpretentious, full of laughter and unaffected by everyone else's measures of success. Her Edinburgh show in 1992, about her real experiences in London as a young woman, *Bob Marley's Gardener Sold My Friend* (a follow-up to her previous hit, *Stevie Wonder Felt My Face*), was hilarious.

We laughed for two weeks in Edinburgh. Simon Fanshawe had his hands full looking after Bea Arthur and Louise and I were like latchkey kids with a new drinking partner who appears to share the same view of everything.

After Edinburgh, Louise became someone I could always call and frequently did. Once, there was a child crying upstairs from my flat in London. The couple above, having had three children in five years in one bedroom, were trapped by negative equity and could not move or, it seemed, buy carpet. I rang Louise:

LOUISE: Oh, you still have my number, then?

ALAN: I rang you last week.

L: Is that enough for a friendship, a weekly check-in, like I'm a dying grandmother?

A: I never ring my grandmother, so you're more important than her, is that better?

L: I'm shocked, not that you never ring her but that you brag about it in this way.

A: She lives in Australia.

L: When did you last see her?

A: Earlier this year, she was catatonic.

L: She must have known you were coming.

A: Listen, can you hear that?

L: That what?

A: There's a baby crying upstairs and I don't know what to do.

L: Why is it crying? What have you done?

A: It's not because of me!

L: Have you been playing your Billy Bragg records?

A: No, it's been screaming, 'Dada, Dada, Dada!' for two hours.

L: Maybe it should try calling for Mama.

A: Should I go up? Is that interfering?

L: I don't know. You could. You'd have to be nice and considerate about another person's feelings, though. Can you do that?

A: —

L: Go up, then ring me back.

A: OK, I'm going.

L: Good luck.

L: Hello?

A: It's me again.

L: Have you got the baby?

A: No, I haven't got the baby.

L: You just left it?

A: I couldn't take it, that would be kidnapping!

L: It's not kidnapping if it's a child, it's abduction.

A: No, that's aliens.

L: Aliens don't kidnap?

A: No, they abduct.

L: And probe.

A: The dad was there. He said they've been told to leave the kid to cry himself to sleep.

L: How's that working out?

A: Kid's traumatised.

L: Obviously. I'm like that when you leave.

A: No, you're not, you're delighted.

L: Oh, don't say that, that's too sad. You believe that too, don't you?

A: Not of you, but when I was a kid, yeah, they were delighted when I left.

L: Who was nice to you, after your mum died?

A: There was a woman called Jenny who made our tea for us, she was nice, but I used to steal money from her handbag. She left.

L: I cannot hold any more information about your childhood. Your show was good, you know. It was funny but you could tell you were trying to articulate something.

A: —

L: As if there was something more that you hadn't got to.

A: I didn't do enough work on it.

L: Maybe get a director next time.

A: How do you do that?

L: Er . . . ask for help?

A: —

L: Are you going to tour it?

A: I don't think so. There's no interest.

L: What does your manager say? What's his name?

A: Malcolm. I think I'm going to leave him, actually.

L: Why? I thought you liked him.

A: I do.

L: Is it the brown suits?

A: No! I thought you might say, 'Is it his size?'

L: I'd never say that! People can't help themselves sometimes, they get big and it's usually not their fault.

A: No, I like Malcolm but it didn't work out in Edinburgh. People were saying I was cancelling all my gigs because I thought I was going to win the Perrier.

L: You weren't, were you?

A: Of course not. I think Malcolm had said we'd wait and see what happens with Perrier or something. I feel bad because Frank left him last year and he'll run out of acts.

L: No one really cares about the Perrier Award, surely? That's too shallow to describe. Malcolm will survive. He's really nice, maybe that's the problem, not agent material.

A: That baby's still crying.

L: Are you identifying with it?

A: Must be.

L: Did you tell the dad you were going to call social services?

A: No, because he was apologetic and he gave me a bit of grass.

L: Cannabis-type grass?

A: Yes, smells strong, like skunk. He said it would help me to sleep. He should give it to the kid.

L: So, you just took the drugs and left the baby crying.

A: I couldn't demand access.

L: No. Is it still crying?

A: —

L: Well?

A: I'm listening, shh.

L: —

A: —

L: —

A: It's stopped.

L: Thank god. So you're going to have a spliff now, are you, in the middle of the day?

A: Maybe later.

L: Think of me when you're having fun.

A: Oh no.

L: What is it?

A: The baby's kicked off again.

L: Go upstairs and demand heroin this time.

Supporting

As soon as I parted company with Malcolm, in the autumn of 1992, the comedy agent and promoter Addison Cresswell, who ran Off the Kerb management, rang me. I'd done a gig for him at the Woolwich Tramshed, but no other work had come my way after I went to Duck Soup and Addison was in fact prone to mucking Malcolm about. He'd do things like tell him he'd sent a cheque when he hadn't, leaving Malcolm to turn his office upside down looking.

Addison referred to his acts as 'family', like a quasi-gangster, but undermined himself with childlike malapropisms. Mark Lamarr was represented by him and used to write them down in a notebook. Things like: 'I'm just another cog in the chain' and 'I've got the Mazda touch.'

Addison offered me two nights at the Bloomsbury Theatre, opening for Lee Evans, and eighteen nights on tour supporting Sean Hughes. It was over four grand's worth of work in one phone call, and in nice theatres. I'd have to do about sixty gigs at the Store to make the same.

Sean and I had known one another for three years or more, since he used to rent Jeff Green's spare room and would sometimes hang out at the Red Rose with Jo Brand and Jim Miller.

One night at Jongleurs, soon after Addison's call, Isabel Silverstone handed me her card and invited me to come into the offices at International Artistes to speak to Bob Voice about management.

I knew that Eddie Izzard had turned International Artistes down. They were seen as old school, nothing to do with alternative comedy, and Eddie's view was they'd 'make you do crap telly'. But I was curious and within days was at their Regent Street offices. While I waited, I heard the receptionist putting a call through.

'I've got Ronnie Corbett on three,' she said.

That was it: good enough for Ronnie Corbett, good enough for me.

Bob Voice showed me round the offices, introducing me to Tony Hancock's former agent, Phyllis Rounce, on the way.

'She doesn't do much these days but we let her keep an office.'

Bob's desk looked out through a large semicircular window, which is part of the listed frontage of Regent Street and was retained when the whole place was later taken over as the Apple Corporation's flagship UK store.

With neatly cut, greying hair and a trim beard, Bob became a father figure over the years ahead. I trusted him without any background checks, reassured by his calmness and confidence.

Another comedian said to me years later: 'Bob Voice? He used to be Mike Yarwood's driver.'

But that wouldn't have dissuaded me, I'd have been impressed, Yarwood was a brilliantly funny impressionist I'd always watched on TV in the seventies.

Isabel had done her job as a talent scout and once in the door I had no questions – about how the agency worked, what they saw in me, what they thought of the other agencies, whether I could think it over.

'Great, thanks,' I said.

In that office, it was as if I'd found a door to another level. Neither Avalon nor Off the Kerb had approached me and it was made so easy, a handshake, nothing to sign, let's see how we go.

'What do you want to do?' said Bob.

'Stand-up and acting,' I said. 'I did a drama degree.'

'Oh, right, anything else?'

'I don't want to do any adverts.'

If I'd known what to look for I might have noticed that this was an agency that favoured high income over high regard and would smooth the way for me to trade in my gun for a badge.

And then I was out on Regent Street and, as soon as this tour with Sean was out of the way, I'd have a new agent. Addison Cresswell never gave me another gig.

Sean Hughes liked to sit in the front, with me in the back. A mate of Addison's, Paul, was our tour manager and driver. Sean controlled the music, favouring obscure indie bands, and would scoff at my every suggestion in his broad Dublin accent. I still maintain that *Spartacus* by the Farm is a great album.

This hierarchy in the car was not what I was used to from travelling with comedians, sharing lifts and petrol money. Sean had rapidly progressed from the circuit via the Perrier Award to a Channel 4 show; and that rise, with me still at Jongleurs, gave him a status and power that he couldn't temper with humility or generosity. Also, he wanted to go home to London after each gig, even when we were in Bristol one night and Swansea the next.

Manchester was a rare occasion when we were staying overnight. Once Sean was in the car, waiting to be driven back to the hotel, Paul grabbed me while we were still on the pavement.

'You and me are going out,' he said.

I gigged every weekend so I'd missed the rise of clubbing entirely. Paul had found a place where everyone was dancing as though they couldn't sit down if they tried. We'd been there about fifteen minutes when he said, 'Do you want to go the toilet?'

'No,' I said.

'Do you want to go to the toilet?'

'No, I'm all right.'

'Yes you do,' he said, and pushed me into the gents. Once inside, he turned me around and put something small in my mouth.

'Swallow it,' he said.

I did. It didn't taste of anything.

'What was that?' I said.

And he gave a wicked laugh like someone turning into Mr Hyde.

I stopped dancing at 4am, when the club closed. I hadn't had a drink all night. Paul had also introduced me to cocaine, so it had been my first time on that as well as on ecstasy, and I'd had no awareness of the time or where I was and hadn't spoken to anyone because whenever I tried to I sounded like a sheep having a stroke. But I felt safe, because I was with Paul.

The next morning, Sean insisted on leaving at ten. I don't know how Paul drove; I could barely see.

Later, we had to stop for petrol. Sean got out of the car and wandered across the forecourt, past all the pumps, through clouds of invisible and highly flammable vapour, smoking a cigarette. By the time he reached the serving window the woman working alone in there was both frightened and livid.

I watched from inside the car as she berated Sean about the insanity of having a lit cigarette, here of all places, before he ambled back to us.

'What's her fucking problem?' he said.

'She thinks you're going to fucking blow us all up,' said Paul.

The only time I sat in the front of the car was after our show at the Hexagon, in Reading, when we were joined for the drive home by a hugely funny northern comic we knew who'd become popular on TV. Sean kept asking me to pass cassette boxes back to them and there was a fair bit of tapping and sniffing among the giggling as Paul blasted up the M4 so we could meet Addison for a late drink on Beak Street in Soho.

I wasn't offered any coke, possibly because one night Paul, Sean and I had shared a wrap and, when it had been passed to me, I'd gone off and snorted the lot.

'Where is it?' said Paul, when I came out of the toilets.

'It's gone,' I said. 'There wasn't much.'

'Fuck me, hoover head,' he said, managing to laugh.

The tour finished in December. I stayed in touch with Paul for a few years, but barely saw Sean again except once in early 1993.

On Christmas Day, I was at my dad and stepmum's house in Loughton, opening presents, when I unwrapped two comedy videos, one of which was a recent release from Sean Hughes.

'Oh no,' I said.

'Have you got that one already?' said Dad.

'No,' I said, 'but I've just spent a month touring with this bloke.'

'Oh really, I expect you're sick of the sight of him then, are you?'

'I am a bit,' I said.

When I bumped into Sean in the New Year, I said: 'You'll like this, I went home for Christmas and my dad had bought me your live video.'

'Have you watched it?' he said.

'Not yet.'

'You should,' he said, in earnest. 'It's different stuff from the tour.'

Viva Cabaret

Anxious people were in the corridor outside my dressing room with walkie-talkies: 'Does anyone have eyes on Eartha?'

No one had seen Eartha Kitt all day. The *Viva Cabaret* producers had brought all the acts to the Riverside Studios early. I'd been waiting for so long I felt like I was in solitary.

When Eartha Kitt finally rehearsed, it was apparent to me that an ambulance ought to be standing by – she was ancient, possibly with minutes to live.

Having looked it up, I can see she was actually in her sixties.

Eartha Kitt's anti-Vietnam War stance, of which twenty-seven-year-old me was ignorant, had effectively led to her superstar career being cancelled. It took me a while to learn that it's polite to familiarise yourself, in advance, with people you are on a show with.

More excitement broke out later when it was time for another old-timer, Tom Jones, to rehearse (he was fifty-three). He wandered on with a few hellos to crew members and then a brilliant guitarist launched into the opening riff from Lenny Kravitz's 'Are You Gonna Go My Way'.

As I nodded along, doing a white-man overbite, the producer approached me.

'Will you go through your set for us?'

'I'd prefer not to,' I said, chuckling, as if that were obvious.

'Why not?' he said. 'It might be helpful?'

'There's no one here, I don't want to perform it to no audience.'

'OK, what do you want to do?'

I wanted to go home. He was starting to annoy me, as if he thought I'd mess up the gig without heavy-handed supervision. The angry boy was twitching, but this bloke seemed angrier.

'I'll just top and tail it,' I said.

'How long is it?'

'I don't know,' I said.

Don't talk to me about how long my set is; you've brought me in to wait for eight hours for no reason.

'You don't know?' he said.

'I've never timed my act,' I said. 'It depends on the gig.'

'If you ever work in the States you'll be expected to have a set that lasts exactly seven minutes,' he said.

Now he was trying to assert himself. No one had said anything about America. We were in Hammersmith for Channel 4.

'Is that what you're wearing?' he said.

'No, I've got a new shirt, from Paul Smith. It's linen.'

'What colour is it?' he said.

'Black.'

'No black,' he said.

'But . . .' I said but he'd walked away. That was how he was going to triumph, a petty ruling about my shirt.

Tom Jones wore a black suit and a black crewneck jumper.

I wasn't allowed to leave the building, so someone from the production team went out and bought me a green shirt such as you might wear on your first day at Wren Kitchens.

I always left my shirt tails hanging out, but the cut of this new one meant that I'd look like a judge in a state of undress during a police raid on a Cynthia Payne party.

Reluctantly, I tucked it into my red 501s as if I was colourblind and yet to be diagnosed.

At the show recording that evening, I was placed on set with a radio mic in hand like I'd used on Jonathan Ross's show. Many of the audience were not looking at me but sitting side-on, facing the larger music stage in the distance, as if I was giving a talk in the aisle of a plane, with the crowd as interested as holidaymakers during an in-flight safety briefing.

I was anxious, thrown by the strange shirt, the sound, the oddly arranged audience. I spoke but couldn't hear myself like you can at a normal gig and wondered if the mic was on; it was hard to tell, since the audience appeared to be waiting for oxygen masks to drop from the ceiling.

I needn't have worried. The editors found so much laughter in the final cut that I ended up nominated for a British Comedy Award as Best Newcomer 1994, along with the majestic Lily Savage from the same series.

I've since watched that *Viva Cabaret* appearance on YouTube. My face was smooth and smeared with foundation, so I resembled the top of the peanut butter when you open a new jar. My emergency green shirt has a baggy nineties cut but a reasonable button-down collar and looks fine. And it isn't shoved into red 501s but a pair of baggier purple jeans from Next. The microphone has a wire attached, which you can see me habitually wrap around my fingers.

The lighting has a hazy feel to replicate the smoky atmosphere of a club in the twentieth century. The audience are sitting at tables, facing me and close to the stage, and there are several cutaways of people laughing. There are two rounds of applause during my act and a big ovation at the end.

Yet I recall only silence.

Something about that whole day of the recording – my anxiety at the long wait, fear of failure, the unsmiling producer, being made to change my shirt – *everything* about it combined to make me feel it was a disaster, but palpably it wasn't. I did my usual set, to time, the crowd enjoyed it, there were music legends onboard and it was a good night all round.

Sometimes I wish my memory functioned differently; it's as if any recollection comes with a label attached: 'Beware, the Past'.

My First Sitcom

Sue Birbeck came to see me at a small gig over a pub in Tufnell Park. There was a curtain behind the stage and I pulled it back to reveal a wall. This brought a laugh so, finding a broken table leg, I began improvising with it as a pointer and talking about a nearby picture.

I liked to put off starting my act; it's always the fun part of stand-up.

Afterwards, Sue introduced herself, in a mid-Atlantic accent, as a producer. She was fortyish, and tall, with longer limbs than mine, which she could only just arrange around our tiny table with its little stools.

'I liked the way you set that stick behind the curtain,' she said, embarking on an uninvited debrief.

'I didn't set it,' I said.

· 'I know comedians,' she said, smiling knowingly, despite self-evidently knowing fuck all.

'It was just there,' I said. 'I found it.'

Now she needed to say, 'Really? My mistake.' Instead she said, 'That material was obviously prepared, but anyway . . .'

I didn't leave at that point, because Sue was the new head of comedy at Red Rooster (a production company) and was looking to develop sitcoms. Was that something I might be interested in?

I was soon contracted to work with a writer called Paul Waite on *The Alan Davies Show* ('to star Alan Davies as one of the main characters').

I'd wanted to write a sitcom about a comedian's life but the emergence of *Seinfeld* had spoiled that plan. Nevertheless, this was still my dream job. We came up with a flatshare comedy in which my landlady was based on Louise Rennison and my best friend would be played by a friend from the circuit, Simon Godley.

The writing was good fun; Paul and I laughed a lot – often at Sue, just after she'd left the room – and we started to become close. I told him a lot about my girlfriend troubles, anyway.

I'd love to go through what happened next in a light-hearted and self-deprecatory way but I've discovered I'm still upset about it.

Our show was sold to Carlton Television for ITV and I immediately disliked the way things began to slide towards the bland.

Eventually, I was told, in writing, that if I didn't work with Sue I'd be in breach of contract.

Paul reassured Sue that he was doing '90 per cent of the writing' (perhaps he meant typing) and that turned out to be that – I was fired, from my own show.

I know, it was thirty years ago, but FOR FUCK'S SAKE.

I spoke to Louise on the phone and she tried to calm me down but I was furious, swearing and ranting about everyone. She stayed on the line for ages as if she was volunteering for the Samaritans and was not allowed to hang up.

'Then,' I said, 'as soon as I was out of the way, Sue apparently announced that our landlady character was now going to be based ON HER!'

I continued my apoplectic monologue but faltered when I realised that Louise was laughing on the other end of the phone.

'Based on *her*?' she said.

'Yeah,' I said, 'they've started to look for a tall actress with long blonde hair.'

'You might be better off away from them, Al the pal, don't you think?'

They made the series, that we'd always called *Just Shut Up* (with that phrase intended to be the last line of each episode), but renamed it *Get Real*. It was immediately canned.

'They should have called it *GET FUCKED*,' I said, as Louise listened patiently again, becoming a little concerned.

In eighteen months, the experience went from my dream job to the equivalent of being asked to go through a door only to find myself out on the street with the key turning in the lock behind me.

I recently found Sue on Instagram, doing tarot readings, alone, with no subject, just talking about cards that she is pulling out herself. She seemed happy.

Looking back on how I coped, when compromise and collaboration were needed, I can see I was bound to fall short. My issues with authority figures remained unaddressed. The angry boy had appeared when things were difficult, but then again, can you blame him?

My Big One

'Is it "Supersonic" by Oasis or "Oasis" by Supersonic?'

On the other side of the BBC studio's glass, three people looked blank. We were playing a prerecorded sketch and then I was supposed to intro the next song. A voice came into my headphones.

'We'll put it on and you can back-announce it.'

The radio edit is three minutes forty seconds long.

As they looked frantically for the CD case, the rest of the *Alan's Big One* cast – Bill Bailey, Kevin Eldon, Alan Francis and Debra Stephenson – chatted among themselves.

Forty-five seconds before going live. This was the downside of not driving the desk (operating the jingles, playing the records and prerecorded tapes) myself.

Thirty seconds. It was second nature to DJs, but not to a comic hosting a Radio 1 show once a week. The helpless shrugging behind the soundproof glazing was now maniacal.

Fifteen seconds. The vocal had finished and now it was just guitars, then they would fade out.

Green light! Green light! GREEN LIGHT!

Dropping my voice low like a mock-rock DJ, I said, in a monotone so it could mean either thing: '*OASIS, SUPERSONIC!*'

Got away with it.

Had we just listened to the song, we'd have heard the twenty-one-year-old Liam Gallagher feeling supersonic and demanding gin and tonic.

*

I had Jim Miller to thank for my presenting chance. He'd been going into BBC Radio Light Entertainment to write for various shows – the standard route for Oxbridge graduates – and he took me to a busy writers' meeting where discussions were taking place about a series of pilot shows for a new slot on 1FM, one of which I was asked to present.

At that point, my radio experience consisted of doing stand-up on *Kennedy's Connections*, a Radio 4 show hosted by the MP Charles Kennedy. His producer wanted some of my comedy-club routines but it was the morning, coffee and biscuits all round, and it's hard to say who was most uncomfortable – me, Charles, the other guests, or the listeners.

The following week, I was asked if I'd prefer to be behind a screen so I couldn't see my audience's discomfort. And that's what I did, performing out of sight of the people in the studio, who would laugh dutifully, just loud enough for me to hear. For my third appearance, standing behind a screen was dropped in favour of sitting at the table with everyone else, almost like a real Radio 4 contributor.

It was a young BBC staffer, Jon Rowlands, who came up with the name *Alan's Big 1FM* for our pilot. Jane Berthoud was the producer and she suggested Alan Francis and Debra as regulars, while I asked for Bill and Kevin – who can make anything funny – to join. We were delighted to go to series.

I sat in the middle as host, always referred to as just 'Alan', while around me hilarious characters were created: Alan Francis did Wags Wilkins for fake travel news and was also Ian Dee, my sidekick from Mad-for-it-Manchester; Kevin Eldon's spoof horoscopes were surreal; Bill Bailey was Jake the Crusty ('Traveller!') and Debra Stephenson could do any voice – Björk was my favourite – listening to the person on tape until she had them. When practising she'd sometimes forget her headphones.

'All my life I've been surrounded by make-up!' she once said, before looking up to see us all staring at her.

'Sorry,' she said. 'Liz Hurley.'

We'd go in on Monday morning at eleven and stay all day, writing and prerecording items, with Jane marshalling various contributors – including Jim Miller, of course – and me helping with script editing.

We also had serials: Michael Redmond's *Eamonn, Older Brother of Jesus* and *The Bradshaws* by Buzz Hawkins, about a northern family.

Alan's Big One went live at 9pm before Mark Radcliffe took over at 10. He was the best DJ on radio so I liked leading into him. Then we'd all go to the Yorkshire Grey.

What with the team on the radio and my group of friends at the Comedy Café, it was as if two families were overlapping. I loved swapping *Bradshaws* lines at the Caff with Mark Hurst (who'd been Mark Miwurdz on *The Tube* ten years before).

Then, one Saturday night before the Monday radio show, I was at the Caff as usual when Jim Miller became involved in a row over the pool table. It was late and Jo wasn't around to intervene.

Jim, who wasn't much of a pool player, had a bet on a game with another comic who wasn't normally there. Then they'd gone double or quits; and now Jim was theatrically burning two £20 notes with a lighter rather than hand them over. Unexpectedly, they fell into a clinch among the balls on the table. Retired Scots punk meets South London sumo wrestler.

Jez Feeney, Mark Lamarr and I watched on, hoping this silly storm would blow itself out; but when one of them picked up a pool ball and tried to smack the other in the head with it, we pulled them up onto their feet and stopped it.

Jim turned on us, ranting that we should have let him go on, even though his fighting was worse than his pool.

'Just shut up, Jim,' I said.

'Why should I?'

'Because you're ruining my fucking night,' I said.

He didn't shut up and the angry boy took over, surprising us all by taking a swing at Jim, catching him above the left eye. He slumped onto the sofa behind him that Jo had bought. Even in her absence she was breaking his fall.

'Oh, bloody hell,' said Jez.

'Oh fuck,' said Mark.

'Sorry, Alan, that's what I should have done,' said Sumo.

'Who hit me that time?' said Jim.

'I did,' I said.

Jim told us that he had new respect for his English friends because he didn't think an Englishman had the bottle to do that to a Scotsman. In Scotland, he said, someone would have chinned him long before.

I offered Mark a lift home to Camden, which was unusual as it was out of my way. He noticed I was subdued.

'He had it coming, the silly sod,' he said.

'I know, but I don't know why I did that.'

Outside his flat, Mark reached across to shake my hand and it hurt. I should have gone for an X-ray but I didn't know where the nearest A&E was and instead went home to bed.

In the morning, the small knuckle on the side of my right hand was in the wrong place. The bone set over the next couple of weeks and has never been the same since. It aches on cold or damp days, there is some discomfort there as I type this; my little finger hangs in underneath my palm like a dog sleeping under a table and never makes a contribution.

The last three people I'd hit had been my sister in 1981, my brother in 1982 and my dad in 1983. I regret that first one; I was fifteen and she was twelve so it was shameful. I'd perhaps misheard or misunderstood what she'd said to me before I bashed her in the face then exploded in a rant at my father about his coming into my room at night. We were in an airport, so it was quite a scene, which I wrote about in *Just Ignore Him*.

My brother and father, each enraged by my sneering indifference to their disapproval, had both attacked me at home, so I put those down to self-defence.

Jim was not the natural successor to them. He could be abrasive and aggravating but he was a friend who had helped and advised me at different times. Something had snapped. I wasn't drinking but I couldn't stand what was happening, in the Caff of all places.

On the Monday, I went to work on *Alan's Big One* at Broadcasting House with a swollen hand and there was Jim, sitting in his usual place, with a huge shiner.

'I've fucked my hand up,' I said.

'That's because you didn't hit me properly,' he said.

*

At the end of the series, we all went to the Yorkshire Grey and then across to the Langham Hotel when the pub shut. Bill marched up to the reception desk and, adopting a military bearing, despite his shorts and heavy-metal hair, he said: 'Bailey, Room 101.'

The receptionist greeted him as if he were an actual guest and then allowed us to use their residents' bar until the small hours.

We were given a second series of *Alan's Big One*; but before that, our producer, Jane, reserved the BBC flat in Manhattan for a week and we went to New York to record a programme with me interviewing the great American monologist Spalding Gray.

The apartment was upstairs in a block close to Greenwich Village. All the kitchen drawers held cockroaches that scuttled for cover when you opened them; the street corner outside had rubbish piled high and rats scuttled around as the sun beat down.

It was great.

We had the place for a week and only a day's work with Spalding Gray planned. The rest of the time I learned in more detail why Jane had chosen me to present our show.

The studio for the Spalding Gray recording was small, with barely enough room to move. I'd seen him perform *Monster in a Box* at the Royal Festival Hall and told him, truthfully, that it was great, fantastic, brilliant. He smiled.

'Shall I just talk?' he said.

'Yes,' said Jane, 'that would be wonderful, thanks.'

And he did. I was not required to interview him; for two hours, we had a private audience that Jane edited into a series called *Shades of Gray* for Radio 3.

At one point, Spalding said of his younger self: 'I felt most alive when I was onstage and pretty dead in my life.'

This was perhaps a portentous remark for me as it wouldn't be long before I felt something similar. But I missed the warning.

A Suggestion

JO BRAND: Have you ever thought about seeing someone?

ALAN: How do you mean?

J: You know, to talk about stuff.

A: No, I haven't. I don't know how I'd go about that.

J: What happened with Angela?

A: We kept arguing, and she was really focused on her career.

J: And you don't like that?

A: I don't mind. I helped her get a telly job but she ended up moving out of London, so that backfired.

J: That was nice of you.

A: You know we went scuba diving in the Red Sea?

J: When you didn't come away at New Year?

A: Yes, we were dive buddies for a week. On one dive I burned my hand on some fire coral and managed to lose my regulator.

J: Your what?

A: The thing in your mouth that lets you breathe. It was flapping around with air pouring out and she swam away.

J: Really? So you'd drown?

A: It was a drift dive so you're going with the current, moving quite quickly, but she didn't look round. I got the mouthpiece back in but I'd lost loads of air and then I swam after the dive leader as fast as I could, so used up even more air, and he had to take me to the surface using his spare regulator since my tank was empty. The burn on my hand freaked me out but it's a bit like a bad stinging nettle. Anyway, when we were back on the boat she was pretty unsympathetic.

J: She didn't say sorry.

A: No, she was pissed off that I was pissed off.

J: I liked her.

A: I did too.

J: What happened with Jim?

A: At the Caff?

J: Yes, when you punched him, do you remember that?

A: I'm sorry.

J: Don't worry, I'm sure you had your reasons.

A: He was being an idiot.

J: I don't doubt it. Were you trying to calm him down with a show of force?

A: It wound me up.

J: Do you often punch people?

A: No, I mean, there were fights at school.

J: Did everyone at your school have fights?

A: No.

J: Would you say the majority did not have fights?

A: Yes.

J: But you had lots of fights?

A: Not loads, a few.

J: I'm not having a go at you, Davies, just seeing how you are.

A: I know, thanks.

J: Think about seeing someone maybe?

A: Yeah.

J: Please.

A: OK.

J: Shall we have a fag?

People Are Looking

One Christmas in the early eighties, we had some visitors from my dad's side of the family come to the house in Loughton. This was unusual and had never happened in the ten years between Mum dying and Dad remarrying. One of the relatives was in a wheelchair after a car accident had left him with quadriplegia. We had to take him round the side of the house to the kitchen as it was too difficult to get him and his vehicle up the steps to the front door. He needed constant attention and struggled to communicate and to eat; everything was difficult. It seemed to me a life of torment. Early in the evening, we all gathered round the television for *The Two Ronnies*. Ronnie Barker and Ronnie Corbett were funny from the start, and one person in particular loved the show. The young man in his wheelchair had been positioned close to the TV with a clear view and was laughing loudly, great honks of mirth that twisted his body back and forth, with a huge smile on his face that lasted for the entire programme.

Bob Voice brought Ronnie Corbett to see my show at the Gilded Balloon Studio during the 1994 Edinburgh Fringe and I later found myself before him not knowing what to say. I didn't mention watching that Christmas show with the family in the early eighties; I wish now I'd recalled it but I was preoccupied with what the great comedian thought of me. I could have told him how much I'd enjoyed his sitcom *Sorry*, but that slipped my mind too.

Before he was taken somewhere else, he offered me praise and this sound advice: 'When you're not working, work on your act.'

Edinburgh's Cowgate is a street with a history going back hundreds of years, first as a route to the cattle market under the castle, then as a wealthy area and then as a slum. By the late twentieth century it came alive during the Fringe as home to one of its most popular venues, the Gilded Balloon.

The Studio, tragically destroyed by fire in 2002, was perfect for stand-up, seating about a hundred and thirty, with tables up the front, raked seating behind and a bar off to the right.

My whole set worked and I set out to be as funny as I could for the full hour. I began the run with fifty minutes of material and finished it with seventy. Every gig was sold out; I was sharing a flat with Alexander Armstrong and Ben Miller, who both laughed constantly, and I began to receive good reviews.

I'd vowed not to read any writeups, since I was diffident enough to take offence at some perceived slight in even the best of notices, but the practice at the Gilded Balloon was to photocopy quotes from the papers and stick them on the walls. There were no stars awarded back then, thankfully, but everybody seemed to love my show. My reviews were plastered along the corridor and halfway up the stairs.

Each night, I'd wear one of three checked shirts I'd bought in Urban Outfitters in New York a few weeks before. After each show, I'd hang the shirt I'd worn next to the other two on a rail, have a chat with Fred MacCaulay, who was on after me, and go out, usually ending up at Late 'n' Live next door until the small hours.

I couldn't have been happier.

After the first week, I was invited to a daytime awards ceremony held by the official Edinburgh Festival, where I received the Critics' Award for Comedy. I was blasé about it; everything was coming so easily to me and it appeared this would be the first of many awards for my stand-up. I'm still waiting for a second.

Bob Voice then trumped the Ronnie Corbett invitation by bringing the great Irish comedian Dave Allen to see me. Afterwards we went to dinner with a few other people. As we settled down in a Thai restaurant, we realised Dave was not with us. The taxi driver had refused to take his money while he'd insisted on paying, so there'd been a standoff. We were in the restaurant laughing until 2am.

*

The talk of the Fringe for comedians was the Perrier Award, for which I was rumoured to be the Hot Favourite. I bumped into Harry Hill one evening and he told me he'd been given the exact same nod and wink, that he had the prize in the bag.

Harry and I decided we'd offer an alternative awards ceremony, a Fringe of the Fringe affair, with quirky categories, called the Hill-Davies Awards. But then the nominations came out and there were our names, and everyone was still saying to each of us that we were going to win, so we dropped our idea in case it looked like arrogance, sour grapes, ingratitude or some combination of all three.

We should have gone ahead, booked a room, sold tickets and banned all awards judges, journalists, PRs and agents. They'd have been desperate to get in; then, when the doors were shut, we could have done an affable Q&A or just issued refunds and gone to dinner. I wish we had.

On the night of the Perrier Awards, if you'd won, someone would turn up during your show and present the trophy onstage.

The door into the Gilded Balloon Studio was at the back of the room. On this night, every time it opened and light came in from the corridor I was expecting the Perrier Award. It didn't come but I had the consolation that it was all over and Harry Hill had won.

But he hadn't. The judges couldn't make their minds up. Bob Voice said we should go to the grand Balmoral Hotel to await the decision, which was supposed to have been made by 6pm. It was now 9.15 and the awards ceremony was at 10. We waited and I drank quite a lot of whisky.

Finally, the news came through that the Australian double act Lano and Woodley had won the award.

There was considerable consternation.

'Who?'

'Not Harry?'

None of that from me, though, because I knew Colin Lane and Frank Wood. I'd seen their brilliant show at the Adelaide Fringe when I'd been over there earlier in the year, visiting family, hanging out with Judith Lucy and Tony Martin and doing some gigs at the Fringe Club.

On the way to the obligatory Perrier Awards party there was some talk of the judging panel (I had no idea who was on it) being split between Harry and me. It seemed many of them had Lano and Woodley in second place, so it had been decided that way, but my favourite explanation for the outcome came from Ruth Wishart in her festival diary in *The Scotsman*. According to her sources, the male judges on the Perrier panel were so irritated by the females swooning over how hot I was that they'd taken their votes elsewhere. Makes sense.

When we arrived at the party, the door staff wouldn't admit us

'I didn't ask to be a fucking nominee,' I said to Bob. 'Let's fuck off.'

'People are looking at you, Alan,' he said into my ear as we finally went inside, like Spock calming down Captain Kirk.

Frank and Colin looked so happy. If I'd won I'd have been cocky, sardonic and pissed, so it was for the best, but that was it for the Perrier Award; you had only one chance of being nominated in those days.

As it turned out, an opportunity came up during that Fringe that was going to take me away from stand-up and onto a different course.

After Edinburgh, I was to do my show once more at the Lyric Theatre as part of the Perrier Pick of the Fringe season.

Bob decided we should record it for my first video and it looked good, despite us not being allowed to light the audience, so that in *Alan Davies: Live at the Lyric* (available on VHS *and* audio cassette) the same three people appear in every crowd-reaction shot. One of them was a friend of mine, Phil Harris from Whitstable, who I didn't even know was coming.

Also in the auditorium without my knowledge was my father, who hadn't been to see me perform since *1st Exposure* in 1989. He'd said he wanted to come and I'd asked him not to.

I couldn't see him from the stage, thankfully, as I mocked his giant underwear and absurd dating tips.

With hindsight I imagine he was relieved I hadn't gone into more detail about our relationship. As with my previous Edinburgh show, I was trying to articulate something but kept veering away from the target, perhaps fearful of a direct hit that could destabilise my whole life and, worse, not get a laugh.

End of the Road

Steven Bawol pointed a video camera at me as I stood before him in Princes Street Gardens in Edinburgh, the castle looming behind me in one of the most beautiful settings in Europe. I began to say the lines I'd hastily learned.

'Stop, stop, stop,' he said, in his broad New York accent. 'Wait for "Action".'

That was my first test and it seemed I'd blown it, but in fact he liked me and as the co-producer (with Bob Altman) of a new comedy series for Channel 4, was on the verge of casting me.

The show was *One for the Road*, a travelogue about a timeshare salesman who sends videotapes of his escapades home to different friends and family each week. There were to be six episodes, set in Israel, Norway, Venice, the Czech Republic, Cannes and the French Alps, all to be scripted by Gary Sinyor, who'd had a recent success with British indie film *Leon the Pig Farmer*.

It seemed too good to be true.

Neil Morrissey, from *Men Behaving Badly*, had helpfully dropped out and they were due to start shooting in September, almost immediately after the Fringe finished. The only downside was that it would clash with *Alan's Big One*. I'd have to miss two of the shows, but that was easily sorted out with Phil Clarke at BBC Radio and John Shuttleworth agreed to stand in for me.

Back in London, I saw Jim Miller at the Caff and he'd obviously heard about the disruption.

'What's this telly you want to do?'

I told him about it and he pulled a face.

'Sounds a bit of a mad idea. Are you quitting *Alan's Big One* for that?'

By 'quitting' he didn't just mean was I giving up hosting; he meant was

I bringing down everything we'd built up, the friendship and camaraderie, all those relationships built on collaboration and laughter.

'Not quitting, just missing a couple,' I said. 'They've offered me four grand a show.'

'You should never do anything just for money,' he said, in an advisory tone, not as admonishment. I was embarrassed. Was his prophecy coming true, and I was beginning the process of turning in my gun for a badge?

'It's not just for money, Jim,' I said, trying to persuade myself. 'It could be a good gig, lots of travel. I want to be an actor.'

He smoked a bit and looked round the room.

First stop on *One for the Road* was Oslo, where I was made to feel welcome by Annicken, the young woman assigned – without qualification, she told me – to make-up duties. Almost immediately, I indulged in fantasies about a fresh start with this softly spoken young woman in the Norwegian capital, perhaps betraying some instinct to flee and hide from what was beginning to happen to me.

I didn't wear any make-up and, in any case, it was too late for Annicken to support me in one big change to my appearance. Before we left for Norway, Steven Bawol had insisted I have my long curly hair cut so I 'looked right for a timeshare salesman'. Then he had me dress in chinos and shirts. Bob Altman laughed when he saw me.

'Steven Bawol has cut your hair like Steven Bawol and now he's dressing you like Steven Bawol.'

It was true, and I mourned my lost locks.

Then came the travelling, in two blocks of filming either side of Christmas. Venice in the autumn was antiquely spooky. My co-star, Zoë Scott, teased me about my 'little Norwegian girl' while I followed the sound of her high heels over little bridges in the fog.

Annicken later flew from Oslo to Cannes and we stayed in a luxury suite overlooking the ocean. In this episode I drove a Ferrari along La Croisette, nearly pranging it on the back of a coach but loving the feeling of power at the throttle.

We were shooting an episode in Cannes only because Bob and Steve wanted to attend the MIPCOM TV conference. Jean-Pierre, our French camera operator, introduced me to pastis, a relationship even more short-lived than mine with Annicken, who, despite being fluent in English, found that humour is hard to follow in a second language. Possibly it was a flaw of mine that a potential girlfriend needed to play the role of audience. In any case, Annicken flew home to Oslo.

Jean-Pierre had previously won an Oscar for a documentary. He said it was: 'The worst thing that *ever* 'appened to me! After zat I do not work for one year. No one called me: "E 'as won ze Oscar he will be too bizzy." I was sat by ze phone for one year!'

And now he was filming this nonsense with me. But he was loving it. In Israel the producers had a desert storyline and were delighted to learn I could ride a motorbike. An old motorcycle with sidecar was produced and I roared up and down on it gleefully, while trying not to hit any goats. Pierre set up the camera and wanted me to grab it as I went by. I managed it and we got the shot but on the final pass I knocked it to the floor and it broke.

'Do not worry, Alan, do not worry!' he said, running up to the bike. That night he retired to his room and over several hours dismantled the video camera and repaired it. Then he found us in the bar.

'It is fixed! It is fixed! One tiny part!'

One night we had to shoot a scene 'on the blink' (during the sixty-second window as the sun drops below the horizon). Our Israeli fixers said there were two ways to get to the location we wanted, one of which was faster but went through 'a Palestinian area'.

'What might happen?' I said.

'You could be shot,' he said.

We took the longer route and made it just in time for a romantic twilight moment with my co-star in the episode, Allie Byrne. We had to kiss, during which I blushed. I hoped she hadn't noticed but my cheeks were like a pair of hot-water bottles.

That night at the hotel, a few of us played the same 'name game' – identifying famous people from the fewest clues – that I'd enjoyed many times on New Year holidays. I was paired with Allie, who was good at it: quick-witted, articulate, constantly smiling. We made eye contact several times as we racked up an unbeatable score in every round. Then we sat together waiting for everyone else to go to bed.

The knockabout style of *One for the Road* didn't feel authentic and my character was morally bankrupt, witless and constantly gurning at the camera. The harder I tried, the less funny it was – a good lesson. The locations looked great, though, and we ended up in Channel 4's 8.30pm travel slot on Mondays instead of 10.30pm on Fridays as we'd expected. I liked the people too, especially Iain Coyle, the assistant producer, runner, dogsbody and provider of additional material, and James the soundman, who counted our forty-two pieces of luggage in and out of every airport.

We didn't get a second series.

I returned to the *Alan's Big One* family and we finished the second series and then a third. Caroline Trowbridge, who was in the Prague *One for the Road* came in and did a sketch and Peter Serafinowicz provided lots of voices. And then 1FM dropped their comedy slot and we were finished. It was a sad day.

Back again at the Langham Hotel after the pub had shut, but this time with no Bill, Jane marched up to reception.

'Berthoud, Room 17,' she said.

'There is no Room 17, madam.'

We smoked a joint on the steps of All Saints Church and then all went back for another party in my flat on Evering Road.

Lie Still

When I was at school, a packet of Polos was 2p, as was the bus fare from Loughton to Woodford when I started at Bancroft's in 1976.

When Polos went up to 3p there was dismay. I liked the multicoloured fruit ones but nothing compared to the classic mint with a hole. I often carried a packet, not least because as teenagers we believed they had tobacco-nullifying powers, so if you sucked one you wouldn't stink like an ashtray when you went into double biology after lunch.

Smoking, it turns out, is one of the main causes of bladder cancer.

The carcinogenic toxins in your bloodstream are filtered out by your kidneys and flushed away via the bladder. Other chemicals can have a similar dangerous effect, so newly diagnosed bladder cancer patients (between ten and eleven thousand a year in the UK) are routinely asked about their working environment. Links have been made to certain chemicals used in dry cleaning, and many other industrial workplaces are now known to pose a risk. Even if I'd never smoked a cigarette, I'd still been in smoky rooms five or six nights a week on the comedy circuit.

I haven't smoked since 2007, when the smoking ban came in, so more alarming still was the news that the lungs and bladder are not considered clear of the risk of cancer for twenty to twenty-five years after you've given up.

A few days after my cystoscopy, I had an appointment at the Royal Free for a CT scan.

When I arrived at the radiology department I was invited to remove any belts or clothes with metal zips, buckles or buttons. I took off my jeans and put on a back-to-front gown. Then I sat in a holding area with four or five other people. Rather like my experience in the waiting area for preassessment a few days earlier, sitting with my fellow patients was a shock. A couple of them looked as if they'd been exhumed for a scan to check they were dead.

A nurse came out into the corridor and yelled: 'Alan Davies!' which made it hard to be inconspicuous. No one looked up.

The nurse began to attach a cannula to the back of my hand.

'I don't know why my colleague told you to take your clothes off,' he said, betraying some internal conflict in the nursing department. 'You can have a scan fully dressed.'

Computed tomography builds a three-dimensional image of your insides with multiple X-rays. The images are formed by dividing sections of your body into slices, like a salami, which are then blended by algorithms into a whole picture.

The more expensive the CT machine, the more slices they can break you down into. The scanner itself looks like a giant Polo mint. It does not cost 2p. You might be looking at north of a quarter of a million for a top-of-the-range one.

A radiocontrast fluid containing iodine was poured into me via the cannula in the back of my hand. The radiographer seemed busy, as if he'd done a hundred scans already that day, so I didn't ask any questions.

The scan involves lying still for a few minutes so is a nice opportunity for a rest. They were going to look at my bladder but also check my kidneys and ureters (the tubes that link the kidneys to the bladder). First I lay on my back, then he had me turn over as if I was being cooked, which in a way I was, since the dose of radiation is stronger than in a regular X-ray. The radiographer leaves the room and can talk to you from his gallery position behind glass. Not unlike working on the radio, except I couldn't see him from where I was.

Twenty years ago, I made a Radio 4 series called *About a Dog*, written by Graeme Garden from an idea by Debbie Barham, a comedy writer who had died in her twenties. Graeme wanted to make the show in her memory. Claire Goose was in the cast and I was looking forward to meeting her. When

I arrived at the studio I was shown into a special booth where I was to sit for the entire recording. My role was to be the voice of the dog's thoughts, so I had to be isolated for sound purposes. The only window was high up, so I couldn't even see out to look at Miss Goose, who I could hear laughing gaily in the company of the handsome actor Darren Boyd. I fell asleep in there a couple of times and had to be woken by increasingly loud calls into my headphones.

It was a funny series, though. I'm sure Debbie would have liked it; she lost her life to anorexia, such a terribly sad story. I didn't even really know her but she came to mind that day at the Royal Free.

What if I died from this? What if they find something in my kidneys? What if I'm riddled with tumours? Then I'll be absent, like Debbie. And my kids won't have their dad. I imagined Fran and Bobby playing football in Regent's Park with me not on the touchline, just a gap there, or Susie singing in the school concert and a place next to Katie where I should be. I could see so many spaces where I was not: at Christmas lunch around the kitchen table, every year the kids just want it the same, the five of us, Katie roasting a big fish with me on my daft (but very comfortable) special seat for my back; there's a space on the chair lift when the kids are sitting there with their skis dangling down; a space on the sofa where I should be watching *The Incredibles 3* with them, when it eventually comes out. Will Fran be able to go to cricket practice? Who will make videos of him bowling people out? Not there for their exam results, or leaving home, or coming back again, or having their own families, who will help Katie? I lay face down for the second scan and closed my eyes and tried not to fear the worst. I have one clear goal from these dark thoughts; I absolutely must live until *The Incredibles 3* comes out. I have to be there with them for that. I have to.

Have You Ever Thought
About Seeing Someone?

ALAN: You used to work with Jo, didn't you? When she was a
    psychiatric nurse?

THERAPIST: Jo Brand.

A: Yes.

T: Yes, I know Jo well.

A: She thought I should see someone.

T: What did she say?

A: 'Have you ever thought about seeing someone?'

T: [laughs] Why do you think she said that?

A: I mean, I've had a bit of a bad run with work.

T: Are you a comedian? Is that right? That's how you know Jo?

A: Yes, I was doing quite well but I lost a sitcom I was doing for
    Channel 4, it hasn't been recommissioned. I was writing a sitcom
    for myself but I was fired from that and now Radio 1 have cancelled
    the slot for my programme there. But something will turn up. Also,
    I punched her bloke.

T: Jo's?

A: Yeah, that was bad, though he wasn't behaving well. Still—

T: You're not proud of it?

A: No.

T: What happened?

A: It was just drink.

T: You were drunk?

A: No, no, he was.

T: I see.

A: I seem to have trouble with girlfriends, and I always dump on Jo when I'm down about that, so maybe that's why she thinks I should come here.

T: Why do you think you struggle with intimate relationships?

A: Well, my mum died when I was six.

T: I'm sorry.

A: Thanks, it was a long time ago.

T: How did she die?

A: I didn't know where she was buried for a long time.

T: That must have been difficult. Was she ill or was there an accident or—

A: Leukaemia, which I suppose counts as an accident.

T: And your father, and any siblings?

A: He's alive.

T: —

A: I have an older brother and a younger sister.

T: How are things with them?

A: —

T: Do you see them?

A: I never see my brother. He hasn't spoken to me really since I was ten. First day at school, he told the other kids I wasn't his brother then ignored me throughout my schooldays.

T: That must have been difficult.

A: I don't really think about it unless I hear that song 'He Ain't Heavy, He's My Brother'.

T: [laughs]

A: —

T: And your sister?

A: I've helped her out with money for her house. I mean I offered to help, insisted really. She was very grateful.

T: Does that bother you? I just wonder why you mentioned it.

A: You asked about my sister, she's not the reason I'm here.

T: Why are you here?

A: —

117

T: It may be a combination of things.

A: My dad used to come into my room at night.

T: When you were a child?

A: Yes, after Mum died.

T: How old were you?

A: The first time, I think I was about eight.

T: What happened?

A: I think it was daytime. I was getting dressed in my room and he came in.

T: Did he often just come in?

A: Yes, I never had a lock.

T: What did he say?

A: I don't remember, but he made me take off all my clothes, I was only half-dressed, and then we lay on the bed and he was only in his Y-fronts. Then he caressed me. I didn't cuddle him, I was like a doll. He didn't say anything, just kept stroking my body.

T: Did he touch you intimately?

A: No, he never touched my genitals.

T: How long did this go on?

A: I don't know, a few minutes maybe, and then he said: 'This is our special cuddle, you must never tell anyone else about this cuddle.'

T: And that's the first remembered attack? But there were others.

A: I don't think of it as an attack.

T: It's sexual assault, but I understand, I think, because you felt cuddled and coaxed, cajoled maybe, not coerced physically.

A: Yes, other people have much worse experiences. I was never raped.

T: 'I was never raped' is quite a low bar to start from, don't you think?

A: [laughs] Yes.

T: Are you OK?

A: —

T: Would you like a tissue? There are some there on the coffee table.

A: Thanks, yes.

T: —

A: —

T: —

A: He didn't do it again for quite a while, I think, then he would come in more often when I was a bit older. The last time, I got an erection—

T: —

A: —

T: Take your time.

A: Thanks. It was hideous. I wasn't turned on, I hated it. I must have been thirteen, because after my erection kind of stuck into his bare tummy he became increasingly aroused, breathing heavily, and then he ran out of the room and I remember thinking he was probably going to finish himself, I'd started masturbating by then. Then he came in and said, kind of tenderly, that I shouldn't worry if any white stuff came out.

T: —

A: I have told some people – not about that specifically, but that he molested me. I've told girlfriends and I told my gran, my mum's mum, she lives in Australia, but she didn't seem to understand.

T: How often do you think about these things?

A: Every day, every day. If I try to write anything, for my act, or if I try to write a script, I can only think of it. So, all my comedy, I just improvise onstage. I have an idea of a story or something funny I want to relate and I tell it off the top of my head.

T: That's quite a skill.

A: Thanks, born of necessity.

T: Have you ever said anything to your father?

A: On holiday in America, I yelled at him in an airport that he was a poof. That was just the language used at school in 1981, I said it a few times. My brother and sister were there, so they both know about it.

T: Did any of them talk to you about it?

A: God no. My brother told me not to be stupid at the time and it was never mentioned again. My dad sat next to me on the plane home and was nice to me.

T: It's obvious why, isn't it?

A: Because he was worried I'd tell.

T: Yes.

A: —

T: You said earlier that you were fired from your own TV show?

A: Yes, by the production company.

T: How is that possible?

A: I was commissioned by a producer to write a script and she introduced me to a co-writer, it was fun at first. She'd been installed by a high-powered TV exec in this new job. Anyway, we had a falling out, the exec presumably backed her up, and I was out. It was like I'd been expelled.

T: That must have been upsetting.

A: The backstabbing? Yes, it was.

T: It's happened to you before, of course.

A: Being expelled? No, I left school after the lower sixth.

T: No, I don't mean literally, but the experience of a group casting you out, holding you to blame.

A: My family.

T: Yes.

A: My mum was not like that producer.

T: No, I'm sure, but the producer did show you kindness at first, she thought you were funny and promising and she wanted to invest in you.

A: Yes, but in hindsight she shouldn't have been given money to invest.

T: And you and the writer, would it be fair to say there was something fraternal there?

A: I'm always a little envious of people who are close to their brothers, who can laugh with them.

T: You could laugh with him?

A: Yes, he loves to laugh, and so do I.

T: Did he seem to care about you?

A: He listened to a lot of stuff about my girlfriend. It passed the time, all writers would sooner chat about anything rather than work.

T: And who was the other chap?

A: The boss? The moneyman, he was friendly to us but I wasn't really privy to any conversations he had with the producer or with the TV company.

T: Parents often keep things from their children.

A: I didn't see them as parents.

T: But the dynamic is interesting, isn't it, Alan? You and the writer develop a fraternal partnership, an upgrade on your relationship with your brother, and the producer and the boss are older. It might be that you began to feel some familiarity here, the word familiar coming from—

A: Family.

T: If a situation begins to feel familial, for you, it's going to generate anxiety about what can go wrong, not consciously, I must stress, but we can expect this possibility. And then, you may find yourself agitating the bonds between you all, testing connections, because for you a family in crisis is familiar.

A: A familiar familial setup.

T: Yes. Some people who have difficult family relationships go towards dysfunction as it feels normal.

A: The thing we fear comes true.

T: That can happen because of subtle shifts in our behaviour, and perhaps unsubtle ones too. You wanted to break the bond with the producer completely, you placed a strain on your relationship with her and therefore on all the relationships, and the bonds between the others were stronger, so you were cast out.

A: *Plus ça change* . . .

T: We are speculating now but what we have learned today, Alan, is that certain relationships in your working life will find echoes in your early family life, and if we can identify those and the associated feelings before you become destabilised you might be able to change course, compromise and collaborate before you begin to look for—

A: The reassuring familiarity of dysfunction.

T: We need to finish now. How would you like to proceed?

A: I'd like to come again.

T: If you're sure. I should say that, if we are going to do this properly,
    I recommend about four years of weekly sessions.

A: Right.

T: Is that something you'd be prepared to undertake?

A: Yes.

Jesus of Montreal

After midnight there was no one about on Mount Royal. You could walk up, either following the road that twists off that way and then back, so you don't know for sure you're heading to the summit, or you could use the steps, a more direct route. The rain made it difficult to see any signs, and all three of us had long brown hair that was straggling into our eyes. Although in our twenties and fuelled by bonhomie and alcohol, standing still for too long might have slowed us down enough that we would turn back, like a battery-powered toy train struggling on an incline. So, we set off blindly, the two Phils and I, with our shared aversion to retiring for the night.

We took the steps, so we didn't have to keep watching our feet and could look upwards for a glimpse of the hundred-foot illuminated cross at the summit.

Phil Kay wanted to do something all the time. On this night, he'd announced he wanted to climb the famous landmark, not the mountain, the actual cross. So, I went with him, as did Phil Nichol, one third of Canadian musical comedy group Corky and the Juice Pigs, who brought his upbeat stage persona on our ramble, which we undertook, appropriately, *just for laughs*, since it occurred in our downtime at the Montreal Comedy Festival of the same name.

The night before, I'd been with Phil in someone's hotel room, with a lot of people, and across the street we could see a roof terrace about six floors up.

'I'm going to get on that roof,' said Phil, his Scottish accent somehow magnifying his sense of mischief.

The whole building was in darkness but a few minutes later, there was Phil, his trousers round his ankles, being chased by a security guard, all for the benefit of his audience in the hotel.

It takes an hour to the top, overlooking the city and island of Montreal. It was lashing down now but if we kept going uphill we were bound to come to the cross – and we did, only to find it surrounded by high spiked fencing with signs that warned of anti-climb paint. Phil Kay found this notion hilarious – a paint opposed to the pursuit of climbing – and his laughter was infectious, as he mounted the fence, getting about halfway up before dropping to the floor and lying on his side giggling like Peppa Pig at the end of each episode.

As we ambled back down the hill, and moments after the Juice Pig had travelled quite far down a muddy bank on his front, screaming, a police cruiser approached. With our hair lengthened by the rain and hanging across our faces and shoulders, we stood at the side of the road, arms outstretched, aping a triple crucifixion and crying out: 'Which one of us is Jesus of Montreal?'

My first overseas festival of the year had been Melbourne in April, where one of Bob Voice's other acts, deadpan one-liner John Moloney, was opening for forty-five minutes before me. The theatre capacity was four hundred and most nights over three hundred of the seats were empty, making for a drawn-out evening.

In the same building was an additional two-hundred seater. Failing to fill that was another mate from the circuit in London, Lee Evans. One night he and I were alone in the back of a car waiting for a lift to the Festival Club.

'Do you hate it here?' he said.

'Yeah, it's shit,' I said, 'and I love Australia.'

'I just want to go home,' he said. 'I fucking hate it.'

At that moment, the driver jumped in behind the wheel and greeted us in his rearview mirror.

'Oh look, sorry about the wait, guys. Everything OK?'

'Oh yeah, mate, brilliant, thanks,' said Lee.

'How's your festival going?'

'Yeah, really good thanks, really good,' said Lee.

At the Festival Club were three people I didn't know playing pool and no one else. I sent a fax to Bob Voice saying I wanted to come home, even though I was supposed to go on to the Auckland Festival next.

'You really can't pull out of New Zealand; you're the first overseas act their comedy festival has ever had,' came the faxed reply.

Two days later, I bumped into Lee's agent, Addison Cresswell.

'Nightmare!' he said. 'I've 'ad to fuckin' fly down here, first class. He's not fuckin'appy. I've had to come all this way, he wants to go home. It's a nightmare. First class, I flew down! Nightmare!'

Two weeks later, I opened at the Watershed Theatre in Auckland. It had two hundred and fifty seats with tables and chairs in front of the stage, some raked seating behind and then a balcony on three sides. Perfect. I was to do my solo hour show, and it was sold out. Paul Horan and Scott Blanks who ran the event couldn't have been nicer.

'How do you feel about extra shows?' they said.

I was booked for six shows but we squeezed in eight. On the first night, a satisfied punter tipped me with a bag of grass so big it would have taken me all year to smoke it.

With all my shows sold out in advance, my promoters took me to an Auckland Warriors rugby match, where Cook Island drummers, standing at the end of the field in traditional dress, pounded out a deafening beat throughout a thrilling game. After that I was taken jet boating, black-water rafting (through caves in an inner-tube), and clay-pigeon shooting. I declined a bungee jump.

It was one of the best weeks of my comedy career – my life, actually.

Montreal was a different affair. *Juste pour rire* (Just for Laughs) was a business convention with agents, promoters, management and PR companies, TV executives, film producers and the like swamping the town to network. Most of the comedians would look for one another like a secret society.

I did have some sympathy for Karen Koren, though, who was there representing Phil Kay.

'Phil's been chucked out of a VIP area for throwing cake at a man in a suit,' she said to me one night. 'He's behaving like a *student*!'

My own agent, Bob Voice, hadn't wanted me to go and have my 'head turned' by promises of riches in America. He needn't have worried about losing his act; no one paid me any attention, possibly because I had no representation schmoozing around the place saying: 'Hi, I used to be Mike Yarwood's driver.'

Each morning, I'd go down to reception to pick up the latest free sheets produced by comics, giving 'information' about festival events. One group of American stand-ups, including Andy Kindler, Blaine Capatch and Sarah Silverman, was going to stage a seminar at noon the next day called 'How to be a Hack Comedian'.

There were industry events all day, but this was the one the comics went to. Every trope we use was exposed: clichés about gender or race, talking loudly at the end of the sentence to cue laughs, and many more. I cringed when they brought up faux-laughing at the end of jokes to suggest spontaneity.

Much as I loved Phil Kay, I didn't just want to be on the outside of the festival, anarchically undermining the event and not meeting anyone new. I wanted to hang out with Sarah Silverman and her clever friends.

There were some US comics, however, who couldn't care less about the cool kids. Among them, Nick Di Paolo was storming all his gigs. He took no prisoners with a provocative anti-PC set. Sample joke: 'I saw a four-hundred-pound woman with a rape alarm, like she's gonna NEED IT.' (Louder at the end of the sentence.)

Phil Kay and I were leaning against the wall at the back of Club Soda watching Di Paolo when I offered Phil a hundred Canadian dollars to go up onstage and moon him.

As I was telling the person next to me about the dare I'd set Phil, a pale-blue moon appeared in the corner of the wide black box that was the club's stage set. It was Phil's bottom against a starless night sky.

Later that night, after a few more drinks, Phil and I loudly celebrated the genius of Norm Macdonald to . . . Norm Macdonald.

The next morning I saw Norm again, in the hotel foyer.

'I'm sorry about last night,' I said.

'Why?' he said.

'We were pretty pissed,' I said.

'I thought you guys were great!' he said, to my relief.

Everyone stayed in the same hotel and at one point two of the elevators became stuck. I was in the first one to be released and there was laughter among the occupants as we were set free. The second lift took longer to open and the first person out was livid.

'She's a really big *agent*,' someone whispered.

I was sure I saw Sarah Silverman emerge and later that evening took the chance to ask her about it. Phil was nowhere around; maybe he had a gig. After a few minutes talking to me, Sarah said she needed to go to her room.

'Oh, OK,' I said, thinking that was that: I was too dull.

'You can come up if you want?' she said.

So, I went with her to the elevator, in which we had a laugh about getting stuck again, then ambled along a corridor until we were alone in her room.

As she was chatting away from the bathroom, I was wondering how to turn this into a romantic liaison (*why not say how funny and attractive she is*) when I noticed some soft-porn magazines on the bed.

'You have a lot of porn mags,' I said.

'Yeah,' she said.

'How come?'

'Read them if you want,' she said.

I picked one up and was holding it when she came out of the bathroom. She was tall, with big, dark eyes, long black hair and a kind of crooked half-smile through which she kept up a stream of witty chat, and there I was clutching a dirty book like a shoplifting teen.

'Me and my friends make up "reader's letters" and send them in,' she said.

'Are any of yours in here?'

'No, not in those,' she said.

I wanted to pay her a compliment on her appearance or suggest meeting up, but she seemed ready to go back downstairs. Bearing in mind I was twenty-nine, not fourteen, it was odd that I couldn't read the room (*beautiful woman with whom you have plenty in common, as twenty-something festival delegates, invites you to read pornographic magazines alone with her in a hotel room*).

My default psychological position filled the void like a factory reset: *She probably doesn't want me here.*

We went back downstairs.

The next time I saw her was late in the evening. She looked upset.

'My agent says I've ruined my career,' she said.

'Your agent says? Don't listen to the *agents*!'

'I don't know,' said Sarah, 'he might have a point.'

'What did you do?'

'I have this thing where I can name all fifty states in reverse alphabetical order really fast.'

'That doesn't sound bad,' I said. 'It sounds funny.'

'Yeah, but I did it while I had my finger in my vagina.'

'Your finger in your vagina?' I said, finding that pretty cool, actually.

'Yeah,' she said. 'I turned around, bent over, put my finger in my vagina and recited all the states in reverse order: Wyoming, Wisconsin, West Virginia, Washington—'

'I don't think that's going to end your career; it'll *make* your career, more likely.'

'Well, he says I'm finished.'

Channel 4 had booked all the British comics in Montreal to appear on a series of stand-up shows for the UK. The producer was having a hard time pinning Phil Kay down on the content of his seven-minute set.

Instead of doing the agreed material, Phil climbed up the side of the stage to the lettering on the *juste pour rire* logo. The *j* came away in his hand and he stuck it back on upside down. Now it looked like the letter *r* so the logo read *ruste pour rire*, which tickled Phil no end.

'Rust for laughs!' he said. 'Haha, rust!'

The audience loved his infectious anarchy.

I performed the same bland set – about events at the Olympic Games – I'd done at the Festival Gala show. It said nothing about me or what was on my mind. I'd been lazy and risk-averse, making safe choices in all directions. Could I ever be as carefree as Phil? I needed to stick my finger in my vagina.

By the time Phil Nichol, Phil Kay and I arrived back in town at the bottom of Mount Royal, the rain had stopped and the sun had come up. We passed a bus parked at the side of the road. I pointed out the destination sign on the front and once again Phil Kay doubled up in laughter.

We all agreed we wanted to get on board, which said something about us; not everyone would want to take a bus that was going to:

NOWHERE SPECIAL

A Producer Calls

Throughout 1995, I'd been seeing more and more of Allie Byrne, though I'd always felt she was slumming it a little.

'I could get used to hanging out here,' she'd said one night, somewhat unconvincingly, as she sat in my basement flat watching me and Simon Clayton share another joint. I wondered whether she was passing up invitations from her old friends at Westminster School and Cambridge.

On Valentine's Day 1996 I was out with her when my phone rang and a familiar, smoky Scottish brogue came on the line.

'It's Susie Belbin.'

'Oh, hi,' I said.

I looked at Allie; she knew I'd been waiting for this call.

'I've got good news,' said Susie.

I had the same feeling of my insides being replaced by cold air as when I first saw my name in *Time Out*.

'You've got the part,' she said.

'I've got the part,' I said to Allie.

'David and I are sorry it's taken so long for them to decide,' said Susie. 'It was Alan Yentob, really; he's the controller of the channel and he wasn't sure, with you being unknown to the BBC One audience, but he's come around. The taster filming we did showed you have something. Scripts will come first and then there'll be rehearsals but that's not until the summer. Any problems you can always call me, OK?'

'Yes, thanks, Susie.'

Allie was waiting next to me as I hung up.

'Nice to meet you, Jonathan Creek,' she said.

Three weeks later, I had a dinner for my thirtieth at Joe Allen's in Covent Garden, from which I still have the photos.

Caroline Quentin, who was going to co-star with me in *Jonathan Creek*, came, along with her then husband, Paul Merton. Louise Rennison was there, as was Simon Godley (who was still in the sitcom I was fired from). Jo Brand brought her friend Christina from their nursing days; Jim Miller, Keith Dover and Simon Clayton were all present, as was Mark Lamarr (who characteristically turned up at the end), Allie brought her equally clever friend from school, Helena Bonham-Carter.

Everything seemed rosy with this new blended family from my comedy past and my TV future.

Three months earlier, I'd taken part in a rehearsed reading at the BBC of a sitcom written by Richard Pinto and Sharat Sardana. They'd met at Forest School, up the road from my old school Bancroft's, though I'd been a pupil a few years ahead of them. After a gig one night they'd thought I'd be a good fit for their latest lead character so they'd handed me a script.

A rehearsed reading is a significant step, one short of a pilot episode. People from the comedy department shuffle in to listen to a cast brought in for the day.

This was what I still wanted to do, undeterred by being fired from my own show: act in a sitcom like the ones I'd grown up with – *Porridge*, *Dad's Army*, *Cheers*, and many more.

The BBC bods laughed in all the intended places. The writers had promise and the cast was good too; a young Rhys Ifans was there, but nothing came of it, at least not straightaway. Richard and Sharat soon made their names on *Goodness Gracious Me*, after which Channel 4 took their sitcom, with the title *Small Potatoes* and the wonderful Irish comedian Tommy Tiernan as the lead.

It was Richard and Sharat, and their producer Anil Gupta, who got me through the door at BBC Television, though no one could have known how that day was going to change my life.

After the reading, one of the audience approached me and introduced herself as Susie Belbin.

'Well done,' she said. 'I work in the comedy department. Do you know David Renwick?'

'No, I don't know—'

'He writes *One Foot in the Grave*, which I produce and usually direct as well.'

'Oh yes,' I said. 'That's hilarious.'

I'd barely seen any episodes, I was always out in comedy clubs and a show about a retired couple hadn't drawn me in, but I knew it had won over several million other viewers.

'David's written a new show, which we're casting, and I wondered if you might like to come and meet with him.'

'Oh, yes, of course, I'd love to.'

'It's not a sitcom as such, more a murder mystery, but still funny. Are you going to the BBC Christmas party?'

'No, no, I'm not.'

'Well, I shall ensure you receive an invitation. David will be there.'

The party was a black-tie affair, my first. I rented a suit from a dress-hire shop in Stamford Hill but on the day there was snow on the ground so I put on my new duffle coat. John Hegley, the eternally wise comic poet, had complimented me on it one night and I'd confided in him that it had cost £85, which he thought a shrewd investment in quality outerwear but I thought *extravagant*.

The party was held in the main studio at Television Centre. There was a carpet and people checking invites. Beyond the entrance, swathes of fabric and coloured lighting served to distract you from noticing you were at a soirée in a hangar.

Hundreds of people were milling about. I scanned the room for the Two Ronnies, Terry and June or Bruce Forsyth and then ran into Bob Mortimer, who I knew from a gig at the Greyhound in Sydenham about five years previously. He was now the co-host of *Shooting Stars* with Vic Reeves. Mark

Lamarr was a team captain on that show but I couldn't see him; next to Bob, in a stylish dress that possibly cost more than eighty-five quid, was their other regular panellist, Ulrika Jonsson. I was about to be introduced when Susie Belbin appeared at my side and led me over to meet David Renwick instead.

I liked David immediately. He has a droll, sardonic quality and it never bothers me that his stated belief is not that the glass is half-empty but rather there is no glass. He asked a few questions and we talked about comedy. He told me that Richard Wilson hadn't wanted to take the role of Victor Meldrew as he was only fifty-five at the time. There was no chance I would hesitate in the same way.

Soon after the party, the first script arrived. There was a drawing on the title page of a small-headed man wearing a long, dark, flared coat. He had a notebook and pencil in hand, but was peering out with round, wire-rimmed specs and just a couple of hairs sticking up. He looked unthreatening, brainy and displeased to be disturbed.

If this was David's sketched vision of Jonathan Creek, he didn't look anything like me, whereas the part of his nemesis, Maddy Magellan, had been written for Caroline Quentin.

Caroline was short with narrow hips like a dancer combined with a big chest and a bawdy and flirtatious sense of humour, like someone from a saucy seaside postcard. She was quick-witted, had been working since her teens, could sing, improvise with the best of them and battled for equal pay on *Men Behaving Badly*. All in all, a confident, formidable character, but vulnerable too, I would learn. I hoped it would help that we'd met before. She'd even appeared in a sketch on *Alan's Big One*.

One scene in the first series of *Jonathan Creek* – where Maddy chaotically cooks dinner, with smoke pouring out of the oven – was based on an actual evening David had spent with Caroline and Paul. David said she was funny all night.

Maddy was a devious ball of energy playing the same role for Jonathan Creek that Dr Watson did for Sherlock Holmes, a conduit for the viewer. No one knows what's going on in Holmes's or Creek's heads, so someone has to ask questions, exasperated at being two steps behind their brainy accomplice.

David knew how that relationship needed to function, understanding all the conventions of television, the storytelling tricks and devices, the clichés he could parody and the opportunities for homage. He would also place the odd cultural reference that only a few viewers might recognise, not minding if only one person understood the joke.

Nicholas Lyndhurst from *Only Fools and Horses* had turned *Jonathan Creek* down. Hugh Laurie had been on board but changed his mind and so the auditions began. I was the thirty-eighth person they saw. All white males, of course; it was still the twentieth century.

When I went in to meet Susie and David, they first asked me about the script and all I needed to say was, 'Brilliant, so clever, loved it,' but I blathered on with some thoughts that nobody needed to hear. I'd expected plenty of laughs but found a complex murder story (that I should have read more than once). The humour was quite understated, with Creek a cerebral and reluctant hero. A frown formed on David's face and I thought I'd blown it.

To my relief, Susie organised shooting a couple of scenes in her office at the BBC, with the furniture moved aside and a skeleton crew cobbled together, all of them doing it as a favour to their producer. Then we moved outside and shot in the *Blue Peter* garden with the bust of Petra (the Alsatian I'd watched on TV as a child) sitting on a plinth looking over Caroline's shoulder.

Susie was going to a lot of trouble and I was nervous, but it was reassuring to have Caroline there as she seemed to be on my side. She'd been waiting for the show to take off for a long time. David told me later that he'd been working on it for five years.

I also learned later that turning up in a duffle coat to the Christmas party, looking as if I was in the wrong place, had been the clincher for Susie and David. That was exactly how Creek would have appeared.

I Won't Be Able to See
You Now I'm on TV

ALAN: I've got a big part in a BBC drama.

THERAPIST: That's nice, congratulations.

A: We start rehearsing next week. After that, I don't know if I'll be able to come and see you.

T: Where are the rehearsals?

A: St Augustine's Church hall in Hammersmith.

T: Is that easy for you to get to?

A: Overground to Liverpool Street and then a tube. It's fine. They have their own rehearsal rooms, the BBC, in Acton but they're now a separate company so they would charge us £350 a day. That's where all the sitcoms used to rehearse in the past, so different casts would meet in the canteen, in their different costumes. I was hoping to go there but the church hall is two hundred quid a week.

T: That sounds a bit barmy. About the BBC rehearsal rooms.

A: Yep. It's only for a couple of weeks, though, and then we start filming.

T: Will you be busy, long hours?

A: Yes, they do an eleven-day fortnight. They've done all the preproduction and the casting, locations, everything. It's five months' filming.

T: Is it a big production?

T: I think so, yes.

T: Quite a different thing for you, then. Will you be OK for five months, Alan?

A: I think so, I don't know. The producer is on my side, so I'll have someone I can speak to.

T: That's important. How do you feel about not coming here?

A: Not good, really. I don't want to stop.

T: You know you can always call, if you need to, it is possible sometimes to do a session over the phone.

A: Thank you. I'm just conscious that I made a commitment to come every week for four years and now I've broken that.

T: Sometimes, events conspire against us.

A: They certainly do.

T: —

A: I'm going to keep a diary.

T: That's a good idea, some journalling.

The Secret Diary
of Jonathan Creek

Day 1 Tuesday June 25 1996

Read-through of episodes 1, 2 and 3.

I don't know if I'll be able to stay off the fags. Producer is a chimney. Some casting isn't done. I've suggested Tony Curtis for a couple of roles. Got a laugh the first time.

I sat next to Caroline Quentin. We have to get on or the show may be no good. She's in remarkably good spirits given her former agent has failed to pass on £250,000ish of hers.

After each reading there is a discussion. BBC Head of Comedy, the producer, director and writer confer. Caroline tries on wigs. Actors smoke and look unhappy.

I think about football and the different girls in the room and then football. It's [the Euros semi-final] *England v Germany tomorrow evening.*

Lunch gets lost but turns up in a cab. I eat biscuits and grin stupidly at people. Caroline gets on well with everyone. So do I. I suggest her husband for a role. Producer says she never thought of him. Very noncommittal, necessarily. Quite an easy slow day, so I don't know why I fall asleep on the tube.

Day 2 June 26

May I not be the Gareth Southgate of this production. All the rehearsing went well and then the Germans won on penalties.

Day 3 June 27

I was late today. Tube strike. I don't blame them, it's not nice on there when it's hot. Caroline was easy to work with this afternoon but this morning things didn't seem to click. Marcus [our director] said he was pleased I'd noticed.

I watched Caroline on Men Behaving Badly tonight. She and Martin Clunes are really good together. I'll just do what I can then, eh? It's hard work not being a stand-up comedian. Working without adrenaline. Just talking, quite pensively most of the time. If I deliver any of these lines like a stand-up it's going to look daft. Really don't like getting up early but I'm disciplining myself. It's not quite like being in the army, as Allie says – I may yet enter her for Private Eye's 'Luvvies' – but it's not like being a stand-up.

Day 4 June 28

Caroline can be extremely warm and tactile. Today we walked arm-in-arm to lunch at a nearby sandwich bar. She paid. Teased me about my ignorance of Italian soft cheeses: 'Is it too grown up for you? Do you like cheddar?'

All true of course.

Stretched out on a makeshift bed in the rehearsal room, she insisted on my snuggling up to her.

'Do you love me very much?' she said, playing with my hair.

'Yes,' I said, wondering if she was larking or bonkers. Both? My trouble is, her mood affects my concentration. I'm a little inhibited.

Day 5 June 29

Just doing the morning today as I've got to go to Manchester to do a Euro 96 show with Nick Hancock. Jo Brand will be there too, which will be nice as Czech/German jokes may be hard to do.

Two hours rehearsing with Caroline, very different from yesterday, she seems irritated and this surfaces after about an hour. 'If he doesn't look at me, I've got nothing to play off,' she said to Marcus, and later: 'I don't give a fuck which way we do it.'

To me: 'I'm not saying you're playing it wrong.'

I wanted to go home then. I do worry about her ever-changing moods. At the moment, I'm just staring at my script and keeping quiet. Allie reveals she's rarely been involved in a production where there haven't been tears in rehearsal. Stand-ups don't do this, you'd last about five minutes. Acting is an insecure profession peopled, ironically, with insecure people and I may as well include myself in that.

Day 6 Sunday June 30

OFF. Hurrah. Hungover all day. Didn't go to the final.

Day 7 July 1

New actors today: Tony 'Gold Blend' Head and Saskia 'Tall' Mulder, both good. Caroline went shopping and bought a handbag for £185. Is that normal? I know nothing of handbags. We came to the scene which, on Saturday, Caroline didn't 'give a fuck' about and she said: 'We did it over there and you got grumpy.'

I said nothing and she ran over and kissed me on the cheek. The rest of the day she kept saying she would slap me or she tried to take my shirt off. Meanwhile, director, writer and producer claim to be 'very pleased' so far.

Day 8 July 2

I had lunch with Rae [Baker] who is 5'11" and playing a model, appropriately. Very beautiful. Absurdly attractive in fact. She told me her life story over lunch, so she's got the makings of an actress. Quite nice to meet someone who is prepared to be furious about overpriced West End shows and the neglect of fringe theatre by an unwitting public. Like most actors, she felt stand-up was terrifying. She's 21 and about to model swimwear on GMTV.

Good Morning Television. What a name. That name is the reason I've never watched it. Caroline reckons I will tomorrow.

Day 9 July 3

Missed GMTV. Sheila Gish arrived to play steely-eyed Serena Shale. I was introduced and she held my hand for a long time and said: 'So nice to meet you.' Well, I liked her straightaway. Everyone did. Tony Head knows her and couldn't wait to embrace her. By the end of the day, Caroline was embracing her as well. I didn't and felt like a small failure.

Caroline insisted I stroke her arm today. Sheila saw a kindred spirit there. I can see a lot of massaging ahead.

Saskia is a Supermodel's sister. Allie knew all about Karen Mulder, I didn't. Saskia's obviously used to being in her shadow. When I asked if she was related to KM, she said: 'The big question.'

Strangely disappointed to find that I wasn't very excited, she said: 'You don't know much about fashion, do you?'

Saskia sometimes seems to be 14 but then she talks about travelling to Milan to model when she was a schoolgirl and about KM's home in Monaco and she seems to be 40. She did a photoshoot today in a little black dress. All the boys casually stared at her. I went to talk duffle coats with Glamorous Annie Costume when word came through that Saskia was in a bikini. I ran out to see this, leaving CQ in mid-sentence, she said, in front of Jo [2nd AD] and Lorraine [script supervisor], who found it hilarious. Really hilarious.

Oh, and Dr Who [Colin Baker] was in today. Not my era, I'm afraid. I'm a Pertweenian.

Day 10 July 4

Caroline in hairdresser's for six hours. Jo, on a mobile to the Dorchester, where the £4 million hairdo is being constructed, kept reporting back: 'She's had four colours put in.'

'It's being washed.'

Rumour has it Paul Merton's going to be hired.

Day 11 Friday July 5

Photos at TV Centre for BBC publicity. Caroline has to stand on a box. Complains about her tits being in the way. In one polaroid we look like we're queuing for a bus.

Day 12 July 6

Last night I saw Bill Cosby [at the Albert Hall]. *Bumped into David Renwick there. We both really enjoyed it.*

Day 14 July 8

Is that doing justice to Cosby? Does it mention the tears in my eyes? The standing ovation? Nothing to do with Creek, though, is it? Except Cosby's doing One Foot in the Grave in the US. So he and I are David's latest leading men. Ha! Ha!

Day 15 July 9

The last day of rehearsal and I'm glad, I want to get on with it now. Getting nervous about tomorrow. Should be all right, I've only got four lines.

Day 16 Wednesday July 10

Ten hours on set today and I did nothing at all. I ate quite a lot of cake. I wish I had a pound for everyone who said: 'That's filming.' Still, it was good to watch everyone at work.

I've been asked by Viv [make-up] *to wear tinted moisturiser. Tried it, saw no discernible difference, and decided against. After conversations with director and producer, this seemed OK. Viv said: 'Oh, you're going to the producer about make-up?'*

Several remarks about how I was going to be 'difficult' and 'starry'.

Day 17 July 11

   Acting!

   'Morning, I was just passing.' My first line.

   Felt sorry for Saskia, who spent the day in underwear or a tiny robe and couldn't get what Marcus wanted.

Day 18 July 12

   Hungover, day off. Played football, went to café.

Day 19 July 13 off.

   Saw Bill [Bailey] *at Store – laughed.*

Day 20 Sunday July 14

   Brick Lane Market 8am. Too many cooks round the camera. Shut up and film it. I don't know what the technical problems are, of course, but I do know it's all taking too long. All afternoon in the curry house next door to our favourite bagel shop. Very hot and uncomfortable. Wish I could have sat there in my pants. Could have really. I was pleased to do a good closeup last thing in the day. Important scenes as it's Maddy and Creek's first proper meeting. Relieved to do them well. We'd rehearsed them a lot. Had a drink after work with Caroline, Brett [1st AD], *Jo and Angus* [location manager]. *Everyone very tired but it was good.*

Day 23 Wednesday July 17

   Marcus and Susie are happy with the Indian restaurant. Colin Baker says he's heard a rumour that we'll have to shoot it all again due to faulty film stock. He's been here an age doing nothing, so I think mischief has crept in. Viv make-up said she'd send him to the set in a long white beard to hint he'd been kept waiting too long. Good to see her laughing.

And that's where it ends. It's all handwritten in pencil and the rest of the journal I'd bought is empty.

The summer went on and we filmed one ninety-minute episode and four sixty-minute episodes, that's three hundred and thirty minutes of television at roughly four minutes per eleven-hour shooting day. It was a long way from storming the Comedy Store at two o'clock in the morning.

One hot afternoon, I was complaining that I really wanted to wear anything but my duffle coat.

'Yes, but just think,' said Caroline, 'it could be Jack Dee and Dawn French standing here.' And we both knew neither of us wanted that.

In that summer of 1996, there always seemed to be coke about. If we were socialising, one or two crew members, whose names I've long forgotten, would chop out lines for people, like me, who didn't buy their own. I joined in a couple of times and then gave it a miss. God knows what Susie Belbin and David Renwick would have said, had they known. 'You're fired,' probably.

The rest of the crew couldn't have been nicer. There were people my age, like Rob Sellars and Darren Wisker, the prop boys, and Jo Cole; and plenty of others with a sense of humour, like Dickon Peschek, the prop master, and Maggie in the production office. During a conversation about horoscopes, Maggie overheard Caroline say: 'I'm a Cancerian.'

To which Maggie responded: 'Oh, that makes me a Librarian, then.'

We filmed in two blocks, with a week off in the middle, during which I moved house to St Mary's Grove, round the corner from Canonbury Square in Islington. Bob Voice was a guarantor to help secure the place before my *Jonathan Creek* money had come through. It was stressful but we did it and it was kind of him.

I'd wanted to live round there since I'd visited the old Tower Theatre three times in 1983, as an A-level student, to see Trevor Griffiths's *Comedians*.

Allie called a third and final strike on our relationship the night before I moved. She'd always been the umpire, and now I was out, which made for a tearful last evening alone in my memory-filled flat on Evering Road. I'd been drunk and shouty a few times, and coped poorly with the filming hours and the stress. I forget what Allie said, but it will have been a safe-for-work, more erudite version of: 'I absolutely do not need any more of this fucking shit.'

One evening, soon after we'd started seeing each other, I'd been at Allie's parents' apartment on Regent's Park, where I found myself momentarily alone with her mum for the first time. Turning to me, she raised her hand high above her head, so it was level with my eyes, and said: 'She has gone from right up here . . .' Now she dropped her hand to the floor. 'To right down there.'

I should have taken the hint.

When I moved into my new house I plugged in my stereo, pulled out a Jimmy Cliff record and sang along to 'Better Days Are Coming'.

The Dead Rose

LOUISE: A therapist? Oh God. Now I'll never hear from you.

ALAN: You will, I'm just going back to seeing him now all that filming's finished.

L: Finally, how was it?

A: It took five months to shoot and I feel like I need another five to recover.

L: Is the therapist helping you with the extremely arduous life you lead?

A: Stop it, he's nice.

L: Not meant to be nice. Whose idea was that? Yours or your subconscious's?

A: Very good.

L: Is he Austrian? 'Lie down on ze couch, Herr Davies, and tell me the most appalling secrets of your mind. Imagine no one, not even I, is here, you are alone. Dare you speak the truth? What is ze worst thing you have ever done?'

A: I once had a wank in a car park.

L: Is that it? Blokes can't get in a car without masturbating, in my experience. You're all disgusting.

A: Not in a car, in a car park.

L: What car park?

A: That's the detail you want?

L: Just for context.

A: Loughton tube station.

L: Oh Christ, where is that? Zone six? How sordidly suburban. So sad. Stop being vulgar and tell me about ze analyst. Do you lie down? Does he sit behind you pulling faces?

A: No, we sit in chairs and what makes you think it's a man?

L: You've got a woman to talk to? How nice, are you going to try to get off with her? Or do you have to be drunk for that?

A: It's a man, and he's not Austrian. He's Welsh.

L: You have a Welsh therapist, I've heard it all now. Like Tom Jones?

A: No, he's shorter, with a beard.

L: A singing therapist! Is it called the Singing Cure? Careful or he'll get you in an Eisteddfod. Where did you find him? Or did you ask for a short, bearded Welshman?

A: Jo Brand recommended him.

L: Oh, why didn't you say? I love Jo. Have you discovered anything yet?

A: The other day, I had some gardeners in and they were clearing a lot of stuff out, weeds mainly . . .

L: Is this in your swanky new Islington pad?

A: It's not swanky. You can wet your finger and wipe nicotine off the window frames. The previous owners were slobs, but really stuck-up snob-slobs. I asked the estate agent to ask them whether you're allowed to install satellite dishes, because it's a conservation area—

L: There you are, swanky.

A: It's just a terraced house. Two floors, built in the sixties. Anyway, the estate agent said he'd asked the seller, who said he 'didn't know anyone in the street who'd want one'.

L: Ha!

A: The houses have all got flat roofs, so I went up through my hatch to have a look, and there are dishes on at least half the houses on my side, just out of sight from the road.

L: I love the sound of your hatch. So, what heinous crime did the gardeners commit that you need the Swansea Freud to investigate?

A: I'd asked them not to cut down this one rosebush. It had been pruned for years so that it was a stem about three feet high with a ball of roses on top, bright-red ones. I was in my bathroom looking over the garden, the gardener had left behind two lads to get on with the work and one of them took a pair of shears, went up to this beautiful rose and just chopped it right at the bottom. I saw him and I couldn't even shout out, I wanted to bang on the window and yell at him to stop but I just watched.

L: Did they know you were watching?

A: No, but I went down and asked them why they did it. They were stoned I think, just hadn't listened.

L: So, what did Tom Jones say about that?

A: Well, I remembered something else, this is the best bit about therapy for me, you never know what you might remember in a session and then you're working out why one thing triggered the other.

L: Have you had a previous bush trimmed?

A: No, in my old flat, you remember, in Evering Road?

L: The one where the Krays had murdered someone.

A: That was in a different flat up the street. In my garden there I had a wall at the end, backing onto the side of a house in Norcott Road. There was a big tree in my garden, which was pushing against the wall, and the couple who lived there said to me they were worried about the wall falling on their granddaughter. Then one day there were two men in my garden trampling on these loose stone steps surrounding the tree, wrecking the paving and smashing the wall down with sledge hammers.

L: They were in your garden?

A: Yeah, but I didn't know they were going to be there, I just saw them through the window.

L: And you couldn't say anything.

A: I wanted to shout out but I couldn't, I just watched, and went back into my front room.

L: What happened?

A: They took the bricks away and put a fence up. I don't know if it was their wall or not.

L: What did your therapist say after this gripping tale?

A: He asked me why I was unable to protect my boundaries.

L: Oh, that's clever.

A: Yes, because I thought of my dad straightaway.

L: Of course, not a respecter of boundaries.

A: Exactly. One of the things that abuse has left me with is not being able to defend myself. In these cases, people literally coming into my property and me watching them doing damage.

L: When your dad came to your room, did you want to cry out?

A: It was all done in such silence. I think of that little boy, being made to take his pyjamas off so he's naked, and it's done by whispering. So my brother and sister couldn't hear.

L: —

A: Lou, you still there?

L: —

A: Lou?

L: I'm sorry, Al, I'm sorry, that just is too awful.

A: I did try to stop him, and if I made enough noise or fuss he'd give up, but I had to make it into a kind of game, like I'd go down to the bottom of the bed. Do you remember having sheets tucked in, not duvets, and you could go right to the bottom?

L: Yes.

A: Sometimes I didn't like to go to the bottom, it was a bit scary, but when he came in I'd go down there and hope he'd go away.

L: Oh dear, this is too awful.

A: Yes.

L: Do you ever see him now?

A: Yes, we still pretend all's well at Christmas. It's as if he never did anything, and I'm away from there now, I have my own life.

L: But your boundaries, Al, how will you protect them?

A: People think it's OK to say what they want to me sometimes.

L: That poor rosebush.

A: I'm still sad about that, and now I realise it's my dad's fault it's even more annoying.

Because Life's
Complicated Enough

At our first-ever meeting, I'd told my agent, genial wealth-generator Bob Voice, that I absolutely did not want to do ads. Although the sixties' countercultural notion of 'selling out' was not in my lexicon, it was still in the air around me among the older, pot-smoking outliers of the Alternative Comedy scene, one of whose number told me the seventies were great because if you were out of work the Labour government 'paid your mortgage'.

I was more familiar with the Sex Pistols album *Some Product*, which had been created as a follow-up to the exhilarating *Never Mind the Bollocks* with the stated intention of making a profit by turning out any old rope and taking money from The Man in that way. Malcolm McLaren had already perpetrated *The Great Rock 'n' Roll Swindle* by producing a Sex Pistols film and album of that name. 'Never trust a hippy' was the mantra; use the system.

But none of these philosophies or worldviews played into my decision-making. I told Bob there was no way I'd do ads, someone would have to pay me 'a million pounds', an unthinkable sum. This was inspired partly by Eddie Izzard, who'd explained to me what he called a 'fuck-off number'. If you don't want to do a gig, deploy a many-zeroed figure and stand clear; let everyone know you're expensive to the point of 'beyond purchase'.

If you were to ask Bill Bailey how much to charge for a gig, he'd recommend that you: 'Say the highest number you can think of without laughing, and then double it.'

In hindsight, perhaps I'd set Bob a challenge: rather than a fuck-off number, now he had a target figure. I'd named my price and he knew what advertisers wanted, at least in the nineties: a likeable, inoffensive leading actor who plays a morally faultless enemy of evil on a TV show pulling in twelve million ABC1s with considerable disposable income. And this one was funny too, taking the viewer way off the bank-y scent with the skills he'd learned over the years as a white male stand-up. Perfect.

I was prone to mock cockney at moments when I was losing confidence. As a boy, I'd been mortified by my father's *Brief Encounter*-style telephone voice.

'Yes, rather!' he'd say, standing by our hallway Bakelite agreeing to play badminton in Chingford on Wednesday, but it sounded like, 'Yes, ra-bo!'

One day I asked him: 'Why do you say, "Yes, ra-bo"?'

'You hate me, don't you?' he said.

I was ten. I didn't answer.

'You really, really hate me, don't you?' he said.

One more thing to feel ashamed about. A part of me did always hate him but I'd do anything he wanted, except empty the dishwasher.

So, to differentiate myself from him, I adopted a slacker, unclipped intonation, like the voices I heard on the terraces at Arsenal; the accent you might think of as 'Essex' today. A collective tone and rhythm, sometimes called Estuary English (referring to the Thames), that developed as locals mixed with the thousands of Cockneys who'd moved out to the green belt in a postwar wave of local-government relocation from London's blitzed East End.

My familiarity with that intonation was what enabled me to shine in a student production of Steven Berkoff's *Decadence*, where two actors play four parts and must swing between toff and oik.

The Abbey Road and St John's Wood Mutual Benefit Building Society was formed in 1874. In 1944 it merged with the National Building Society, which began life in 1849 as the Metropolitan Freehold Land Society.

In 1997, Bob told me that Abbey National were prepared to hire me for three years at the rising rate of £300,000 for the first year, £325,000 for the second and £350,000 for the third: £975,000 in all for six, maybe ten days' work a year. These sums would dwarf what I earned as Jonathan Creek, as a stand-up comic, as everything I'd ever been put together – ice-cream seller, sandwich-board man, dishwasher, greengrocer, radio host, sacked sitcom writer . . .

Bob was beaming at me through his white beard, over his middle-aged spread and beyond his big desk, a modern-day Mephistopheles tempting me, poor old Faustus, into selling his soul.

But I was no Faustus; I was an entrepreneur from Thatcher's Enterprise Allowance Scheme. I'd said I'd never do ads but caved at the first offer.

'It was too much money to turn down,' I said, twenty-five years later, during an interview for *Richard Herring's Leicester Square Theatre Podcast*.

Richard tried to stifle the grin that was appearing on his face as a derisory murmur spread around the three hundred or so comedy punters.

'I didn't have the backbone,' I said, placating those in the crowd who didn't want to hear excuses for the sellout.

I had earned a regrettable security.

But, how might I have behaved if I *had* turned it down?

I've seen comedians telling their audience they've rejected ads, as if to say: 'I'm still one of you!' and drawing cheers and adulation.

Might I have succumbed to that kind of humblebrag?

I wanted people to know how much I was paid, so they'd understand me and sympathise with my choice to side with the financiers, the lenders and the megarich City boys.

But life doesn't work like that. You can't make people think of you as you'd like them to. Your every action reveals something about you, never more so than when writing an autobiography. There's no point in me hoping that I'll be viewed in a particular way because of how I present myself in this book; my true character will slip through the gaps, between the lines, in defiance of me. Might as well be honest, then. I did it for the money and then felt eternally guilty.

After four years of my ads, Abbey National was swallowed up by Spanish mega-banco Santander and the famous brand disappeared from the high street forever. Oops.

*

But no one saw that coming when I received the first scripts. We were to shoot them in Cape Town and the director would be John Lloyd, who specialised in making funny ads for Barclays (with Rowan Atkinson) and Red Rock Cider (with Leslie Nielsen), among others. More significantly to me, he was the producing genius behind *Not the Nine O'Clock News*, *Blackadder* and *Spitting Image*, three of the best comedy series of the previous two decades, of which I never missed an episode.

I was frowny and brittle in my first meeting with John. I thought he'd come up with the scripts and I didn't like them.

Deploying the calming tone I would become used to, John reassured me that, while his production company was to shoot the ads, he wasn't responsible for the scripts: they'd been written by the advertising agency hired by the client, and he'd been told I'd 'signed off on them'.

So, we began to read through, come up with ideas and make changes. Recognising that I was anxious about being there at all, John said he'd deal with the agency creatives.

In Cape Town, John and his producer, Caroline Warner, felt like a security blanket to me, and viable candidates for pseudo-parents as I renewed my quest for a replica family.

The crew seemed to be drawn entirely from the world of movies.

The ads were shot on 35mm film for cinemas and the camera operator had worked on the last *Batman* movie.

The costume designer had dressed Sean Connery.

The make-up artist worked regularly with Madonna. When she learned I was going to Marbella on holiday she asked me to find a flamenco dress for Lourdes, the Queen of Pop's then five-year-old daughter. (I did.)

The storyboard for the first ad had me cycling with a kitten. I wondered how they'd make that work.

I was astonished when an actual kitten was put in the basket on the handlebars of the old-fashioned bike I'd been given. The animal wasn't secured in any way but I was told to start pedalling.

The tiny cat shat and pissed repeatedly and made several attempts to leap into the road, which I prevented, nearly killing us both. We arrived at a pub full of Cape Town Hell's Angels, who had to be positioned carefully since many of them had tattoos revealing our true location when the ads were meant to be set in rural England.

Over dinner one night I surprised myself by trusting John and Caroline with the story of being abused by my father. Perhaps I felt this would bring me closer to them, I obviously needed to tell someone.

Or maybe my changing public image was prompting me to come closer to breaking cover, out of discomfort at the fraudulent façade that was building up around me.

I now had fame and money, both of which had seemed like a good idea only two years previously, but I didn't know who I was or what I was presenting. I still had hidden pain and this was now complicated by my new status, with which I was increasingly preoccupied. In short, I think I might have become a bore.

Fame is irreversible and if you don't like it you should have thought of that in the first place.

Caroline was a good listener and had a different view of the possibilities of our time in Cape Town. While certain folk from the agency went looking for the city's adult entertainment, Caroline went to a township church and saw a gospel choir. I wished I'd gone with her. I became interested in the history of Cape Town's District Six, one of the areas where defiance against Apartheid rule had been most vigorously suppressed but where illicit music venues and drinking clubs thrived. I bought a set of prints depicting scenes from the area.

In this way, I perhaps saw myself not as part of the money-making machine but someone lured into temptation while really being concerned with life's underdogs.

The South African crew were mostly white but there was a black member, working as a grip. I said 'good morning' to him one day, as everybody did to everybody else. He looked startled and didn't reply.

The first AD said to me: 'You'll have to forgive him, he's been in this industry for a long time and it's only in the last few years that white people would even address him.'

We were in Cape Town for the weather, for the budget and because it could double as England; but as we looked across the city from Table Mountain at dusk one evening, we all knew this place was not like home and it made a lasting impression.

The ads went out soon afterwards and then I was on ITV in the breaks during *Coronation Street*, *Emmerdale*, *Blind Date* and every other ratings monster, amounting to tens of millions of viewers each week, and in 1997 you couldn't pause and fast-forward live TV.

I was no longer recognisable only to the largely white BBC audience of *Jonathan Creek*. It was noticeable, living in inner London, that all strands of the city's multi-ethnic population were spotting me in the street and it seemed none of my new viewers knew my name. To some people I was 'Jonathan' and to everyone else I was 'Nat West' or 'Nationwide'.

'Oi, Nat West!' they'd say.

Or: 'Halifax! It's you, innit?'

'No, I'm not Halifax.'

'What are you, then?'

'Abbey National.'

'Oh, yes! Get the Abbey habit!'

'That's not the slogan now.'

'Isn't it? Get the Abbey habit' – and he sang the last bit – 'wiv Abbey Nat-ion-al!'

'No, it's changed.'

'What is it, then?'

'Because life's complicated enough.'

'No, what's the slogan now?'

'Because life's complicated enough.'

'The old one was better.'

Perhaps he was right. What's more, I didn't even say the slogan properly, adding a mockney-ish glottal stop: 'Becoz life's complick-ated enuff.'

At the time, I'd begun banking with Abbey National; and when I wrote a six-figure cheque to pay the income tax due on earnings from the ads, they bounced it, which certainly made life complicated for a while.

As I entered the second year of the ads, I was given the opportunity to take my stand-up show, *Urban Trauma*, into the West End at the Duchess Theatre, where it would be recorded for BBC One and DVD release.

I asked the set designer to incorporate my name, so bothered was I by being recognised by people who didn't know me, which is why 'Alan Davies' appears in the centre of the backdrop.

Things have changed a little now I'm less high-profile. These days, I'm often mistaken for James May or Hugh Fearnley-Whittingstall.

I told John Lloyd about people calling out 'Perm!' to me in the street or at comedy clubs, so dubious were they about my corkscrew curls being real.

So, we did a spoof hair commercial claiming that the Abbey National's handling of my finances was beneficial to my shiny locks. John can be heard calling 'Perm!' off camera, causing my smile to drop. It was funny, and I found I wasn't embarrassed by the campaign despite my misgivings. When the chance to do a fourth year came along, I once again failed to resist the three hundred and fifty grand on offer.

This time, though, the agency wanted to make a change. They had a new director in mind, Tom Hooper, and forwarded his impressive showreel. But I told them I'd only work with John Lloyd.

To me, the ads said I was spineless; to the average punter, they said I was doing well. To the leftie comedians, I had brought shame on my profession. I remember Mark Steel sarcastically repeating the campaign's slogan to me at a BBC Radio party. I recall nothing else from that evening, which shows how wounded I was to be a version of power for Mark to speak truth to. And

I really liked Mark, even though whenever I gigged with him he'd never, *ever* stick to his time. He *always* went over. Still, I felt I'd earned the scorn.

Nowadays, Mark and I go to Lord's with Miles Jupp to watch Test cricket, days you wish would never end. But I always knew he was right about the ads. The catchphrase threw a veil over the complexities of a banking system soaked in avarice and driven by greed that took the world under a few years later in the global financial crash, frying our admirably principled prime minister and chancellor of the exchequer in the good times, Gordon Brown.

Tears for Fears

16th October 2024.

A couple of days after I'd learned I had a tumour in my bladder and a few days before I was to have surgery, I had a voiceover to record, with the hilarious musical comedian and actor Isy Suttie, who by then I'd known for fifteen years.

We were voicing a radio ad for Sky and Netflix. This would have been unthinkable back when Rupert Murdoch's sacking of printworkers led to strikes and picket-line conflict in the face of mass policing. The father of one of my best friends at school was 'in the print' and lost his job and pension aged fifty-eight.

A boycott of Murdoch's papers and his Sky TV service continued for years. I caved in 1993, when Sky bought the Premier League, and after that I took the shilling writing articles for *The Times*.

This voiceover was the type of thing I'd have turned down in the past, not on principle but because they were offering only a few grand.

After I'd done the Abbey National ads, I kept a costly vow for several years not to do any more commercials. This led to a couple of crackpot decisions.

First: I was offered £70,000 to make a TV commercial for baked beans in New Zealand that was only going to be shown there. A free trip to NZ (I could probably have done some gigs, too, while I was there, and visited all my friends and relations in Australia), and I love beans. Turned it down. *Twat*.

Second: I was approached by the agency making the TV ads for Direct Line Insurance. For years they'd had a red telephone on wheels whizzing around as their spokesperson. Now they were adding an online service, so they wanted to pair the phone with a talking computer mouse.

Would I be the voice of the mouse?

They'd asked Stephen Fry to be the phone, so by hiring us both they'd get an ad apparently endorsed by *QI*. I turned it down, saying: 'There's no way Stephen will do that.'

Not long afterwards, a Direct Line ad came on the TV, Stephen was the voice of the phone and news satirist Paul Merton was the mouse.

Voiceovers somehow feel like a lesser crime on the sellout scale, since you can't easily be identified, and I'd said yes to this one with Isy in part because she's such good company.

When Sean Lock died in August 2021, Isy had sent me an email to express her shock about his passing and offering her condolences.

I thanked her, but in truth I hadn't been close to Sean towards the end. All the news about his condition came to me through our mutual friend Bill Bailey.

Sean chose to keep his cancer private and didn't talk about it to many people. Part of my reply to Isy read: 'Not the way I think I'd do it, but I suppose we don't know until it's our turn.'

I thought about that exchange on my way to meet Isy in a Berwick Street studio. I contemplated telling her about my cancer scare and realised I didn't want to. I'd told only three people, other than Katie, and had come to understand why some people don't want to tell the world.

There seemed to be a cost involved. I just wanted to have fun in a recording studio.

Why risk upsetting people? If you don't feel their sympathy will strengthen you, why spread the news? Leave them alone; they have health problems of their own, or in their families, or friends who are ill, or they've lost someone. So, my view of Sean's private final months changed; you really don't know how you'll react.

Isy and I were asking after each other's children and started talking about what they liked to watch on TV. I mentioned *The Incredibles*, assuming that everyone has seen it.

'I've never seen *The Incredibles*,' said Isy.

'Shut the front door,' I said.

All the ad people liked that line and put it in the script.

'Where's it come from?' one of them said.

'Common usage,' I said. 'No one knows who said it first.'

Isy and I went for a coffee afterwards, sharing stories and catching up, while my tumour was silent within.

Two of the three friends I'd told had become tearful with the news. I scared them; it was apparent I was really worried, not knowing how long the tumour had been there, how quickly it was growing, and still awaiting the outcome of my CT scan.

I told Katie I was becoming preoccupied with not being around any more, absent from everything. We held hands across the kitchen table and our eyes filled with tears.

'No one wants that,' she said.

I'm a Celebrity

On one side of me was the ventriloquist Paul Zerdin, who was chatty and amiable, but Stephen Fry, sitting beneath the window on my right, seemed anxious. His hands were shaking and he was fumbling with a miniature bottle of spirits. I watched him in the large mirror before us; we'd never met but it occurred to me he might be better off with a puff on a joint made with the grass I had in my pocket. We chatted but there wasn't much time to pass, as we had the dressing room for only half the evening; it was occupied the rest of the time by Frank Bruno and Willie Carson.

When I was called down to the wing of the Palace Theatre, Manchester, I was told I'd be following Phil Collins, who appeared to be singing 'Where's my hat?' even though he was wearing a hat, so that was preoccupying me and then I was on. Phil and his band exited stage right and I came on stage left. No MC, just an announcement from somewhere.

On the ITV broadcast months later, there was a commercial break after Phil Collins and a Voice of God intoned: 'Still to come, Alan Davies, Jennifer Aniston and the Spice Girls.'

Those three names have never been in the same sentence again until now.

After the ads, there I was, on the 1997 Prince's Trust Gala, doing some material about charity mailouts and then various impressions of our family Alsatian, Sasha, who was always hungry. My last joke was a mime of her trying to walk on the slippery kitchen floor in her final weeks when her crippled hips meant she could barely stand. I slipped to the floor, a failsafe for me in many stand-up routines.

Sasha had been put down only a few weeks beforehand. I'll always regret not holding her while she was injected. The vet took her into a room and Sasha craned her neck to see me and my stepmother, keeping us in view until the door closed.

Outside, I tried to hug my tearful stepmother but she stiffened like an ironing board. We'd accepted the vet's transport service, which turned out to be forty quid for them to put the dog in the back of a van that we followed. I could have put her in my car, as I'd done many times in the months when she lived with me in Stoke Newington.

My dad was still ranting about the cost when my stepmother and I got back to their house in Loughton.

'Forty pounds! Forty pounds to put the damn dog in their van?'

His wife looked devastated before him; I was also upset. But other people's feelings never influenced his behaviour. He was astonishingly insensitive and parsimonious. He hadn't even paid the forty quid.

'Forty pounds!'

It was becoming an attack on his wife. I went home as soon as I could.

I loved that dog. There is a framed photo of her a few feet from where I'm sitting now, as I write.

For the finale, all the performers gathered onstage behind the curtain. At the back was the Manchester United football team, with David Beckham among them wearing a different-coloured suit from the rest of the squad. At the front were the Spice Girls, including Victoria 'Posh Spice' Adams. The other girls were calling out for Beckham to come to the front and join his new girlfriend. It was like a huge, star-studded school playground.

The Prince of Wales came onstage to thank everyone and told the audience that he could never match the brilliant wit of the wonderful Stephen Fry, who had given such a hilarious evocation of the value of the Prince's Trust (the charity we were all there to support but that no one mentioned in any conversation backstage all night).

After the recording, we waited while the prince shook hands with each of us.

'You've got plenty of ideas, haven't you?' he said to me, but before I could reply I noticed that he was already looking at the next person, even though he was still shaking my hand.

Later, Joanna Lumley was hesitating alone on the threshold of the stage door. There were crowds of photographers. I used to have a picture of her on my bedroom wall when she was Purdey from *The New Avengers*. I walked her to her car. Despite scouring countless publications looking for a picture of us leaving together, I never found one.

The party afterwards was at a hotel. I didn't know anyone so began drinking as my usual coping strategy. I wanted a spliff but was out of Rizlas.

While I was wondering what to do with myself, Jennifer Aniston approached me.

'I love dogs,' she said, smiling.

'I do too,' I said, and she made a slight tilting movement with her head, putting her weight on one side in a way that suggested a connection we might build on.

I could scarcely believe how beautiful she was; shining eyes, dazzling white smile, bare tanned shoulders with a long blue gown hanging from the thinnest spaghetti straps over flawless skin and with that famous hair on top.

'*Friends* is so popular here,' I said, and noticed a flicker of disappointment. (*don't mention* Friends, *you idiot fanboy; ask her something, about the dress, the earrings, where she got those shoulders from, and that skin, no, not the skin . . .*).

'I had German Shepherds,' she said.

At least I think that's what she said, because people from *Coronation Street* were calling to me: 'Alan, Alan! Introduce us!'

I didn't know them but instead of waving and leading Jennifer away to a quieter spot, where we might plan our elopement, I took her over and there was a chorus of friendly Mancunian adulation that Ms Aniston smiled through politely.

Just as she turned back to face me, clearly hoping I'd whisk her elsewhere to begin our lives together, a hunky American man appeared, glaring at me as if he might have to squash my head between thumb and forefinger and, with an apologetic smile that was *so* Rachel, she was gone. Three years later she married Brad Pitt, so she'd been looking for love. I'd had a window, a chance.

Pop star and songwriter Cathy Dennis was good company in Jennifer's absence, but she left too and soon the party was thinning out and I was back at the bar knowing no one. It was time for bed but I had no brakes and an accelerative drinking pattern, so each wine lasted me less time than the last. Soon there were only a few agents and a bunch of unhappy journalists left.

Several of them had already asked me about Caroline Quentin.

'How's Caroline?' they'd said.

'I don't know; fine I think, why?'

And they'd wandered off, no further questions.

It turned out there was a rumour going round that Caroline and I were having an affair and that was why she and Paul Merton were splitting up. No truth in that, as they doubtless verified with a routine phone hack.

I still hadn't gone to bed and I really wanted a joint, so I turned to the bloke next to me at the bar and said: 'Haven't got any skins, have you?'

'No,' he said.

He turned out to be Stuart Higgins, editor of *The Sun*. They didn't run anything about me hanging around the Prince's Trust party trying to skin up, though, so perhaps he thought it was a practical joke.

For my part, maybe I wanted to get caught, to end all this and go back to the Comedy Café; this place didn't even have a pool table.

A *Sun* journalist subsequently offered to advance my career with a double-page interview in Britain's biggest-selling paper. Over lunch, she told me about spending the night with recording equipment in a hotel bedroom while a famous snooker player was next door, in bed with a woman who'd already been paid by a tabloid.

Afterwards I went to see Bob Voice and told him about the journalist.

'She said *The Sun* would pay for a conservatory on my house,' I said.

Bob frowned. 'There's no such thing as a free lunch,' he said.

Successfully warned, I rang the hack to say no thanks. I was put through and could hear her talking to someone else. Just before speaking to me, she said, 'Hang on, I'll just get rid of this,' and then her voice went up an octave: 'Alan, hi!'

I said goodbye and paid for my own house refurb.

*

A month or so later, I was a guest on Ruby Wax's chat show with Glenys Kinnock and Anna Massey, as the comedy circuit slid permanently out of view and another life took its place.

After the recording, we went out for dinner and I found myself next to Alan Rickman, a friend of Ruby's. He didn't know me but Anna Massey told him he simply must watch *Jonathan Creek* and that I was 'wonderful' in it. He seemed unconvinced by Anna's effusiveness, but she was a great Shakespearean actor (as a drama student, I'd seen her in *King Lear* with Anthony Hopkins in 1985) so Alan paid attention to her and turned to look properly at me, as if I were an option for his main course. Then he took an empty Silk Cut packet (it was the nineties; everyone smoked, especially in Chinese restaurants) and wrote on it the title of a book he recommended: *Respect for Acting* by Uta Hagen.

'The best book about acting,' he said.

'Thanks, I'll get that,' I said.

Stupidly, I didn't read it.

The following year, when my stand-up show *Urban Trauma* was on at the Duchess Theatre, Glenys came to see me with her husband Neil, my political hero in the eighties.

We went for dinner to Joe Allen's, where Glenys did an impression of Margaret Thatcher: 'Come and meet Captains of Industry.'

Neil had been to Wembley to watch Wales beat Scotland at rugby before making his way to the show. After we'd eaten, he sat back and said: 'I've had a great day.'

Three years later, I needed somewhere to stay in Brussels with my friend Jez Feeney as we were going to see England play Germany at Charleroi in Euro 2000. Even though the Kinnocks weren't home, they arranged for us to stay at the house they lived in while she was an MEP and he was a European commissioner. A note left behind said: 'Help yourself to the wine cellar.'

There were riots in Charleroi, but Jez and I made the stadium, saw England win 1-0 and avoided the local water cannon to get back to Brussels. After all that, we set off the Kinnock's burglar alarm and thankfully just remembered the code word when the phone rang seconds later, or else we might have had a visit from a diplomatic SWAT team.

All of these memories of the strange turn my life took – meeting Prince Charles, Jennifer Aniston and Joanna Lumley, befriending the Kinnocks and being tolerated by Alan Rickman – have stayed with me because I was as impressed by fame as anyone else.

Now, having a modicum of celebrity myself, it was as if a layer of formality had gone and I could legitimately address the famous. I was fortunate to work with Bob Monkhouse on *Jonathan Creek* around this time. Everyone recognised him so, to minimise awkwardness when meeting new people, he'd smile, thrust out his hand and say: 'Bob Monkhouse!'

It put me at ease when I first met Bob, so I thought I'd try it myself. I did it just once, when I met the popular Olympic medal-winning athlete Kriss Akabusi at the BBC. Thrusting out my hand, I said: 'Alan Davies.'

He frowned, not having a clue who I was.

'Hello Dave,' he said.

Showbiz Party

Channel 4 aired the episode of the US sitcom *Ellen* in which Ellen Degeneres's eponymous heroine comes out as gay on 28th April 1998. To celebrate, they showed coming-out-themed programmes and held a televised party, hosted by Graham Norton, at the Cobden Club in West London. Ellen, who attended with Anne Heche, said that her own network back in the States had downplayed the whole event.

For younger readers, 'coming out' in the late twentieth century meant to publicly acknowledge that you were gay, which was still commercially risky in the entertainment industry. This might appear anachronistic but, at the time of writing, homosexuality remains criminalised in sixty-four countries, as it was for decades in Britain.

Consensual homosexual sex between adult men was illegal until 1967, by which time my father, a secret addict of 'teen boy' pornography and clearly homosexual, was married to my mum and had two sons. His homosexuality, it should go without saying, was not the cause of his abuse of me. That sprung from his tendency to criminality, manipulation and an oblivious disregard for the feelings of others.

Despite an absolute silence on the existence of homosexuals throughout my school years – something the Tories tried to preserve in law as late as 1988, with its Section 28 legislation – coming out was common in the safe space of higher-education drama departments in the 1980s. Though we can't rule out some of the women at Kent making a choice because there were only two straight men on the course and I was one of them.

In 1998, coming out was a cause for celebration on television. I went along to the party despite being beset by the notion that any event would go better in my absence. Presumably I was invited because I was a comedian – like Ellen – and because *Jonathan Creek* was being watched by twelve million viewers on Saturday nights.

My new girlfriend, Cath, was on the West End stage that night with Hannah Waddingham in *Saucy Jack and the Space Vixens*, so I was on my own. I worried that over-familiar strangers would approach me, and that there might be unwanted touching, things I'd begun to dread. Perhaps this would be a safe zone, though, since it was a showbiz party, a weird kettling of minor celebs.

The Cobden Club had high ceilings and grand doorways and was decked out in bright colours, like an overgrown chat-show set. There were trays of fizzy wine, and I began to drink.

In the centre of the room was a raised platform with a couple of sofas where interviews would go on between programmes.

On one of the sofas, a squat man with a bare backside and thick hairy legs had contorted himself into a face-down ball and was thrusting away doing an impression of a couple shagging. As he pulled up his trousers with a maniacal grin, to nervous chuckles from those nearest to him, I saw that it was Keith Allen, one of the regulars at the original Comedy Store, before I'd started.

After this warm-up act, I was relieved to bump into Caroline Aherne. I hardly ever saw her as she lived in Manchester, where she presented a hilarious spoof chat show playing an old lady called Mrs Merton. She'd also married Peter Hook, the bass player from Joy Division and New Order.

At the Edinburgh Fringe in 1995, Mr and Mrs Hook had come backstage at the Gilded Balloon's Late 'n' Live, which featured Bill Bailey's band, Beergut 100, playing every night.

The Beerguts were drawn from the comedy world. Bill played lead guitar and Kevin Eldon was usually the frontman. Everything was a punked-up version of something well known, like the theme from *Rainbow* or Morecambe and Wise's 'Bring Me Sunshine'. The other members were Jim Miller, who was living his punk dream and kept asking for his guitar to be turned up while Bill was having it turned down; Phil Whelans on bass, often bare-chested, which made a mockery of the band's name; and Martin Trenaman on drums and fags.

I attended most of their gigs but resisted joining them onstage, which many other comics did for various cover versions. I'd just roll joints and make trips to the bar like a quasi-groupie, although I did go onstage one night when a video camera was handed to me to record footage of the band. I took pride in managing to do so without ever putting down my pint of Guinness.

That night at Late 'n' Live, Hooky (as he was known) joined the Beerguts onstage to play 'Love Will Tear Us Apart', the Joy Division anthem recorded just before their singer Ian Curtis took his own life.

Bill knew the song and helped Hooky remember how it went. There was a touching scene afterwards when the normally straight-faced Hook was asking how the band knew the song so well and Bill told him that for about three months when he was a teenager it was never off his turntable.

Hooky embraced Bill, saying: 'Thanks, man, that means so much to me, man, thank you.'

'No, thank *you*; you've made my day,' said Bill

'Ask him about the one who hanged himself,' said Caroline a few times. 'He doesn't mind.'

Three years later, at the Cobden Club, Caroline didn't seem to be with anyone so we knocked around together drinking as she kept up a stream of witty comments on passers-by.

A young woman in headphones asked us if we'd come up to the sofas for a bit of live chat. This was the free-wine trade-off. Caroline whispered that she'd only do it with me and up we went. Across from us on the other sofa was Keith Allen, who I'd never met.

'Didn't I see you up here earlier?' I said, trying to be friendly.

'I'll fucking have you when the cameras are running,' he said.

'No you won't,' I said and left three seconds after we'd sat down, with Caroline holding the tails of my shirt saying, 'Don't leave me!'

Perhaps I appeared sarcastic. Caroline and I, still giggling, found a seat and some wine.

'I might snog you in a minute,' she said and I laughed and we didn't snog, not then or any other time.

Then she said she needed the loo and we couldn't see the ladies' so I said I'd take her into the gents' and find her a cubicle. I didn't consider how that might have looked to the roomful of television personalities and industry people: TV's Mrs Merton and Jonathan Creek stumbling around a Channel 4 party pissed and going into the toilets together.

The gents' were busy; both cubicles were occupied, apparently with two people in each one.

I loudly called out to the occupants: 'What are you doing in there?'

No one shouts in the gents', especially not at people doing coke. A gruff 'Fuck off' came back through the cubicle door. It was Keith Allen again.

'Why are there two of you in there?' I said.

Referencing my TV-detective persona, he shouted: 'Why don't you fuck off and find something out, you fucking cunt?'

'You're a fucking cunt,' I said. I'd been trying for a laugh up to then, but now the angry boy was at hand and he came with a sense of humour failure as standard.

'Let's go,' said Caroline.

We turned to make our escape and, like a nineties Laurel and Hardy, opened a door to an actual broom cupboard, full of mops and buckets. This was hilarious to us and also made us panic a bit, since my adversary would be out of the cubicle any second. We found the exit and went back to our sofa; neither of us had used the toilet, that was forgotten. Seconds later, Keith Allen was scowling over us.

'Why wouldn't you fucking talk to me on camera?'

'We can talk now, come and have a drink with us,' I said.

But he just walked away.

'You were all nice to him then,' said Caroline, eyeballing me. 'All shouty in the toilets and then nice to him out here.'

'Yep,' I said.

And we laughed again. I recall nothing else of the night, certainly no one mentioned Ellen at all, and it became just another evening when I couldn't remember how I got home.

Before I began writing this chapter, I thought I'd be recalling a night out with an old friend and a daft episode in the broom cupboard of a club at a forgotten

TV party, but the process of setting it down has surprised me. I did a bit of digging online about the cast of characters and it just seems sad now.

Anne Heche's relationship with Ellen ended a couple of years after the coming-out party and she published a memoir, *Call Me Crazy*, in 2001 in which she disclosed the sexual abuse she'd suffered at the hands of her father.

A few weeks after the party, Caroline Aherne tried to take her own life by overdose.

I listened to Peter Hook's book *Substance*, where he described Caroline's jealousy and his unhappiness and also said:

> In comedy they have a big green-room drinking culture, it's a very boozy, incestuous world. They drink together, sleep together, bitch together about one another behind their backs, while going out of their way to tell each other how great they are to their faces. They're insecure, paranoid and hyper-sensitive to criticism. I met the lot of them. I fitted in perfectly. You name them, the so-called cream of British comedy at the time. I thought they were a right bunch of jerks.

Possibly fair but he means the ones from Manchester, right?

But when I think about the bewildered assistant producer, or of the people around that cubicle door, the drunken yelling and obscenity, it's grotesque. I imagine my present-day self appearing alongside thirty-two-year-old me like the shopkeeper in *Mr Benn*, saying: 'Time to go! You're making a fool of yourself and shame lasts a lifetime. Next time, do something to make your future self proud.'

People who find themselves prone to conflict, to arguments and shouting, somehow find one another, as if there's a sixth sense at play. Whether they're driving or drinking or just queuing for the loo, their antenna is alive to the charge of that contact, usually with a similarly afflicted stranger.

It tells you they are never, ever at peace, and that seems like a terrible burden to carry, which is perhaps why we all want to be Mr Benn, with the magic shopkeeper preserving his dignity every time.

How Much Are You Drinking?

ALAN: Some nights a couple of bottles of wine.

THERAPIST: And you say your girlfriend is living with you.

A: Yes.

T: Does she drink?

A: No, hardly anything. She lives off diet supplements and vitamin pills, the drawer in her room is full of bottles like she's shoplifted from Holland & Barrett.

T: You have separate rooms.

A: She doesn't sleep in there.

T: So what does she do when you're drinking?

A: She goes to bed.

T: And you watch TV and drink?

A: I usually play on the PlayStation, and smoke some weed.

T: How often do you smoke weed?

A: Every night.

T: Does it calm you down?

A: I suppose so. It's quite addictive. I play *FIFA* and I want to win the treble: League, Cup and European Cup. I've mastered the game now, I'm at World Class level and I win pretty much every match.

T: Can I ask you, Alan, and I'm aware this is difficult for you to answer since you were so young when your mum passed away, but do you know whether you were breastfed as a baby?

A :　I think I was, actually, because I used to suck my thumb and I remember being told not to because I'd get buck teeth, but I used to put my forefinger against my nose and rub it and suck my thumb.

T :　The finger would be to simulate the feeling of your mother's breast against your nose when you were latched on. Babies go in to an almost trancelike state when feeding.

A :　They feel safe.

T :　And it's possible that for some heavy drinkers the quest, if you like, is to return to that state. The sipping of a sweet liquid that has a numbing effect, which you further supplement with marijuana, and in addition a repetitive action on the computer game that is rewarding and not difficult, so relaxing, not frustrating, possibly suggest an attempt to create an environment that is reminiscent of breastfeeding, a return to that peaceful, safe place.

A :　One night, I was on my own in the house, and I was sitting on the sofa stoned. I'd had a bit of wine and I could hear some scratching noises, I didn't know where it was coming from, I'd only recently seen *The Blair Witch Project*, do you know it?

T :　That's a low-budget horror?

A :　Yes, terrifying, and in the film all kinds of noises in the dark freak the kids out, so now I was getting a bit freaked out. I got up and looked in the garden but there was no one there, I was a bit unsteady and I went into the kitchen. The front door was open and there was a bloke standing there. He grabbed my bag off the chair and ran, didn't even close the door behind him. I looked outside and he was already at the end of my street and then I noticed my car was gone.

T :　He'd taken your car?

A :　No, some other kids had taken the car. The police told me there'd been a documentary on TV about thieves putting coat hangers on bamboo poles and using them to hook people's keys through the letterbox and since it had been on, every kid in Islington had been doing it. There were bamboo canes on the front lawn. I got the car back but they'd hit something in it. I never got the bag back, it was empty, too, so useless to him.

T: How long have you been drinking and smoking every night?

A: About a year or more.

T: Did you used to drink when you were on the comedy circuit, working in pubs?

A: Not really because I drove everywhere. So I tried to stick to a two-pint limit. I used to take cans of low-alcohol beer with me sometimes, since most pubs didn't serve it. Once I was doing a gig called the Oranje Boom at De Hems in Chinatown and the barman kicked me out for bringing my own cans in. I had to listen out from the street and when the compere introduced me I ran up the stairs and onto the stage to do my set.

T: Did he realise you were on the bill?

A: I told him I was but every time I spoke he became more pissed off.

T: Do you ever have a drink to calm your nerves before a show?

A: I never drink before gigs.

T: But now you're drinking every day?

A: Cath thinks I've changed since I became famous.

T: Does she? What does she say?

A: 'You're not the same since you became famous.'

T: I see.

A: I say, 'I haven't changed, everyone has changed towards me,' and she says, 'It's not your fault, but you *have* changed, you're grumpy and smoking weed and you never come to bed.'

T: Why don't you go to bed? Are you attracted to Cathy?

A: Yes, yes, absolutely. I think everyone's attracted to her, but maybe I'm biased. Sometimes, though, people change around me, old friends act differently. Four of us went to the FA Cup final recently and we hired a stretch limo to take us from my house in Islington to Wembley. We thought this was a masterstroke but we counted seven other limos going up the Holloway Road. It was good fun, but I was tense because I wanted Arsenal to win so much. Maybe it's tied in to my dad being a Spurs fan.

T: Is he? Your great rivals?

A: Exactly. I don't know if winning means more to me than the
    others, certainly not Keith, but it's just an extra-personal layer.
    So we got to the ground, there were Newcastle and Arsenal
    fans mingling but no trouble. I was wearing a hat to hide my
    hair because I didn't want to be recognised. The Arsenal fans
    were singing: 'We've got Dennis Bergkamp! We've got Dennis
    Bergkamp!' He's our hero, even though he wasn't fit to play.
    And then one of my mates starts singing, 'We've got Alan
    Davies, We've got Alan Davies!' really loudly, as if trying to
    draw attention to me, the last thing I wanted. He couldn't seem
    to understand why everyone else was telling him to shut up. At
    halftime he went off to do a line of coke, which I didn't get, we
    were all on the edge of hysteria as it was. Anyway, I don't know
    why I'm talking about that.

T: People have changed towards you?

A: It feels that way, but Keith, who's loyal and protective of me, which
    I really appreciate, says I can't see half the things that are going
    on when I'm walking through a crowd because so many people
    point or pass comment when I've gone by, so unless you're walking
    behind me you wouldn't know.

T: And Cath must see that as well.

A: She didn't know who I was when we met, things have gone a bit
    weird this year.

T: But most nights you'd rather drink, smoke weed and play than be
    with Cath?

A: It's not that I'd rather. I'm tired, I'm trying to unwind.

T: But she's worried about it?

A: Yes, but I think maybe she's changed too. People speak to me
    sometimes when we're out and they just ignore her completely,
    which is even worse if they're women. I wasn't really well known
    when we met, *Jonathan Creek* hadn't been on yet. Now people stare
    and want to shout things. It can be tricky to go to the pub, and I love
    to go the pub, I've been doing it since I was fifteen.

T: You've been drinking a long time, then.

A: But I didn't used to drink at home. And I never smoked weed or did any drugs when I was a kid. I can remember hearing my stepmother saying to my dad, 'I think he's on something,' but I wasn't. I don't know if he believed her, but it could only make things worse.

T: So you've started smoking weed a lot since you started to get recognised.

A: I suppose so. I'm at home more. I'd like to go out but I'm a bit paranoid. Even at home I'm a bit paranoid, since Cath checks my answerphone messages and goes very quiet in the next room if I'm on the phone.

T: Why do you think she's eavesdropping?

A: She thinks I'm interested in other women.

T: Are you?

A: I did have a crush on an actress I worked with, but I seem to always get a crush on actresses I work with.

T: Has anything ever happened?

A: No. Maybe we're both a bit paranoid, can't relax.

T: Perhaps.

A: Just because you're paranoid doesn't mean they're not out to get you, right?

T: There can be some truth in that, certainly. Fame is bound to be difficult and the prevailing attitude to it is that it's desirable.

A: Some young people now have the stated ambition of being a celebrity. What do you want to be when you grow up? 'Famous,' or, 'Rich and Famous,' without thinking they need to master any skills. So celebrity is becoming a pejorative term. I always wanted to act and do comedy and fame is a measure of success in some ways, if that is your chosen field. I enjoyed being recognised at first but, even though the majority of people are indifferent, every now and then one person wants me to be something that fits with their view and I can't and they get annoyed. Most of the time, though, the possibility that someone will be unpleasant is always there, that makes it hard to relax. A while ago I went to Copenhagen with

Steve Cram for Channel 4. It was to preview the World Cup in France and we were going to watch Denmark play Norway with John Jensen, who played for Arsenal. It was a nice trip, I used to love watching Steve Cram racing and breaking world records and he was easy to get on with. In the afternoon before the game, I had some free time and I wandered round the city by myself. It was relaxing and stress-free and then I realised that no one was looking at me, not a single person knew who I was, and that change back to anonymity was calming for me.

T: Do you think your unhappiness is because of fame?

A: Do you think it might be a red herring?

T: There are things in your life that must be very difficult: the bereavements, the abuse . . .

A: I sometimes wonder why I enjoyed being recognised, was it a validation or something?

T: The desire for attention might be related to – in ways we haven't thoroughly explored yet – your state of mind during and immediately after childhood.

A: But my siblings don't do comedy, or seek attention.

T: But they weren't abused, Alan, they weren't scapegoated in the family. They had enough attention and, for a combination of reasons, you have an aptitude in your field.

A: So I want to be famous because of the events of my childhood and I can't tolerate being famous because of the events of my childhood. Fundamentally, it's my dad's fault?

T: You could arrive at that conclusion.

The Overrated Pretty
Boy of Comedy

Susie Belbin told me that she was retiring before we shot series two of *Jonathan Creek* in 1997. When she started out at the BBC, as an assistant floor manager, one of her jobs had been to keep the elderly cast members awake during studio recordings of *Dad's Army*. Now she'd become my champion and I owed her everything.

Verity Lambert had been the first producer of *Dr Who* in 1963 and had held many important posts in television for three decades, and now she was to be Susie's replacement.

If Verity had produced the first series, had she been more persuasive with Nicholas Lyndhurst or Hugh Laurie, I might never have become Jonathan Creek. As it was, we became friends and she counselled me often, about work, agents and relationships. She had no children and I had no mother so perhaps that played a part.

Maybe that's what a parent can be: considerate and on your side. I'm sure Mum was those things to me. I never remember her being cross, only her laughter.

Verity also loved to laugh and make jokes. On one car journey with her and David Renwick, I was moaning about some 'ridiculous line' I'd been asked to say for an Abbey National ad and how there'd been a standoff in the studio as I'd acted all pouty and stubborn.

'Did you say it?' said Verity and David almost simultaneously.

'Yes,' I said, and they both laughed loudly.

'John Lloyd had me do it in a way that they couldn't use,' I said and David said, 'Oh,' and Verity, 'I see,' and I looked out of the window thinking about how these two had been in the frame to be my surrogate parents and now I saw they thought me ridiculous, or rather they'd noticed I am, as I accumulated hundreds of thousands of extra pounds off the back of David's brilliant TV show.

Before we started shooting series two, we were told there would now be two motorhomes on location for the actors, one for men and one for women. Caroline and I asked if we could share one and the second could be used by whoever else was in each day. We'd become closer and our relationship was better.

After series two was broadcast in early 1998, we were invited to the BAFTA Awards where series one was up for Best Drama.

It was 18th May 1998. I'd been out to Hugo Boss and purchased the exact same outfit that Arsène Wenger and the Arsenal players had worn when I saw them win the FA Cup at Wembley two days before: black suit, grey shirt, grey tie.

When *Jonathan Creek* was announced as winner, Sandy Johnson, one of our directors, said, 'Come on,' to me and I went up with him, David Renwick and Marcus Mortimer.

After they'd handed David the award, I turned and went back down the steps to my seat in the stalls, next to Ellie Renwick, who was chuckling at me. The others had exited into the wing for photos and I'd left them looking forlornly out into the auditorium for me. I didn't know the protocol so I didn't have a picture taken with the famous mask.

I haven't won another BAFTA and I put that down to looking ungrateful when I received the first one.

A few weeks later, I was up at Edinburgh for my first show there for three years. Shooting *Jonathan Creek* the previous two summers had meant I couldn't attend the Fringe, but I'd managed to head over to Ireland for the Kilkenny comedy festival in June each year.

The comics all love Kilkenny. There are no critics, no reviews, no PR and barely any agents. I went four years in a row for blissful weekends playing to packed rooms in the back of pubs.

Before heading to Kilkenny in '98, I'd toured New Zealand, where *Jonathan Creek* was the number-one rated show and my gigs went down a storm. A newspaper in Christchurch described me as 'A runaway laughter-making machine.'

I was loving stand-up and looking forward to a run in Edinburgh at the Music Hall in the Assembly Rooms.

Arriving at the venue on the first day, I saw hundreds of people queuing down George St and realised it was my audience. At a different time in my life, I might have gone along the line saying a few hellos.

'I'm keeping my fingers crossed it won't rain on you before you get inside!' I'd have said, to general mirth.

I knew I was going to enjoy my hour onstage, but I also knew that I didn't want to be spotted. These punters had booked to see me out of the thousands of events at the Fringe, and yet I was relieved to feel drops of rain so I could put up the hood of my blue waterproof coat and cover my hair, recognisable at two hundred paces.

I soon realised that I didn't know many of the new comics around the Fringe; it was like going back to school after you've left. So I was pleased to bump into Boothby Graffoe, a regular on the circuit when I'd been there before.

'Here he is,' he said, 'the overrated pretty boy of comedy.'

Just a throwaway remark from a grinning comedian, but it seemed to confirm my fear that I'd separated off from my past life. I'd go up late at night to the Gilded Balloon Studio to watch Rich Hall as Otis Lee Crenshaw and sit at the back, rolling joints.

'I know you kids are smoking out there,' said Otis.

Maybe, once again, I was hoping to get caught.

Back in London, I bumped into Bob Mortimer at the BBC.

'Are you all right?' he said, by way of hello, that familiar soft smile on his face.

He meant was I all right with the stress and lack of anonymity. He was one of the few people I knew who might understand.

'No,' I said, 'not really. I've had chest pains.'

'Oh,' he said, 'that's not good.'

'Doctor says it's not cardiac,' I said.

'Me and Jim want to take three years off,' he said, using Vic Reeves's real name. 'Everyone thinks we're joking but we're not.'

A Bad Loser

My next attempt to create my own sitcom came on BBC Radio 4. *Alan's Big One* was over but I still loved doing radio, so Jane Berthoud introduced me to two young writers, Ben Silburn and Tony Roche.

In *The Alan Davies Show* (not my choice of title but I couldn't think of one), I played an actor who longed to be taken seriously, resented jobs going to comedians with no training and claimed he'd never do an advert but became Mr Strawberry, the face of a synthetic fruit drink that was so bad for kids it came with a health warning. He also had a new girlfriend each week, since no one would stay with him. It seemed like a role I could manage.

Debra Stephenson played all the girlfriends. Alan Francis and Ronni Ancona played my kooky best friends and Kevin Eldon or Dave Lamb played every other part. It was a reunion of most of the *Big One* family.

By way of research, I spoke to David Renwick about *One Foot in the Grave*. 'How do you go about putting an episode together?'

'I just try to think of six funny things,' he said.

'Six!'

'Yes.'

'We're just working with three plotlines,' I said. 'A main one for me and subplots mirroring or linking up for the two supporting characters.'

'That's fine; there's no right way to do it.'

So, we stayed as we were, with me script editing and suggesting storylines. Perhaps our best episode was the one when all three characters were locked in separate rooms for different reasons. I also enjoyed asking Alistair McGowan to do all the voices in a scene at a film premiere where Tony Blair met William Hague and Hague did an impression of Blair to Blair. Alistair didn't flinch at the request and it was funny. Other than at exceptional moments like that, my mantra was always 'steal from life'.

We all greatly enjoyed the recordings in the Radio Theatre and at the end of 1998 we were nominated for a British Comedy Award.

For the first time ever, the awards were fancy dress, with everyone invited to embrace a Latin theme.

That week, I'd been filming for a BBC pilot called *A Many Splintered Thing* and asked the make-up designer, Tori, to help. We went for it: a matador outfit for me and a kind of Carmen Miranda for Cath, which consisted of a spangly yellow bra and plastic fruit on her head. Helped by her musical-theatre smile and impressively flat stomach, she pulled it off. I looked in the mirror and saw a man who'd had the wrong costume delivered but couldn't escape wearing it.

On the red carpet outside the studios we received a lot of attention – because no one else was in fancy dress. Once inside, I became aware of the musty storage smell from the fabric of my matador suit and wondered who had worn it before. The show was going to be a couple of hours, at least, and my hat was already itchy on my head. I reached for a glass of wine and said, '*Olé!*' to myself.

At the end of the show, Dana International, the transgender Israeli singer who'd won Eurovision that year, picked me out as Best-Dressed Man from a field of one, for which the perennial host, Jonathan Ross, kindly coaxed applause from an audience who would all have taken their own lives rather than swap places with me. My prize was a case of champagne (when it was delivered, several bottles were missing, which neatly sums up the Comedy Awards).

It was the only thing I won all night.

After the live TV broadcast, as the studio began to clear, I received a hefty whack on the back of the head. I looked round to see Addison Cresswell on the raised seating area at the side, cackling away. He and someone I didn't know (turned out to be Lily Savage's manager, Brendan) were throwing unused rolls of streamers at me, trying to knock my hat off.

Little did they know I had about fifty pins in my hair. The streamers were tightly packed and made for weighty projectiles. Another one came over and I snapped.

'Why don't you fuck off, Addison?'

'You're a bad loser,' he shouted.

There followed an expletive-laden back and forth before Brendan took Addison away, aware that this prank had gone horribly wrong but unaware that it had brought out in me an angry boy forged in childhood.

Richard Wilson, star of *One Foot in the Grave*, came over.

'That was quite an outburst,' he said.

'They were trying to knock my hat off,' I said.

'Oh,' he said, 'I see.'

Richard stayed with me for a few minutes and I calmed down. There are some pictures online of him laughing with a haunted-looking matador and a fake Carmen Miranda before Cath and I went to get changed for the after-show party. I couldn't see Addison anywhere.

The next day, Matthew Wright wrote in his *Mirror* gossip column that I'd been thrown out of the Comedy Awards for fighting.

The Sun also ran a similar full page of fiction about me being ejected. Both papers had devoted considerable space for pictures of me ready for the bull ring. I suppose I could have sued but instead I moaned about the articles to various friends, none of whom knew what I was talking about.

Years later, Addison approached me to offer an apology for that night at the awards show, acknowledging that he'd provoked the whole argument and planted the story in the tabloids. Oddly, he claimed he'd been under pressure at the time from comedians in his stable, peers of mine who weren't doing so well, and so hadn't much cared about damaging my reputation or career by lying to those gossip-column hacks. It was an apology that evolved into a confessional, reminiscent of someone from Alcoholics Anonymous 'making amends' as part of the Twelve Steps. I told him not to worry about it; the Comedy Awards brought out the worst in people, including me.

Everyone knew the *TV Quick* Awards was the fun one to go to.

*

Despite the horrors of 1998, I couldn't resist going back to the Comedy Awards the next year. *Jonathan Creek* had a chance, since David Renwick had excelled himself with my favourite-ever episode, 'Black Canary', which starred one of my comic heroes from *The Young Ones*, Rik Mayall, as Inspector Gideon Pryke, a sleuth who was a match for Creek.

Months earlier, Rik had fallen off and under a quad bike, sustaining head injuries. This was his first job back; and although his giggly sense of humour remained and he looked fine, he couldn't remember his lines. He was frightened his brain might never recover and needed all the patience we could offer.

We were rewarded with a lot of laughter between takes. Caroline Quentin was at her playful best and we had a lot of fun with a pair of old-school actors, Murray Melvin and Francis Matthews.

Although we filmed it in September, the story was set in the snow and I was back in the duffle coat for some 'cold' acting.

Once, on a particularly chilly shoot for an Abbey National ad, the wardrobe department gave me a pair of Ugg boots previously worn by Sean Connery. I put them on despite the costume designer telling me how much the great actor perspired. Years later, I reluctantly threw them out as they had become the mothership for a moth infestation at home.

When it was Connery's closeup, he'd sometimes remove his trousers in an effort to stave off sweating under the lights. Rik and I pictured James Bond over an ice bucket into which he would lower himself, imagining a hissing sound as first contact with his undercarriage turned a solid to a gas, and then he'd say:

'I'm ready for my closhup.'

And the first AD would call out:

'Just waiting for the steam to clear and . . . ACTION!'

We had the giggles like children. I'd only have to open my legs and bend my knees slightly as if lowering hot tackle into cold water, or stand behind Rik and say, 'Hiiisssss,' and he'd double over.

At the 1999 Comedy Awards, I found the *Jonathan Creek* table and sat down with Verity Lambert, Geoffrey Perkins, Sandy Johnson and David and Ellie Renwick.

'We haven't won,' said David.

'How do you know?' I said.

'I was on the judging panel,' he said.

'I hope you voted for us.'

'No,' he said, 'I didn't.'

'Why not?'

'When it came to our category, I said I thought I ought to step outside, which I did, but some other people more prudently stayed where they were.'

'So they could vote for their own shows?' I said.

'Yes,' he said.

'Sensible,' I said.

'So it would seem,' he said.

I looked across the room as the tables filled, silently cursing David's moral correctness, with which he'd also imbued the character of Jonathan Creek but that I seemed not to share. For the only time at the Comedy Awards, I knew the result in advance. When our category came up, a camera was pointed at me to catch my reaction. While the successful cast went up to receive their lump of perspex, I can be heard booing in the background. Thankfully, I couldn't be identified on the broadcast, the director cut away. Too much wine, again.

Jonathan Creek never won a Comedy Award, which is probably for the best. When we won a *National Television Award* the year before, one of the presenters on the night was the American model Caprice. Having struggled on the steps to the podium, she said, 'I have six-inch heels.'

When we went up to accept our award, I said: 'I have a six-inch penis.'

'Now say something they can use,' said David.

Looking for Somewhere

ALAN: I was in a group of friends at university who all met in our
    first term, and when it came to looking for somewhere to live in the
    second year someone said it would be great if we could find a house
    big enough for seven.

THERAPIST: Rented accommodation?

A: Yes, because in the first year you're in halls.

T: I understand.

A: One of the group, Betty, told me she couldn't stand the only
    other girl, Nell, who was also the girlfriend of the group's sort of
    leader, Dean.

T: In what way was he the leader?

A: He just had a big personality.

T: I see.

A: His room was on the ground floor by the entrance to our college
    and he'd sit by the window calling out to people, playing music,
    he had lots of hair and was always grinning, everyone knew him.
    Anyway, Betty hated Nell, saying she was annoying and doing
    little impressions of her voice as if she were part rodent, and I said
    I understood what she meant and maybe we should find a couple of
    smaller places near to one another.

T: Did you tell the group?

A: We all met up to discuss the plan.

T: What did you say?

A: I said I didn't want to live with Nell.

T: *You* didn't want to?

A: Yes.

T: Not Betty?

A: Yes, me. I don't know why I said it, Nell was pretty, she had dimples when she smiled.

T: You were attracted to her but you said that? Was she there at the time?

A: Yes, all of us had met up and I said that at the start and Betty said nothing.

T: Betty didn't say she didn't want to live with Nell.

A: No, she just looked panicked.

T: No mouse noises?

A: No, and Dean was scowling.

T: Did Nell say anything?

A: No. It all broke up. I went to see Dean in his room to say sorry.

T: Not to see Nell?

A: No.

T: It seemed more important to pacify the leader of the group.

A: I suppose, I did go to see Nell afterwards.

T: What did you say to Dean?

A: That I was sorry, I didn't know why I'd said that, Nell is lovely . . .

T: You didn't mention Betty.

A: I just kept saying sorry.

T: What did he say?

A: 'I'm very disappointed in you, Alan.'

T: Did he? 'Disappointed'?

A: 'Very disappointed, very, very disappointed.'

T: What did you say?

A: I started crying.

T: —

A: It was embarrassing because I couldn't stop blubbing and sobbing and he just sat there staring at me, it was the first time I'd ever seen him not smiling. It felt like it went on for ages. Eventually I left.

T: He didn't say anything else.

A: We never really spoke again. I went to see Nell and said, 'I'm so sorry, I don't know why I said that, I didn't mean it, you're the nicest person out of all of us.'

T: Was she disappointed in you?

A: No, not at all, she'd been upset by what I'd said and was very pleased to make up straightaway. But the group broke up really.

T: You lost your friends?

A: Not quite. Me and Betty found a place with Vince, who was a friend of Dean's, but it was all a bit awkward. It can happen in first year at university, I suppose, you make friends and feel like you've known them forever.

T: Like a family?

A: Sort of, yes.

T: With Dean and Nell as the parents?

A: I hadn't thought of it like that.

T: We've talked before about coming to terms with losing your mother, not that long before this?

A: Thirteen years.

T: Of childhood.

A: Yes.

T: Maybe you feel abandoned by her, even angry with her for leaving you – I can see you're frowning, and this is a difficult idea to accept when the lost parent has become idealised – it's probably not something you would be aware of consciously but it might make you fearful of this type of mother figure. But more likely, perhaps, is that Nell didn't represent your mother here at all. The mother is absent and all the authority in the situation is invested in one man who is, inevitably, taking the father role, a very difficult one for you. What you were feeling regarding your mother might be described as the Presence of Absence. The absence is so strong it can be felt.

A: Almost tangible.

T: Therapy does not tie things up with a nice bow, but part of it is trying to understand our responses. The situation with Dean is clearer: he's the dominant male, so, to you, a very dangerous figure, like a father, and you need to please him. Were there any other men in the group you could have turned to?

A: Just Vince and a lad called Bryn, but they stayed out of it.

T: Like your own siblings compliant in the rule of the father?

A: Maybe, it blew over really. Vince only lived with me and Betty for a bit then he went to live with Dean, so Bryn came to live with us.

T: So, you're sharing a house with Betty and Bryn now.

A: Yes, it was freezing in winter, ice on the inside of the windows, but cheap. My room was £15 a week.

T: But no more trouble from Dean?

A: He never spoke to me again, which was a shame. They took me for my first-ever curry, I was eighteen and they couldn't believe I'd never had Indian food. I tried to explain that my dad didn't like foreign food, and that included rice. Dad never tried Indian food, of course.

T: Did you tell them any more about your dad?

A: No.

T: But you were settled in the house, what happened?

A: Bryn's girlfriend moved into his room, so they were paying £7.50 each and I suggested they should contribute more to the rent. Betty agreed with me but, of course, when the subject came up she kept quiet again, and Bryn was furious about it and I lost my friendship with him and he left.

T: Were you conscious of breaking up the group?

A: I didn't mean to. After that, Betty moved her boyfriend in, then she broke up with him but he and I became friends over the next couple of years.

T: Are you still in touch?

A: No, he had an affair with my girlfriend that went on for three years. Everyone knew except me.

T: Really?

A: Yes, I was the last to know.

T: That must have been very difficult.

A: [laughs]

T: [laughs]

A: It was humiliating. I'm not over it. [laughs]

T: I can see. [laughs]

A: At one point he had a serious car crash.

T: The boyfriend?

A: Yes. He was in hospital in Nottingham. I was in Manchester, I think, gigging, and I drove there in the pouring rain, in the dark, to see him, all the time thinking about his Ford Fiesta being wrecked and was I about to go the same way? When I got to the hospital he looked terrible, immobile in bed, wires sticking out where they'd put his bones back together, stitches, just awful. He was grateful that I'd come, he didn't expect many visitors, being so far from home. After a while he said he needed the toilet. I helped him along this big wide corridor, he could walk but only if someone supported him, he was wheeling a drip with his other hand. He went in the loo and I waited outside. After a few minutes, he called out to me and I had to go in and help him pull his trousers up since he couldn't manage. Then I got him back to bed. Eventually, I had to go back to London. He made a full recovery, and when he was well he started sleeping with my girlfriend again.

A: Did you ever confront them?

A: No, I had some pretty violent fantasies, especially after he wrote me a letter suggesting I should be grown up about the situation or some self-serving horseshit. I didn't reply, never saw him again. We'd been friends – best friends, I thought – for several years, and shared a house. I think they're still together now, I don't know.

T: How do you feel about that?

A: Good luck to them. I just wish they'd told me sooner. Who knows who I might have met or what I might have done? It was as if three years of my life had been stolen. I'd ask her to move in with me and she'd fob me off. When I look back and tally it up, some people were not very nice to me. Do I invite that? Is weakness and vulnerability too tempting a target? I never told any of them I'd been abused, they never asked about my mum.

T: It was a pseudo family, perhaps, and a family is alien to you
   unless there is a fracture in it, discord, disharmony, so you, quite
   unconsciously, set out to bring that about.

A: But if that's what my subconscious was pushing for, why was I
   unhappy?

T: Were you not already unhappy? And this situation showed it?
   On top of everything it appeared to shock you that your opinion –
   regarding Nell, or asking for help towards the rent – carried
   weight, that people would be impacted by the things you said, and
   again, we can look back to see how your voice had been denied
   throughout your whole life after your mother died. Growing up
   feeling that your voice has no power might have contributed to the
   impact you had on this friendship group.

A: So, it's my dad's fault?

T: You could draw that conclusion.

Pilot Cleared for Take-off

BBC Television liked *The Alan Davies Show* and would we consider making a TV pilot?

Everyone involved wanted to jump from Radio 4 to TV. It was a well-trodden path that peers of mine like Steve Coogan (as Alan Partridge), Rob Newman and David Baddiel had made with success.

The money would be better, but I'd learned that television was not as much fun to make as radio. It could be arduous and stressful. What if we made a crap pilot? The show would be dead and we wouldn't be able to revive it for radio. It would just be lost, like a ship sunk in deep water.

I hoped it would still be fun because the process would be similar: the same people, a week in a rehearsal room, a couple of days' filming on location and a studio day. We wanted to make a sitcom for a live audience even as they were going out of fashion after the success of Caroline Aherne's show *The Royle Family*.

Our main problem was that we took our characters all over the place on the radio, because you can. The list of locations from our six episodes would be beyond the budget of any sitcom apart from *The Simpsons*.

So, we created an internet café called the Sea of Tranquillity, to provide storylines with the customers and the possibilities of the characters finding things online. It would be very different from the radio show.

The pilot was due to be made in March: read-through on the 9th, studio recording on the 24th. It was too soon. I was on tour all through February and making a three-part documentary series at the same time, called *Stand Up with Alan Davies*. This involved a camera crew following me on the road with stops on the way to interview the best comedians in the UK.

There were also six episodes of *Jonathan Creek* to film that summer with Caroline Quentin, who had perked right up since she'd got off with a runner twelve years her junior on *Men Behaving Badly*.

Squashed in the middle would be my sitcom pilot, which was the most important project to me, the thing I'd always wanted.

I didn't yet have access to email when I was away on tour, so Tony and Ben had to fax me pages of the script. One hotel receptionist in Leeds saw virtually an entire roll of shiny paper reel out and fill her workspace, like the office equivalent of too much bubble bath.

I wanted to postpone the pilot, but there was some issue with the BBC calendar and the available budget in the tax year, or something.

So, they pushed on without me.

It occurred to me that I'd feel much safer making my pilot if John Lloyd would direct. He and I had a good rapport on the Abbey National ads. To my amazement he said yes.

Geoffrey Perkins could hardly believe this coup.

'Really?' he said. 'We've asked him so many times to come back to television.'

John hadn't worked on a show for a decade, since *Blackadder Goes Forth* (a real masterpiece), and was now willing to help me. We didn't need a director for the radio, but TV was different; to have an expert like John managing all those cameras and shots would be perfect.

Soon after he'd agreed to come on board, John called.

'Hi, Al,' he said. 'Look, I've been up since six trying to get this script to work and I just can't do it. It's not that there aren't funny bits, it's the setup. A sitcom needs a situation where the characters are trapped, they can't escape; whether because of money, or marriage, or their own inertia, they have to return to zero at the end of each episode. These characters could go anywhere and I don't really get this café location – why would they be in there every day?'

And I recalled that John wasn't the director of *Blackadder Goes Forth*; he was the producer, involved throughout with the writers Richard Curtis and Ben Elton.

'I just feel you need to start again,' said John.

But I couldn't meet up with everyone as I was back on the road with a string of interviews to film.

These Fellas Don't Mind

We had Victoria Wood and Jo Brand lined up for *Stand Up with Alan Davies* alongside nine white male stand-ups.

Ken Dodd arrived at the Adelphi Hotel in Liverpool forty minutes late and disappeared immediately to change out of the suit he was wearing.

When he came back he was in a different, almost identical suit. Then he talked for two hours. He wanted to keep me laughing throughout, but I managed to ask some questions. I thought we should just broadcast the whole thing.

Bob Monkhouse was equally generous with his time, speaking to me in his back garden. When he appeared in *Jonathan Creek*, I'd noticed his script was covered in doodles. He kept a large sketchpad in his trailer and drew a cartoon of me, which I still have, depicting my head being split in two by an axe. Maybe he'd had an early start that day.

As we left Bob's house, Vanessa Engle, the producer/director, noticed he was going out to the shops in his slippers.

'Should I tell him?' she said.

'No,' I said, fearing embarrassment.

'Bob,' she said, 'did you know you have your slippers on?'

'Oh, thank you, my dear, that's old age.'

I'd interviewed Dave Allen before, for *The Observer* in a 'Dave Allen meets Alan Davies' feature they'd cooked up by telling each of us the other person would only speak to him.

I told Dave I'd seen him live in the West End in 1991 and it was the funniest stand-up set I'd ever witnessed. My face and sides were hurting from laughing.

'You have to be careful with people,' he said. 'You have to give audiences a rest, I had a guy break a rib in the front row of a show.'

'From laughing?'

'From laughing.'

He said this with no trace of arrogance.

I'd sent Victoria a handwritten note saying an examination of the best of British stand-up without her would be worthless. We met in a teashop in Highgate and she talked about the nerves she'd suffered early on, when she'd stand in the crook of the piano so she could lean against it to stop shaking. She hated her gender being mentioned so often. She outsold everyone, so why wasn't she just a comic instead of a female comedian?

Jasper Carrot had come up through the same kind of folk clubs as Billy Connolly (who, I'm sad to say, was the only comedian who'd declined our invitation to appear), so gave an insight into another world of comedy. I asked Jasper about his stage name and he said he was really called Bob Davis and that he thought there could be no more boring announcement for an MC to make than: 'Please welcome to the stage, Bob Davis!'

I now have a son called Bob Davies and consider it an excellent name.

We interviewed a string of my peers: Ardal O'Hanlon, who'd found success in the brilliant *Father Ted*; my friend from Montreal, Phil Kay, who met us at Preston station, direct from Glasgow, and improvised being repeatedly thrown off a stationary train. We saw Harry Hill in an old-folks' home since he was talking a lot about mince at the time. It worked somehow, helped by a passing resemblance between him and one or two of the residents.

Eddie Izzard met us at Wembley Arena, where he was about to do a show. He had a big screen above him and wanted a locked-off camera so no director could interfere with the audience's view. The consequence of this control freakery was a performance area about two yards wide, on a stage that must have been a hundred feet across.

I stood at the mic so Eddie could go down onto the floor for a look while I sound checked for him.

'Say something funny!' he shouted, from page one of the heckler's handbook. I couldn't think of anything.

During his interview, Eddie mentioned losing his mum at six and said that he knew I'd had the same experience. He shared his theory that our performing, and seeking approval, is an attempt to replace the lost love of our mothers. I hadn't thought of that and struggled to accept it. Years later, I became convinced he was right.

Jo met us in a Little Chef, synonymous with so many years of gigging on the road. Off camera, I found myself unloading on her once again. She always listens, is loyal, forthright and leavens everything with silly jokes. My relationship with Cath was ending and I wasn't meeting up with our mutual friends.

Before she left, Jo checked that I was still seeing the therapist she'd recommended (I used to go round to her house afterwards) and then told me to ring her any time, obviously worried about me. I was low and lonely, despite playing to packed theatres every night.

Our last interviewee was Bernard Manning. Since he was an incorrigible racist, Vanessa had set us up in an Indian restaurant. I'd watched a couple of his videos, a stream of gags expertly delivered. But some racial slur was always inevitable.

'Why do you do it, Bernard?' I said. 'You don't have to, you're funny.'

'I know I am.'

'So why the racist stuff? You could just drop it.'

'They're good gags, and they're just gags, everyone knows that. These fellas in here don't mind.' He looked around at the Indian waiters: 'You don't mind, do you, fellas?'

Afterwards, Bernard climbed into his Roller and left. As the crew were packing up, one of the waiters came over.

'Can you not put that stuff in about how we don't care?' he said.

'About the racist jokes, you mean?' I said.

'Yes,' he said, as one or two of his young colleagues came over to join him. 'We do care, we don't like it.'

'OK. We won't leave that in.'

Vanessa and the crew bemoaned the fact that the waiters hadn't spoken up on camera, but it didn't surprise me. Those old racist attitudes are intimidating, daring you to oppose them so you can be derided for having no sense of humour. Or, worse, you end up in a row with an intransigent bigot.

When Vanessa edited the show, she finished one episode with a clip of Monkhouse and Manning singing 'Me and My Shadow' on some variety show from the seventies. It was poignant and almost chilling. Bob wasn't pleased.

'You put me together with Bernard, didn't you?' he said.

I could understand it: Bob was no racist, but Bernard could taint anyone. In some people's eyes, we shouldn't have interviewed him at all.

In between gigs, Vanessa would ask for my thoughts about stand-up and the series is peppered with me, half-awake, answering questions in a serious tone, unable to muster so much as a quip.

'Why are you interviewing me again?' I'd say. 'We've got great footage.'

Being on the road is dull, even though I had company in my support acts Keith Dover and Ian Stone.

But I trusted Vanessa, and had confided in her that my relationship was falling apart, so I was put out when she interviewed Cath, who was out of work and accepted the £150 appearance fee.

Cath told a story about the day she knew I'd become famous. We were walking down the street when a burly man aged about forty came up, took my face in both his hands, kissed me, and said: 'You are one comical bastard.'

The series was edited over several months, shown once on the BBC and then gone. Three years later, Bob Monkhouse died. I contacted Vanessa and asked about the interview he'd given us. Maybe we could put something up online by way of tribute.

'It's gone,' she said.

'You don't have any of those interviews?'

'You didn't want to keep the masters,' she said.

'I didn't want the footage of *me*,' I said. 'I just assumed the interviews would be kept.'

Cath moved out soon afterwards and wrote a song called 'Crazy' about someone with a Jekyll and Hyde character. She entered the Song for Europe with it, a New Yorker hoping to represent Britain at the Eurovision Song Contest. One of the tabloids printed the lyric in large font across a double-page spread, saying:

THIS SONG IS ABOUT YOU, ALAN.

Too late to help with ticket sales for the tour, unfortunately.

I'd Rather Lie in a Field

All was not well with *The Alan Davies Show* pilot. Supposedly Jane had left thirty-eight messages in one night on Tony Roche's answerphone and what's more, it appeared that she and John Lloyd couldn't be brought together on the script. Time was running out.

I don't know what was going on with Tony and his answerphone. Presumably he was getting through a lot of tapes but I felt sorry for him and especially for Ben Silburn, who was unfailingly good-natured and I'm sure would rather have been cycling round Richmond Park than going through this. But I also began to feel sorry for myself as another sitcom vehicle was falling apart. We had about a week and a half before the read-through, filming days and studio were booked, as were the cast and presumably the crew. We needed a meeting, to clear the air, sort out the weaknesses and try to improve the script and the atmosphere. Really I wanted Jane to listen to John a bit more and for Tony and Ben to benefit from his experience. It was only a pilot, a step towards a series.

But the meeting never happened. The second-draft script was delivered on 1st March and was not substantially different; Jane and Tony seemed dug-in. Maybe I needed to release John from a tricky situation and try to make the best of it, but instead I torched the whole thing by walking away, heading off an appearance by the angry boy, while wishing we'd never left Radio 4, where we'd felt like a family. I rang Bob Voice.

'I'd rather lie in a field than do this,' I said.

'I'll get you out of it,' he said.

*

Geoffrey Perkins, in his capacity as BBC Head of Comedy, visited the set of *Jonathan Creek* later that summer. He asked me about *The Alan Davies Show*. I told him what had gone on.

'If we'd sorted it out, would you have made the pilot?' he said.

'Yes,' I said. 'It's all I've ever wanted to do. But it wasn't ready and I didn't want it to be bad and not get commissioned.'

'I didn't know that,' he said.

'You didn't ask me.'

'I was in contact with Jane.'

'Yep.'

'I'm sorry,' he said. I was glad someone was.

'Don't worry,' I said. 'I think it was going to be rubbish.'

'I'm sure it wouldn't have been,' he said and I felt sad again, as I do whenever my lost sitcoms come up.

It's strange reading Tony and Ben's pilot script now, twenty-five years later. Below is a scene at a gym where Alan's latest girlfriend, Sandra, and her friend Jo, both described as having 'that unattractive end-of-workout look about them', are discussing his/my appearance:

SANDRA
  His role model isn't Brad Pitt,
  it's Bagpuss.

JO
  Maybe he's destined to be a saggy old fat
  bloke that nobody loves. You know, looks
  okay to begin with, then as soon as he's
  settled down let's [sic] himself go?

SANDRA
  You've met him. What did you think?

JO
　　Only briefly. The only thing I thought was – bit
　　flabby round the waistline, poorly defined
　　stomach muscles, slightly sallow complexion,
　　probably not getting enough protein, poor
　　posture, not a particularly stylish dresser and
　　the boots didn't go with the jeans. But, you
　　know, I wasn't paying much attention. Nice
　　hair, though.

SANDRA
　　It is, isn't it?

JO
　　Pump and curl?

SANDRA
　　Curl booster.

A while ago I saw Tony Roche at a screening of one of the best television dramas for many years, *Succession*, on which he was both a writer and executive producer.

He's tall, must be six three, and as I looked up at him I could still see the young man I knew in the nineties. Maybe we could raise the wreck of *The Alan Davies Show*.

'Fancy putting the band back together and doing some Radio 4 shows?' I said.

'Ha,' he said, 'as if you'd work for radio money.'

'I would, actually.'

'Yeah, right,' he said.

And off he went. Maybe I should have just left a message on his machine.

The Tears of Jonathan Creek

I'd never seen Caroline Quentin crying so much. After all she'd been through, with her agent stealing her money, her marriage breaking down and then spending nearly six months of 1997 stuck in a motorhome with me, it was surprising that things could get any worse.

It was a sun lounger that did it. In the summer of 1999, Caroline was heavily pregnant and exhausted by the filming schedule for *Jonathan Creek* series three.

She'd been upbeat at first, as she was happy with her handsome young partner, but now her ankles were swollen and a difficult shoot was made worse by her outrage at the stand-in who'd been hired to let her rest.

'She doesn't look anything like me, look at the size of her arse!'

Everyone stared at the blissfully unaware stand-in, whose costume, hair and height were identical to Maddy's, a fact that had (despite the disparity between bottoms) led to several instances of mistaken identity, each one a dagger in Caroline's heart.

I suggested to Darren and Rob, our loyal prop boys, that Caroline needed something more comfortable to rest on than the foldout chairs they carried on their van. They excelled themselves with a wooden, cushioned, reclining lawn chair.

Caroline broke down when she saw it, shaking and sobbing and hugging Darren and Rob. There wasn't a dry eye on set.

'I just thought you'd be more comfortable,' I said, blinking, but she didn't respond.

'. . . I'd seen you on our crappy chairs, and I said to the boys that maybe we should find you something.' No response.

'. . . They came up with it so quickly, I only suggested it yesterday.'

'Yes, *all right*! I know it was *your idea*!' she said.

In a memorable episode in series three, a Jonathan Creek fan club convenes. Lots of men appeared on set in duffle coats and curly wigs, their leader played by Tom Goodman-Hill.

I'd recently met the kids' TV presenter Kirsten O'Brien in the office at International Artistes. We were texting a lot and she was teasing me about playing a wizard who lives in a windmill. One day, during a week away on location in Oxfordshire, a package arrived from her at the hotel. I opened it on the way to set, sitting in the back of a car next to Tom.

'That's great!' he said, chuckling at Kirsten's sense of humour as I unwrapped a joke-shop wizard's hat.

Caroline was in the front seat.

'Some people will do anything for a fuck,' she said.

The rest of the journey was silent. Once we were out of the car, Tom said: 'Does she always talk to you like that?'

'Not *always*,' I said.

My sister came to see me on set while we were filming exteriors at Shipley Mill in Sussex, as she lived about half an hour away.

The handsome windmill, once owned by Hilaire Belloc and marked as such on some maps, is evocative of a different era and our unit base was set in lush green grass surrounded by hedgerows. I had happy memories of filming the first series there, when the mill's interior was dressed in the most detailed and extraordinary way by the design team led by John Asbridge. All of Creek's files and folders had precise titles and subject headings that you'd be unlikely to see on camera; the magician's posters and props were chosen with the same care that David Renwick took over every punctuation mark.

My sister had driven over for lunch on this sunny July day despite being even more heavily pregnant than Caroline.

Poised over a barbeque was our muscular new caterer, Colin, shirtless with just an apron over his torso, like a handsome cross between Ainsley Harriott and Mike Tyson. It was the only time I saw the make-up department go back for seconds. Although that may have been because the burgers were delicious, my sister had two of them, one for her and one for the baby, and when she went home that evening her waters broke, a fortnight early.

Much to his amusement, I held Colin responsible; but it was a happy accident as I was close enough to meet my new nephew, Louis, when he was a few hours old. His middle name's Alan and he towers over me now. As I write this, he's twenty-five years old and backpacking in Bolivia with his brother, Connor.

A few weeks later, Caroline was taken to hospital. Her baby had also come early, and by more than two weeks. There was concern among her friends on the crew; we'd spent four summers together, so everyone was relieved to hear, eventually, that mother and daughter were healthy.

Verity Lambert took control and we carried on shooting as the schedule was moved around. Caroline came back to finish her remaining scenes towards the end of the year, and we completed the series, but she would never play Maddy again.

I don't know what happened to that sun lounger; I hope the stand-in has it.

Stand-Up Sits Down

I needed new material. All the touring, the DVD, the BBC1 special, meant that the routines in *Urban Trauma* were now deceased.

I can't come up with stuff without gigging and I always feared that I'd never think of anything funny again.

Jonathan Creek took me away from the circuit but once filming was over I'd try to keep my hand in at the Comedy Store, where Kim Kinnie was always welcoming.

In the dressing room, Ed Byrne said to me: 'What's this thing you're in on Saturday nights? My ma watches it and she fookin' loves it.'

'He's a magician's assistant and creator of illusions who is able to find clues to solve murders,' I said.

'Jesus, who came up with that load of old shite?'

You could always rely on the dressing room at the Store to keep you grounded but things had changed around the place. I'd heard about good comics I'd gigged with for years getting hooked on coke and making a mess of their careers.

One night, I went into the dressing room and one such comic was in there chopping out a line on the counter next to the kettle. He hadn't even gone in the toilet, four feet away.

'Hello, Al,' he said. 'Do you wanna a line?'

'No,' I said, 'I don't. What are you doing? Aren't you going on next?'

'Yeah,' he said, 'this is for when I come off.'

Addicts are pathological liars.

'No it isn't,' I said. 'You were just about to do that when I came in. Don't do that, you're at work. Who does coke at work? Save your money. How much was that wrap? Fifty? You've got kids; put your drug money in a box marked "Christmas".'

He'd stopped what he was doing. Someone else was bound to come in at any moment.

'Yeah, yeah, I will,' he said, looking down. 'You're so right, no one's ever spoken to me like that about it.'

'Really?' I said. 'Listen, this is your job, don't piss it away; you'll lose your family, you'll lose your kids.'

'Thanks, man. I'm going to stop, you're right; I appreciate it.'

'Yeah, well, good luck,' I said.

He lost his wife and kids.

I dropped in at the Comedy Store one weekend in late 1999 to see if they'd let me just wing it for ten minutes to see what came up.

Arriving at the venue reminded me of the theme tune from *Cheers*. Sometimes you do want to go where everybody knows your name. Everyone was pleased to see me, the bouncers, stage manager, box office and cloakroom staff and Don Ward, the owner, who said: 'Yes, of course, Alan,' when I asked if he had room for me.

Tim Clark was the compere and watching him on the monitor in the dressing room, with his smart suit, shaved head and soft Liverpudlian accent, it felt like old times. He was preparing the audience for a special guest.

'Now, this next act is a bit nervous, he's new to the game, so give him a chance, please welcome Alan Davies!'

The door from the dressing room is at the back of the small stage. As soon as I put my head out, a huge cheer went up. Tim looked at me with a wry grin, as if to say: 'Was that a good intro or what?' and patted me on the arm as he went by, a touch that said: 'Have fun, son.'

It's only three strides to the microphone and the applause and cheering was still going strong – easy to milk, in fact, with a gesture to one side of the room to whoop louder than the other.

Years before, I'd arrived at the Store for a gig when Kevin Day, who was compering, stopped me on the way in.

'There's someone in the dressing room,' he said, before deciding not to tell me any more. 'You'll see.'

Standing in there, alone, was Lenny Henry, then at the height of his television fame, looking like he was going to crap himself. He went on to a massive ovation. The Store audience, always on a promise of the star drop-in since Robin Williams turned up one night thirty-something years ago, are delighted to see a famous face. Lenny brought his familiar energy and a few gags he needed to try out before scarpering back into the dressing room relieved that he could still hack it but with no wish to do *that* again.

Now it was my turn and the shouting soon started.

'It's a perm!' said a voice up the back, to huge laughter, so a couple of other people, doubtless with a drink inside them, shouted 'Perm!' and then, to my right, a woman stood up to defend me.

'Oh, shut up!' she said.

I was mumbling something but had no opening line; and my comedy car was in neutral or, worse, had been off the road so long, the battery was dead.

'What's Caroline Quentin like?'

'Have you shagged her?'

'Yeah, have you shagged her?'

No reply came to mind.

'Yeah, he has shagged her!"

'No, I haven't shagged Caroline,' I said. 'And no, it isn't a perm.'

No comedy so far.

'Perm!'

'Perm!'

'Leave him alone!"

Still nothing, just grinning at them.

'Just shut up, so we can hear him!'

'Perm!'

'Shut the fuck up!'

The idea of 'just winging it' was abandoned on take-off. I tried to pick out a routine from my touring show, but that was ninety minutes long and all of it had left my head. The ceiling is low at the Store and most of the audience are in the dark, but you can see enough of them to gauge how you're doing. The gig had already gone awry. They did quieten down when I talked about the crowd heckling one another being a new experience, but I couldn't think past that. A few little laughs followed remarks that were generated by something I said as if by muscle memory. I was like a first-timer open spot floundering in the deep end and needing to put my feet on the bottom. Where's the shallow end?

Oh yeah, there isn't one.

The clock was ticking. My in-built laugh counter, which lets me know when the next one is due, does not tolerate long stretches like this and had shut off. If this was a high-wire act, I'd fallen off and was in the net.

'Do you know what?' I said. 'I think I'm gonna go. Goodnight.'

And there was a groan of disappointment.

'No!'

'Stay!'

'NO!"

But by then I was on my way to the dressing room, my back to the crowd. It would be ten years before I stood on that stage again. Tim Clark came through the door as I approached; even a seasoned pro like him had been caught out by such an abrupt departure. He'd regained his composure by the time he casually stood before the mic and addressed the audience.

'Oh dear, what have you done?' he said.

Laughter and more groaning.

'That was Alan Davies,' said Tim, the master craftsman drawing applause where there was none.

'More!'

'No,' said Tim, 'he's not coming back, and can you blame him?'

This was the Store, my favourite club, no one went down better than me there, or so I'd thought. I'd taken it for granted and now doubted I'd ever be able to go back. Where would material come from if I wasn't gigging and how could I gig if it was going to be like this?

I saw Ian Stone a few days later.

'I hear you had a shit one at the Store,' he said, with a consoling grin on his face that I scrutinised for signs of hidden glee. Of course everyone knew.

No more *Cheers* for me. It seemed the unintended consequence of the wealth and fame I'd sought was to lose my creative outlet, my sanity-restorer and the thing I used to do best.

If I wasn't a stand-up comedian, what was I?

Who was I?

Part Two

Not Waving or Drowning

Late in the year 2000, I told an estate agent in Islington that I wanted a place with a swimming pool and they'd said that was almost unheard of in the borough, but – and it was funny I'd called, actually, because – they did have something and maybe I'd like to see it.

At the time, I lived two minutes' walk from the excellent public baths at Highbury Fields.

A viewing was arranged and I arrived at a corrugated shutter alongside a converted factory on Corsica Street. There was a narrow doorway and then a reinforced-glass entrance leading to a long wooden staircase that went up into a large atrium with further stairs, at the top of which the owners were brewing fresh coffee in their stainless-steel kitchen.

He was a multi-award-winning international hairstylist with a string of salons, she a feng shui consultant and interior-design guru. Their furniture was not available on the high street.

There followed a tour: palm trees on the roof, raised sleeping platform with blackout blinds, three mosaic-tiled bathrooms, softly carpeted bedrooms, and parking.

Then the pool itself. The building's steel framework had once supported industrial machinery but now suspended a vast body of water on the first floor, behind large windows alongside a fifty-foot maple-floored living room. As I gazed through the glass at the shimmering blue, the owners whispered that Catherine Zeta-Jones, one of the world's most desirable women, had once swum naked in there, for a scene in a film with Eric Idle (who was certainly looking on the bright side of life in that job, nudge, nudge, wink, wink, say no more).

And Right Said Fred had made a video in the kitchen.

I wanted to buy it. This was going to be the home that Abbey National bought. I'd heard that Rik Mayall called his house Nintendo Towers after making ads that weren't even shown in the UK. Perfect.

My attempt at striking a deal began by offering the asking price, a move the owners fell for immediately, but then everything went quiet. There'd been a bigger offer, from a banker who worked for Credit Suisse.

The owners said they'd prefer to sell to me, but preferably at the Credit Suisse man's price point.

I agreed that I was the best available buyer and we shared an unspoken understanding that our creative life choices made us better people than some financier from *The Bonfire of the Vanities*.

After a phone call pleading for an even bigger loan, I continued my hardball negotiating tactics by matching the offer.

We overlooked the fact that the money I was about to spend on their mega-apartment had come because a bank had purchased my cheery persona, my 'everything's all right with the world if you just smile and enjoy your pets' attitude, with my face being used as a distracting mask over who knows what corporate investment. Deforestation? Fossil fuels? Cluster bombs? Banks weren't vocal on helping with inadequate social care, or the underfunding of the arts.

It didn't occur to me that I could use my status as a public figure to help anyone. This was an act of self-preservation. Hadn't I worked hard? My loss of privacy, sacrificed to fame for the enjoyment of others, meant that owning a gated palace was not only nice but a necessity.

It was a big commitment, especially given there was no *Jonathan Creek* series that year, the Abbey National ads were not something I wanted to do any more and future stand-up touring seemed unlikely.

On top of that, I'd quit *The Best Show in the World . . . Probably* and my own sitcom, immolating the one thing I did want to do.

In the last show I'd done, a sitcom called *A Many Splintered Thing*, I'd played a married 'jingle writer' who wants to run away with Kate Ashfield's delightful flower girl.

At one point I had to get out of a bath and wrestle in the nude with my screen wife, the tall, cheek-boney Simone Bendix, who was stylishly dressed throughout. It was February and I was naked, wet and freezing for an entire day at the arctic 3 Mills Studios in East London. I had a triangular flesh-coloured modesty patch covering my privates, though, by the afternoon, I was so reduced by being sprayed with cold water, I could have squeezed the complete works into the wax covering from a Babybel cheese.

We lasted one series and were lucky to get that. I was not funny at any point in any episode and had no work for the rest of the year.

At home, I'd become reclusive and paranoid and a return to stand-up comedy is not possible in that frame of mind, which was a shame because I could have shifted a lot of tickets. Yet I was nonetheless prepared to hand over a fortune for a groovy new pad and moved in on 1st December 2000. I kept and let out my little house on St Mary's Grove, perhaps because it all felt like a risk.

I found myself back out in Loughton at my dad and stepmother's house for lunch on Christmas Day. My sister had her one-year-old and my brother had two young sons who I watched at play.

And then I went back to the apartment. The pool had a noisy fan running twenty-four hours a day to stop condensation. For the water to be pleasant, it had to be heated by a gas boiler to twenty-eight degrees, which was already feeling costly.

I spent several days in the apartment between Christmas and New Year without speaking to a single soul. I went out for an Arsenal home game but most of my friends had gone away over the holidays and I'd arrived home again to the same loneliness. I wasn't screening my calls, there just weren't any. And it was all made worse by being unable to sleep at night.

One day I stood in the swimming pool, which was forty feet long and uniformly four feet deep, and stared in silence at the far end, which was the only place to get in and out. I was motionless for maybe two hours, or four? Unable to walk back to the other end, I just couldn't move.

I'd been in therapy for five years by then and had some idea of how to identify feelings and attempt to articulate them, but this situation was defeating me. Ultimately, I was invested in the idea that there might be an actual cure from the so-called talking cure.

At the end of the therapy road, I hoped, lay a life of tranquillity, equanimity and carefully strategised associations with only those people I respected and who were respectful back, in which I made considered choices to avoid hazards (catch nets under leaves, concealed spike pits) with no horrors of the past creeping up from behind to ensnare me with a monstrous psychological tentacle.

And that, perhaps, was the depressing problem. I still misconceived life as being linear, to be progressed through to new destinations and further away from previous experiences.

The past recedes only in memory, not in influence. The fact that certain incidents are forgotten, or can no longer be accessed in memory, doesn't stop them from having an effect.

It's a difficult concept, the idea that lost events are shaping our choices, every day, but it's possibly best understood by considering that we're all formed by the long-forgotten first eighteen months of our lives.

Firstly, there's the genetic accident of conception. A personality formed by the combination of our parents plus the influences exerted on a foetus; noise, stress, diet all play a part. It seems responses to old dangers have been internalised too, over millions of years of evolution. When we fall asleep sitting up, we sometimes wake with a start; it's suggested this is because when our ancestors slept in trees they'd grab a branch immediately they woke to not fall out.

Perhaps a baby is innately ready for the trauma of birth in the same way some elderly people declare themselves ready for death. My gran would say: 'I want to be in me box.'

Do babies know what's coming but can't stay squashed in the womb for another minute? Does the baby fear the birth? Is it thinking: 'This is a squeeze, where's that draught coming from? What is this head-clamp?'

Or during a sudden C-section: 'Back off! Who is moving me? Aaaarrrggghhh!'

With all this innate behaviour, followed by the first year and a half of emotional learning, we are set for life; the only thing that can blow the doors off your personality, put a kink in your pipe, a hole in your bucket, is trauma. Malnutrition, violence or illness in early childhood can be included here, as well as impactful sudden events, like bereavement, or prolonged betrayals of trust with concomitant, exploitative secrecy, such as predatory sexual abuse by a family member.

Those things will change your personality later in life. But otherwise, you're formed in the dreaming, pre-memory, without having any recollection of the behaviours and events that continue to act upon you.

You need some self-acceptance, some self-love. I lacked those skills at the time, and the angry boy certainly wasn't at any point of understanding. I was just miserable, but what I did know how to do was construct a cheery façade.

So, I decided to have a party on New Year's Eve!

I wouldn't tell anyone I'd been unhappy, even Kirsten, who was back from Christmas away. I'd act like a millionaire playboy sharing the trappings of my sellout. The estate agent had said this was a fabulous space for entertaining.

Lots of friends came. Old ones from the comedy circuit, like Bill and Kris Bailey and Keith Dover. And new ones like Mark Tonderai, who I'd met that summer when I was in his film *Dog Eat Dog*.

Mark, his girlfriend Zoe and another friend sat down to roll joints on one of two huge custom-made leather-and-suede sofas, next to the Bang & Olufsen stereo left by the previous owners. Mark was also a Radio 1 DJ and kept the music going all night, despite my unpromising CD collection and solitary disc player, with some alchemic wrangling that turned a pile of filla into killa. The only issue was that he insisted on full volume, so I couldn't hear the front door.

'Mark,' I said, 'people are trying to get in; we can't hear the buzzer.'

'They'll get in,' he said.

'PARDON?' I said, and he smiled, exhaling clouds of marijuana smoke that I tried to breathe in so as not to waste it.

Hattie Hayridge was among the other comedian friends who turned up, along with a young Ross Noble, who brought a large inflatable hamster wheel that he blew up using only the lung power of a youthful non-smoker. It had a printed warning on its side: 'Do not use in or near a swimming pool'.

Once I was floating in that wheel, I did not want to get out; could this party not go on forever?

Bill Bailey was in the water wielding a champagne bottle in a parodic display of rockstar excess for all the dry-side revellers. There were speakers in the pool room (of course) and under the water. Andy Linden jumped in and then Kris's friend Sasha appeared looking so finely toned and proportioned that no other woman at the party would swim.

No matter: in the open-plan kitchen there was food and drink and plenty of weed all around and at midnight it was 2001 AD, the year of Stanley Kubrick's *Space Odyssey*, where an astronaut has only a talking computer for company. Could be worse.

It occurs to me now how like a bleak interstellar journey my last week of 2000 was. If only I'd had some means of accessing diagnostic status reports.

A couple of months after the party, Kirsten and I broke up. We'd laughed a lot together, not least on a holiday in the Cayman Islands where we'd spent most of the week placing an Austin Powers action figure in daft locations and photographing him.

I have Kirsten to thank for one night in a Brighton club when I reconnected with Damian Harris, also known as the Midfield General. To me, he'd been the teenage brother of Phil (my friend from student days in Whitstable who'd come to my video recording in 1994).

Damian had alwys wanted to be a DJ, referring often to his Wheels of Steel. When we met in Brighton, I hadn't seen him in ten years.

'So, you're doing it then?' I said.

He's a big boy but gentle to the point of notoriety.

'How do you mean?' he said.

'Making a living as a DJ?'

'Don't you know what I do?'

'No.'

Kirsten had told me only that she'd bumped into someone in the music industry who'd said he knew me.

'I don't know anyone in the music industry,' I'd said to her.

'I run Skint Records,' said Damian now.

'Skint?' I said. 'Why do I know that name?'

'Fat Boy Slim,' he said.

'Oh!' I said. 'Wow, even I've got that record, you are doing well, then.'

We both had season tickets at Arsenal and in 2006 when the club moved to a new stadium we merged our two sets of friends and eleven of us have sat together ever since. This group includes Oliver Scott, Tayo Popoola and Alistair Wotton, who still go to games along with me and Keith Dover.

It would be neglectful not to mention them in a book where the search for family is a recurring theme. Now I think about it, I'm not short of brothers. As an example of why I enjoy their company, I was telling Oliver how, when we named our second child Bobby, I hadn't thought about all the famous Roberts and Bobs there have been.

'De Niro, the Bruce, Dylan, Marley, Moore, Pires . . .' I said.

'Mugabe,' he said.

The Day of the Jackal

20th October 2024.

Once you know you are having a trans-urethral resection of a bladder tumour, it is hard not to search for information online. There is plenty, much of it useful, particularly from the NHS and Macmillan websites.

The examination of the bladder is performed with a flexible cystoscope but a TURBT, or turbot, as I kept calling it, to no one's amusement, is performed with a rigid cystoscope. This thing looks like something rolled out in a leather bag containing items used to torture a man tied to a chair in a movie. It's a contraption with finger grips, a long barrel, a sight and the potential to wound.

Just before my operation, I repeatedly saw trailers on TV for a big-budget new series, *The Day of The Jackal*. Eddie Redmayne plays an assassin and the trailer showed him assembling a bespoke sniper's rifle by dismantling a wheelie suitcase into components with holes, spaces and unusual angles, then snapping it all together until what he had in his hands looked less like a gun than it did a rigid cystoscope.

There were images all over London of Eddie Redmayne looking down the barrel of a cystoscope as if he was going to fire a specifically commissioned tumour-busting round through my penis and straight to the target. I imagined being awake as Eddie put my growth in his crosshairs. This guy never misses, right?

Right?

Quite Interesting

'You don't get points for being right; you get points for being interesting,' said John Lloyd.

'Sounds great,' I said.

'Really? Everyone else I've spoken to thinks it's a terrible idea.'

'I prefer it if the question is a jumping-off point,' I said, 'so that the panel have to work together off the cuff. Much more fun than trying to crowbar in prewritten material, so it's a collaboration, not a competition.'

'I've been researching for years, Al,' he said. 'I've already got a database of interesting stuff that isn't taught in schools. The show could be the most interesting lesson you never had with the best teacher and funniest pupils.'

'I can't understand how anyone could not think that's a good idea, especially after everything you've done before.'

'Would you be up for doing a pilot?'

'Yes,' I said, 'I'd love to.'

'I was thinking of asking Eddie Izzard, is that a good idea?'

'Yep, he's funny, if he's over not doing telly.'

'Who else is good?'

'Bill Bailey,' I said.

'I don't know him, is he funny?'

'Yep,' I said.

In 2001, as our time on the Abbey National ads was coming to an end, and two years after we nearly made a sitcom before I jumped out of the window in a panic, John Lloyd had come up with an idea that would allow us to continue working together. I was delighted.

The host was to be Stephen Fry, which was a coup because while he was familiar to viewers he wasn't actually on television very often.

Kit Hesketh-Harvey was the fourth panellist. I'd seen Kit and the Widow opening for Joan Rivers and knew him to be hilarious.

John had been planning to have a Toffs vs Oiks setup, with me (middle-class drama graduate) cast as the downmarket opposition to Stephen on the other team. The idea had been that Michael Palin would host, except he didn't fancy it. And Eddie wanted to go to America so had no appetite to commit to a series.

We recorded a non-broadcast pilot scripted by John, in which Stephen continually dished out points. Bill, Eddie and Kit were funny throughout. I was trialling an open-mouthed halfwit persona, laughing too much at everything, which seemed to help the feelgood factor if nothing else.

John had talked to me beforehand about Arthur Koestler's notion that great scientists and comedians are similar in that they make unpredictable connections that can move thinking in surprising directions. John has a great capacity for flattery but I doubted I was what Koestler had in mind; I'd read his *Darkness at Noon* and its brilliance came from an intellect that dwarfed mine and possibly even Stephen Fry's.

It didn't take long to hear that BBC Two had commissioned a series of *QI*. The panel game was a staple of the entertainment-department output. A simple setup with two teams behind desks answering questions from a likeable host.

Usually, whether it was *Have I Got News For You*, *Call My Bluff*, *A Question of Sport* or various others, there'd be two permanent team captains, with guests making up the numbers on either side. But John said he wanted me to be the only regular, alongside Stephen. This was a different model, more like an American talk-show, where the quick-witted host might have a sidekick to be the butt of a joke whenever the laughter thinned out.

That I was the class dunce didn't really dawn on me until about four years later, by which time I'd suggested a loud klaxon for anyone who fell into the trap of spouting widely believed but false information, such as Bangkok being the capital of Thailand or the Earth having only one moon. That sound has featured in my dreams.

A couple of years in, Patrick Marber remarked one day that the relationship between Stephen and me was 'the best sitcom on television' and that a spinoff flatshare series was inevitable. I asked if he'd write it but he declined.

As I was still off stand-up, *QI* became the place where I could be in front of an audience (six hundred and fifty of them, at London Studios), often sharing the stage with people I'd known from our early days on the comedy circuit like Jo Brand, Bill Bailey and Sean Lock.

Off camera, John Sessions was the funniest guest. Usually before the show, we'd congregate in Sue Sian's make-up room, where Stephen would welcome people with fulsome praise for their work and gratitude for their existence and the atmosphere was unfailingly convivial.

One night, John (or 'dear old Johnny Sesh', to Stephen), wearing a mischievous grin, said: 'Do you know about the famous argument between Richard Burton and Elizabeth Taylor in the foyer of a Los Angeles hotel during which she shat herself?'

'No,' said Stephen, laughing already, 'I haven't heard about that.'

'They were both pissed,' said John, setting the scene before he began a dialogue between Burton and Taylor, taking off their Welsh and mid-Atlantic voices hilariously and interspersing the conversation with loud raspberries to indicate Ms Taylor's predicament.

'You're such an asshole!' she said.

'You're a drunk and a whore!' he said.

'You bastard!' she said.

[sound effect]

'You're disgusting!' he said.

'How dare you?!' she said.

[sound effect]

'Stop shitting yourself, you crazy bitch!'

'Stop, please stop,' said Stephen as we both held our sides.

The subsequent recording was a good one but the studio audience must have wondered why we all found things so funny as the residual joy lingered on.

Bob & Rose

ALAN: I'm going to be away again, for three months this time.

THERAPIST: Where will you be?

A: Manchester. I've got a part in an ITV drama.

T: Congratulations, is it something you want to do?

A: The scripts are great. I might have got off on the wrong foot, though. The director of this new show, Julian Farino, invited the cast to his house one evening before we get started.

T: That's a nice thought.

A: Yes, it is, but I refused to go. I said to my agent, 'Why should I go to his house, why can't they come to mine?'

T: Did he pass that on? Your agent?

A: She, yes.

T: Oh, you have a new agent?

A: Yes, I left Bob.

T: Why was that?

A: I wanted more acting opportunities, and I found a letter on his desk to the advertising agency trying to get a fifth year of Abbey National ads and I'd said I didn't want to do them.

T: You found it?

A: Yes, honestly, I was alone in his office and it was just there on his desk. I asked him about it and he said he was writing to get me out of it.

T: That must have been awkward.

A: A bit. When I left he was disappointed but he hasn't tried to make things difficult. I've heard of comics getting sued by their old agents, which is unbelievable. Some agents really seem to think they deserve all the credit. Bob couldn't understand why I'd go because we'd made a lot of money, but the main thing was I wanted more acting opportunities and Michelle Milburn had joined the agency.

T: Is she good?

A: I hope so. She's younger, more connected with casting agents, she represents two new comedians she rates very highly called Mitchell and Webb, who I hadn't heard of, so I'm feeling a bit out of touch.

T: So, this meeting with the director, could Michelle not have advised you to go?

A: I wouldn't have listened. I said I wanted them all to come to my flat, I was grumpy about having to meet up at all.

T: Did you feel threatened, perhaps, by Julian offering to host? Is there sometimes a power struggle between the director and the leading man?

A: Not from my end. It wasn't something I was conscious of.

T: No, but perhaps still a factor. And they came to your flat?

A: Yes, and I showed off my swimming pool, and how I live in this Austin Powers-type penthouse. God knows what they thought of it. Anyway, it was fine. I think really I was anxious about the part.

T: Why's that?

A: Because he's gay.

T: Do you worry that people might think that you're gay? Is that why you're anxious?

A: I don't think so. I remember at university I was at a party one night, just ten or so people from the drama department, and one of the women, who was about three years older than me, just kissed me on the mouth, out of nowhere. But she had her lips clamped together so it was a bit of an odd kiss, and then she said, 'Open your mouth,' and pushed a piece of tangerine in with her tongue and backed away looking at me. I had no idea there was this game going on and my job was to pass the segment to the next person, who was a gay man, also a few years older. I put my mouth against his and passed the bit of tangerine, and his stubble rubbed on my face. It really reminded me of when my dad used to molest me. I suppose the last time would only have been about five years before I went to university. Anyway, the gay man was teasing me for being uptight, as if I was a bit homophobic, and I didn't feel able to say, 'You remind me of my dad in bed.'

T: But you didn't mind putting your mouth on his?

A: No, I didn't care about that, though passing the fruit around was weird, I don't know why they were doing that.

T: There's quite a well-known cartoon, you may have seen it, set in a gentlemen's club, with a few old duffers sitting about in leather chairs, silently reading newspapers or smoking cigars or dozing. In the middle of it all, one man has jumped to his feet and is shouting: 'That's it, I can't hide it any more, I'm gay and I don't care who knows it!' And no one around him has moved a muscle.

A: No one cares. That's funny.

T: Exactly.

A: Part of it is just professional anxiety. I don't want to be bad at being gay, you know how sometimes you see people on screen smoking and you can tell they've never smoked before.

T: I'm sure you've been cast because you're more than capable.

A: I met the writer. He's really nice, good fun, he's Welsh, by the way.

T: —

A: Russell T Davies. He did a series called *Queer as Folk*, which was excellent, and very gay, lots of sex scenes. This one is less riotous and explicit, partly because my character, Bob, falls in love with a woman called Rose. Anyway, he says he's always thought there was an ambiguity about me.

T: He thought you might be gay.

A: I suppose so, but I've never had any experience at all, never experimented, so the first time I kiss a man will be on camera, apart from Satsuma Man, of course.

T: And your father.

A: Yes. I hadn't thought of that as a sexual experience, but yes,
      I suppose so. The other thing that bothers me is not making a mess
      of the thing because the scripts are so good. They sent me three
      and I read them all one after the other, spent a whole evening with
      them until one in the morning. They're so well constructed, and
      touching, with lots of humour. Everyone in it is not quite happy
      with their lot.

T: And that appears authentic to you?

A: Yes, I suppose it does.

T: Well, even though you can't be here for three months, don't forget
      you can call and speak on the phone.

A: Yes, perhaps I will, thank you.

I never rang him, even though my anxiety was such that I did not sleep for
a single minute the night before the first shooting day. I'd been put in an
apartment in Manchester and just lay there worrying. Kirsten rang me at
eight in the morning to wish me luck, which was thoughtful, but I felt had to
respond in a certain way and couldn't, so ended up biting her head off.

Bob & Rose was being made by Nicola Shindler's Red Productions, a company
with a growing reputation for high-quality, popular television. Lesley Sharp
was playing Rose. Like me, she felt a responsibility not to make a mess of the
wonderful scripts. She was considerate, with a sense of humour, and I was
always delighted to see her on set, which was good, because one of the first
things we had to do as Bob and Rose was shag in a train toilet.

The tiny lavatory was built as a set. Standing outside the window, while
Lesley and I were snogging and pulling at each other's clothes, was a big 'spark'
who had to pass a piece of board in front of a light repeatedly to suggest the
train was moving. We conducted the (fully clothed and rapid) intercourse as
an unfolding consensual negotiation, all shot from the waist up. Afterwards,
Lesley said, 'Thank you,' which has never happened to me in real life.

In one episode, Bob goes home with a handsome chap (played by Jonathan Wrather) he's just met in a club. There was to be some fast undressing followed by tumbling-onto-the-bed-snogging. I asked the gay make-up designer if there was anything I needed to know about kissing a man. I didn't want to do it wrong. He frowned and said: 'Just kiss him.'

Obviously.

Mr Wrather's forceful passion pushed my head back so I disappeared out of shot.

'Cut! We'll go again.'

For take two, I braced myself.

It did make me wonder whether girls are forever being pushed off balance by assertive males. The scene was fine; two straight actors had a snog. I imagined the man in the gentlemen's-club cartoon yelling: 'I've kissed a man!'

Bob's best friend Holly was played by the brilliant Jessica Stevenson (now Hynes), who had a different approach to Lesley. She's bright and funny and talked continually up to the call for the camera to 'turnover'. A few seconds later when we heard 'Action', I'd look at her to find Jess had gone and Holly was standing there, like someone switching between personalities. She would now be unmistakeably the character, with all her vulnerability and misplaced scheming. At the word 'Cut', Jess would return. It was eerie.

At first I lived in central Manchester, but the city was in preparation for the 2002 Commonwealth Games and builders would sit in trucks with the engines running (to keep the heating on, since it was freezing) under my window when I was going to bed at 9am after night shoots, so I moved out to leafy, suburban Didsbury. It was pleasant there but I was lonely, not knowing anyone to go for a drink with after work. Lesley would rush back to London to see her two young sons, who she was missing terribly, and Jessica was living in North Wales with her mum.

So, I'd go to the off licence by myself and was initially surprised to find all the shelves of drink and the counter behind security cages. I hadn't seen that before.

Soon I was not fit for socialising in any case, as I contracted an exhausting chest infection, which left me short of breath and coughing up a different colour each day.

Never missed a minute on set, of course; that was unthinkable.

After a while, I met some crew members who would go to the Press Club in Manchester for karaoke nights, meeting up with people from another Red Productions drama, *Clocking Off*. I enjoyed watching but never went up; I've only done karaoke once, at the Comedy Café in a duet of 'Tracks of my Tears' with Mark Hurst. Halfway through, he shouted, 'rap break' and was off: 'The tracks of my tears are falling down . . .' followed by a succession of hilarious off-the-cuff rhymes as if Mark Miwurdz had been reborn. I stood against the back wall and made a mental note to retire from karaoke.

Our director for the second *Bob & Rose* filming block was Joe Wright. He was in his twenties and, like me, up from London by himself. Now I had someone to knock around with. We'd go out in the Gay Village around Canal Street, where we also filmed several scenes. It felt more hospitable than the 'straight end of town', as the city centre is described in the show.

Joe and I tried absinthe together in one bar and I wondered if I was hallucinating before we realised that, in that place, Thursday was 'Trannie Night'. I don't suppose they have that these days. We were made welcome and learned that many of the people there bought their make-up from Avon ladies as they were too ashamed to go to the counters in department stores.

We went to a club where women were not usually let in and I was asked whether I was gay or a tourist by a man who brought to mind the Right Said Fred video shot in my flat. I said, 'T-t-tourist,' and shut down goodness knows what avenues of pleasure. Joe persuaded them to admit the actress Sarah Parish and the three of us stood meekly by a wall, the only people there with our tops on. I put it down as an evening dedicated to research.

Once a week, in a bar called Spirit, we'd see the Salford ladies' handball team.

'How many of you are lesbians, then?' said Joe.

'Half,' said one of them, making us all laugh.

*

One day we were shooting a club scene and several drag queens working as supporting artists were called to the unit base for 7am. They were loud in their three-way trailer, with the radio blaring and lots of traffic in and out of the little rooms. One of them stuck their head out of the door and shouted:

'Oh my God! We're on the radio! We asked for a shoutout and they've only fookin' given us one! Aaaaaaaahhhhhhh!!'

'They're on good form for an early start,' I said to the second AD.

'They were working in Leeds last night,' he said. 'They've had forty minutes' sleep.'

There were twelve hours of shooting ahead.

For the sixth and final episode, Lesley and I had to shoot a tumultuous argument scene in a burger restaurant. We'd been finding quiet corners to run the lines for days. Now we were sat across a table from one another on plastic chairs bolted to the floor. It was 3am and we ran the lines one last time while lighting went on around us. Eventually Joe came over and said, 'Shall we try one?'

Lesley put her arms on the table and buried her face into them. I wondered if she was OK; I didn't know what to say so I left her alone. It was already completely quiet when we heard: 'Turnover.'

Lesley sat up and looked at me with tears running down her face. Recalling it gives me goosebumps. I don't know where she went, perhaps she was imagining her far-off little boys, but wherever it was, when Joe said, 'Action,' she tore into the scene. It was as if she were a tennis serving machine, firing straight at me, and I had to keep returning the ball. *Do not forget your lines; look at her, listen to her, say your words even as tears fill your eyes.* It was harrowing and moving and brilliant. At the sound of 'Cut', you could tell everyone had felt the emotion because there was a reverential silence in the room.

We were filming in a pub when Joe Wright said it was his birthday (although the internet says that's in August, so maybe I missed something). He bought a bottle of champagne and I toasted him. Later he opened a second bottle. I was sipping some out of a plastic cup, sitting next to Annie Harrison-Baxter, our producer.

Annie and I had bonded early on, when she'd asked me if it was true that I'd insisted on having a caravan to myself and that no one else could use it on my days off.

'That hasn't come from me,' I'd said.

'I didn't think you were like that,' she'd said.

I offered Annie some champagne but she was staring straight ahead.

'You shouldn't be drinking on set,' she said.

I'd been ill and lonely and no one seemed to care; one weekend I'd asked several of the crew to go to Blackpool with me, on our day off, to ride the Big One (it's a rollercoaster). I went on my own. In between our screams, the boy next to me called out exactly when to smile for the camera, as we hurtled past, and I bought myself a keyring with our photo in it.

At the first sign of a telling off, the angry boy appeared.

'Go fuck yourself,' I said, and immediately regretted it.

'You go fuck *your*self,' said Annie.

My last scene was on 16th June. I went back up to Manchester a few days later for the wrap party but it seemed I'd left things on a sour note and the head honchos weren't talking to me. So, I got drunk with some friends on the crew. It was good fun, despite a diversion to casualty to patch a couple of people up, and I ended up at my flat with the boom swinger's sister.

The next day, I tidied up and left Didsbury forever.

Two days later, in London, I went to a hilarious show featuring two Australian lads who my friend from university, Jackie Clune, was opening for.

Jackie left after a few drinks and I found myself up until dawn with a bunch of Aussies in a hotel room in Swiss Cottage. They were great company but I was taking more cocaine than I'd ever had before.

I left at about 8am, went home and drank three cans of Heineken for breakfast, standing in my stainless-steel kitchen staring at my pool.

Then I had an alcohol epiphany and, in defiance of the angry boy, decided to pour all the booze in the flat down the sink.

I found bottles in the fridge and at the back of cupboards and dusty old ones behind condiments on a countertop, ancient booze, including some ouzo someone had bought on holiday. I didn't think it was me.

Then I was yanking back ring pulls, unscrewing bottle tops and uncorking wine for what must have been fifteen minutes, tipping and pouring, with all the empties packed together upside down in my huge bespoke sink.

The smell of aniseed lingered for days afterwards but I'd stopped drinking and it was a relief.

The first episode of *Bob & Rose* was due to go out at 9pm on 10th September 2001. I'd just got home from the first day of shooting a *Jonathan Creek* Christmas Special when Jessica rang.

'Where are you watching it?' she said.

'At home.'

'Who with?'

'No one.'

'You can't watch it on your own; come to mine.'

So, I went to her flat and watched it with her partner, Adam, and her sister, I seem to remember.

The programme was excellent in every department, including the music, which Jess and I had never heard; it was all so assured, both moving and funny.

As the credits rolled, Jess's phone rang. I could hear her mum's enthusiasm from the other side of the room. Jess put me on the line mouthing, 'Sorry,' and then stood by to relieve me of the call, but I was happy to be praised.

My phone didn't ring that night but some friends did text to say: 'We LOVE *Bob & Rose*!' And then some more alerts pinged on my Nokia and several messages came and I knew the show must be good. If your programme's bad, the silence is deafening.

Sometime later, my dad said he'd also watched the show.

Uncharacteristically, he praised everything – the script, the editing, things he knew nothing about – but without mentioning me and what he thought about my kissing that handsome chap.

Bob & Rose was the first primetime ITV drama to have a gay lead, though some people suggested it was commissioned only because Bob 'goes straight', as if that implied sexuality is a choice. Russell was forced to defend his show, which he did by telling the truth: it was a love story based on a couple he knew.

I later met the real Bob at the BAFTAs, where we were nominated for Best Drama.

Five million people watched each of the first five episodes. I then learned that the climactic last show was to be moved to 10.40pm. I phoned David Liddiment, who was responsible for ITV, and was amazed when he took the call.

'I love *Bob & Rose*,' he said, 'but I've got to go to an advertising conference this week and speak to a thousand people to explain why we're not delivering the audience numbers they expected.'

'I'll come with you,' I said. 'We can say we've made a quality product, among the best television programmes they could hope to be associated with, and that the viewers were loyal and discerning.'

It was pointless. ITV scheduled a blooper show at 9pm the next Monday. An hour of studio cock-ups and onset accidents. Seven million people tuned in. The last *Bob & Rose* was watched by 3.2 million people in its later slot and has never been shown by ITV again, which is a shame (not least because I'm holding out for my repeat fee).

Months later, Annie Harrison-Baxter rang to say *Bob & Rose* had been nominated at the 2002 Monte-Carlo Television Awards, for Best Drama, Actress and Actor, and did I want to go? Of course I did.

Lesley and I met up with Julian Farino and Joe Wright on the French Riviera. It was nice to see them all without being knackered and freezing on a winter's night. Instead, we were being celebrated and took home all three awards, known as Golden Nymphs. I really couldn't believe it.

Another winner that night was John Spencer (Leo McGarry in *The West Wing*), who I spoke to briefly as a gushing fan. I met the creators of *Sex and the City*, too, who all loved *Bob & Rose*. I'd never had such respect for my acting; at home I wasn't put up for any awards, being just a stand-up comedian with impostor syndrome, but to these people I was Bob from 'Such a great show!'

Afterwards, we met a hero: Monaco resident Sir Roger Moore, the James Bond of my childhood. He was patient as we gathered round him for a photo and from there we went on to the awards party, taking with us the actress Anne-Marie Duff, who also had a Golden Nymph.

The party was lavish. The wealth! The opulence! We ate at long banqueting tables before the live entertainment began. Prince Albert of Monaco was at the top table, like, well, royalty.

At his side was the diminutive *Baywatch* star and *Playboy* model Carmen Electra. Many other women in expensive gowns floated around the prince; we were told they were known as the 'Albertinis'.

Stages kept moving and sliding about before us as new musicians rolled into view and others drifted away. And then the roof opened, literally, to reveal the stars. The headline act was Supertramp and they unexpectedly stormed it, as we used to say on the circuit.

Before we left Monaco, Julian surprised me by saying I'd been 'a revelation' on the trip, as if he was amazed that I could be good company.

I remembered a scene we'd shot at two in the morning in Manchester when I'd disagreed with him, mildly I thought, about when I should stand up from a table. I wanted to do what Russell had scripted, since there was a beat in the action we were missing. Julian had surprised me then, too, by taking me to one side and saying: 'Don't undermine me in front of the other actors.'

I was bemused but then we were all so cold, so tired and so strung out, and maybe I'd upset him by refusing to go to his house all those months ago – something I now regretted.

I was glad to part on good terms with them all in Monte Carlo; they're as good as any actors and directors I've worked with and better than most. I'm proud of *Bob & Rose* and remain grateful I had the chance to do it.

I Have Whoopi Goldberg for You

'Am I speaking with Alan Davies?'

'Yes,' I said.

He was American and leaned on the *e* in Davieez. Glenys Kinnock had told me that Davies is a Welsh spelling and the *e* is silent. Contrary to everything I'd been told as a boy, there is no Welsh heritage in my family so the spelling is an anomaly.

'I have Whoopi Goldberg for you.'

It was another chilly day in Manchester. I had my Bob clothes on and this phone call appeared to have come from another world.

'I'm sorry but I'm just about go on set,' I said.

'Would you like to tell her that yourself?' he said, as if to leave Hollywood royalty with any kind of snub was unthinkable.

'Yes, that's a good idea, thanks.'

The crew, in their wet-weather gear, were setting up a shot.

'Hello, is that Alan?' Whoopi's gravelly voice was unmistakeable. 'It's so great to speak to you,' she said.

'Thanks, yes, you too.'

'I understand you have to go to set.'

'Yes, I'm sorry,' I said.

'I love *Jonathan Creek*, it's such a great show,' said Whoopi, 'and we looked into you and found out you're a comedian and we'd love to bring you over to New York.'

So removed was I from my first love of stand-up comedy, and so low was my confidence, that this amazing opportunity came as a disappointment.

I was hoping she was going to offer me a part in a made-for-TV movie or something, anything.

I hadn't done stand-up for fifteen months and had no act now that *Urban Trauma* was in the shops. But it wasn't available in America; I could just relearn my old show. Fortunately, I didn't say, 'No thanks,' and hang up. I was flattered and liked her on the phone, so I said that I'd go to New York to meet her and her associate Tom Leonardis once the *Bob & Rose* shoot was finished.

I bought my ticket and flew out almost as soon as *Bob & Rose* was over, landing on the 4th of July, amazed at what was happening to me. Who knew what a run of shows in NYC could lead to, even if it was only more gigs in other cities? Could I possibly do a spot on *Late Night with David Letterman*?

Having walked the streets near the hotel for a while, not sure what to do alone in the Big Apple on Independence Day, I went to bed.

The next day, Whoopi sent a car for me and I was driven an hour upstate to her house on a lake. We had lunch, she told me about her life and we talked all afternoon.

Then we boarded her tour bus and drove two hours to Uncasville, Connecticut where the Mohegan Sun casino was the venue for her latest tour show. It was a vast property built on land reclaimed as a Native American reservation after being used for years to build nuclear reactors for submarines. It was now owned by the Mohegan tribe and was bringing in revenues of over a billion dollars a year from gambling.

A crowd of four thousand greeted Whoopi, more than she normally played to, she said. After that she took me to the slot machines, along with her amiable bus driver, a man vaguely reminiscent of John Ratzenberger, who played Cliff Clavin in *Cheers* (without the postal-worker uniform and confident stupidity).

The casino had given Whoopi $3,000 credit but she'd first had to produce ID, even though seemingly *everyone* who saw her said: 'Whoopi!'

The legal technicality just made her laugh. We sat on stools putting $100 chips into two of the resort's six and a half thousand slot machines.

'Thank God they gave me credit or else I'd be putting my own money into these,' she said. 'Do you gamble?'

'No,' I said, 'it's never done anything for me.'

'You're very wise,' she said. 'Still, this is better than a few years ago, when I'd have been putting this money up my nose.' And she laughed again.

The tour bus had beds and cooking facilities. She showed me all the precooked food her daughter had loaded onboard since she knew Whoopi couldn't be trusted to eat well.

Back in New York, Tom arranged a meeting for me with an agent, since I'd finally left International Artistes and had no representation.

It was Whoopi's name that had opened this door for me. Tom stressed the rarity of the opportunity, but once in the room I felt too lowkey and unfocused for the big American agent. He asked what I wanted to do and I really didn't know. Was I a stand-up now? Was my acting good enough? Could I suggest I'd write my own sitcom having been fired from one and then scuttling another?

Nothing came of the meeting, though I liked the people, not least because they took me to a Mets vs Yankees Subway Series game when I told them I loved baseball.

I saw Whoopi perform two more shows, most memorably to an all-African-American crowd at the Apollo in Harlem. It seemed the only white people there were her agents and me.

It was a big night for Whoopi, surprisingly her first-ever show at the famous old theatre. Backstage afterwards, various people were telling her that 'New York is buzzing' after her performance. I said something that made her laugh and a couple of strangers looked at me as if I'd not been reverential enough. I decided to slip away and said a quiet goodbye.

'How are you getting back to your hotel?' said Tom.

'I'll just get a cab,' I said.

'No, you won't,' said a few people at once.

They all thought it unsafe for me to be out in Harlem at night so they organised a car to pick me up.

Whoopi doesn't fly, so the next day we were going by bus again to Washington, DC. Before we set off, I had a chat with the bus driver. He told me about a friend who'd lost both legs when they served together in Vietnam.

'When he came back his girl and his mother were going to visit him in the hospital and he made me put pillows under the sheets because he'd told them he'd lost one leg, not two,' he said. 'He wanted me to make it look like he still had one leg. I told him they're going to find out! And he said he thought they might not come to see him if they knew, so I encouraged him to tell the truth. And he did, and they loved him, of course. But then I saw him a few weeks later and he said to me that him and his girl hadn't done it since he'd got back. He was afraid he was too ugly with no legs. So I said: "You just gotta try it."

'Anyway, I went to see him again a while later and I could tell by the way he looked at me, I didn't even need to ask, and he said to me: "You know what, with no legs you can get right on up there!"'

As he laughed at the memory I wondered how I'd ever thought he resembled Cliff Clavin.

It was a five-hour drive. Whoopi and I talked about comedy and books and she even welcomed a couple of thoughts I had on her act.

In Washington various dignitaries came to see the show; among them was Gloria Steinem, who I wouldn't have recognised if Whoopi hadn't pointed her out. If Bill Clinton had still been in the White House we might have been able to visit, but it was George W Bush by then.

It was a different atmosphere from the Apollo, where Whoopi's material about gun crime had brought murmurs of, 'Mm-hmm,' and, 'Thass right,' and, 'You tell it, girl,' as if the crowd were responding to a preacher.

At one point Whoopi tried something that I'd suggested on the bus and when it worked, she had time during the laughter to turn and nod at me watching from the wings. I gave her a wry English smile and nod, but inside I was thrilled.

We said goodbye in Washington. I flew home from there, mulling over the suggestion that Whoopi might be up for a US version of *Creek* with her as my sidekick. I wanted that to happen.

*

The following month, I took the opportunity to do twelve shows at the Music Hall in Edinburgh, as I'd done in 1998. William Burdett-Coutts, who runs the Assembly Rooms, had invited me at short notice when another show cancelled.

'I haven't got any new stuff,' I said.

'Don't worry,' he said, 'it's the twenty-first anniversary of Assembly and we'll say you've been asked to bring the old show back.'

It was a chance to work up some material for New York but I hadn't done a single warmup gig, not even ten minutes in a small club. I was told lots of press wanted to come.

'Tell them I've been invited to do my old show,' I said. 'Certainly no reviewers on the first night, please; I haven't done any gigs for nearly two years.'

On the second night, thirty-five press tickets were handed out and my show was not up to the standard I was capable of.

I didn't read any papers – that way madness lies – and set about improving. By show nine of twelve, new ideas were coming and I was really back on form. I hugely enjoyed my festival, sharing a flat with Jackie Clune while still not drinking at all and hanging out with a harpist called Hattie, but I still wasn't sure I had a show for New York, so I decided to return to the Edmonton Fringe.

I took my old friend Sue with me to Canada; she was extremely low as she'd had a miscarriage and was now resigned to a life without children. 'Come with me,' I said. 'Don't be on your own.'

We stayed with another old friend, Don, who was mid-divorce, so also below par. I bought him a Hawaiian shirt and insisted he wear it. They are two of the best people I know and I wanted to help; it's what Whoopi would have done. Between us, we managed on affection, dark humour and a trip to the highest slide in the West Edmonton Mall water park. Then I learned my show had been described in an Edmonton paper as 'side-splittingly funny', a description I'd last had in Edinburgh in 1994.

I was still nervous about doing gigs in NYC, though. What if no one came? I spoke to Tom Leonardis on the phone.

'Somebody's getting cold feet,' he said, but we were still talking about shows towards the end of that summer when something happened that changed everyone's future, in the US and beyond.

Jonathan Creek 2.0

The phrase 'left in the lurch' has its roots in a sixteenth-century French game, similar to backgammon, known as *lourche*. A player can be left behind and this is called *lourche*.

David Renwick was in *lourche*, not to say deep *merde*, when Caroline Quentin turned down an offer for the 2001 *Jonathan Creek* Christmas special. Despite all our attempts, led by Verity Lambert, to change her mind, she was gone.

This was catastrophic news; David had spent months on an intricate and now ruined feature-length script and twelve million viewers awaited. His solution was to create a new sidekick character called Carla Borrego that he hoped would be played by Julia Sawalha.

But Julia wasn't available, being committed to a series with David's old writing partner, Andrew Marshall.

Over a hundred actresses were seen and I read with several of them, including Sally Philips, who would have been excellent but inexplicably did her audition in an Italian accent, the memory of which now reduces her to near hysterical laughter whenever we meet. And then, unexpectedly, Julia was free again, and she was cast without hesitation.

The script was now two hours long with all the extra work David had been forced to do, but he'd salvaged the show. At the readthrough, he looked as if he hadn't slept for a month. But Julia's arrival lifted the rehearsal room, and we all benefitted from the laughter and the feeling of relief.

The harmonious atmosphere continued when shooting began on 10th

September. The only time Julia expressed any displeasure in the entire month was when the caterers put a big lump of butter in the peas.

Our location on the second day of filming was the Queen's Theatre on Shaftesbury Avenue, with Stuart Milligan and Bill Bailey on set. Our stills photographer, reformed paparazzo John, was coming in to take pictures. When he appeared, he was not his usual laidback self.

'A plane's just flown into the World Trade Center,' he said.

John led Bill and me to the black-and-white portable TV by the stage door. As we watched the first tower smoking and burning, another plane swung into the second.

Two days later, I had an AOL online chat with Whoopi about what was to become known as 9/11:

W: it is so fuckin strange, i cant get to anyone i am freaked.

A: No-one can get thru on phones, too scary

W: it is beyond conception, and i wonder what comes now. we here in la are in a state of emergency

W: what are you getting there

A: They've evacuated buildings in London

W: so it begins the world wide madness

W: are you ok

A: trying to work out who it might be, thousands dead

A: Ok. at first it seemed comical . . .a hole in a building, but the collapse . . . been filming, people stunned

W: the pictures are beyond belief. to see the twin towers collapse was a stunningly numbing sight

W: thousands trying to get away, people jumping from windows, not to mention the people on those planes

A: beyond belief, like an earthquake & the pentagon. the president cant get to DC . . .weird. 260 at least on the planes

W: how strange to see this not on a movie screen but to realize that this is the new reality

Of course, filming for Jonathan Creek continued, as did normal life everywhere. Raby Castle in County Durham was to be used as the home of an eccentric millionaire film director played by an actor and writer I had revered as a student, Steven Berkoff. I was looking forward to meeting him, resisting the temptation to bring in play scripts and programmes from the eighties to be autographed. When he appeared on set, his powerful, stocky frame, balding head and piercing eyes were instantly recognisable.

Sandy set up a shot showing the vaulted interior of Raby decorated with antique shields and swords as Creek arrives there for the first time. On entering the large hall, Berkoff looked all around, high and low, as if in amazement.

'Cut!' said Sandy. 'Steven, when you come in, just walk through and put your coat away.'

'But this is an amazing place, I should look around!' said Berkoff.

'Steven,' said Sandy, some distance away behind the monitor, 'you live here.'

As the shoot went on, Berkoff found himself in conflict with David Renwick over learning his lines. David tolerates no deviation from the script.

'This ridiculous *scheisse*!' said Berkoff one morning, wielding his script in his clenched fist. I wondered if he'd expressed similar sentiments during the filming of *Beverly Hills Cop*.

As we waited for another take, since Berkoff was, at best, paraphrasing throughout, he yelled at David: 'You're no fucking Shakespeare, mister.'

David recalled that moment many times over the next fifteen years that we worked together, never failing to make me laugh.

At the wrap party there was a feeling among the crew that surely Mr Berkoff wouldn't turn up, but he arrived all smiles, ignored Julia and me as usual and offered gifts for the writer, director and producer. David, Sandy and Verity unwrapped them graciously. He'd given them copies of his own books.

Central Perk

October 2024 (between the 14th and 21st).

A telephone appointment was scheduled for me after my CT scan and I was hoping to hear the results and perhaps get a date for my operation, but it turned out to be another round of preassessment questions that took a while and left me none the wiser.

My fourteen-year-old daughter, Susie, came in.

'Who was that?' she said.

'Someone from the hospital,' I said.

'You OK?' she said.

'I'm going to have an operation. It's a small thing; I'll be in and out on the day.'

I'd had a cyst removed from my back a few years ago.

'It's like the thing on my back,' I said, 'only it's inside.'

She adopted an upward inflection – as she might say, 'giving Jennifer Aniston in *Friends*'. 'Is it cancerous?' she said.

'Hope not,' I said.

From Reagan to Bin Laden

In November I persuaded Julia to come with me to visit Whoopi at her house in Malibu. On our way up the Pacific Coast Highway, it seemed every lawn and most of the cars flew the Stars and Stripes, post 9/11.

The next day was Whoopi's forty-sixth birthday and Julia and I watched as she had a star laid in the Hollywood Walk of Fame.

That evening we were invited to a party held for Whoopi in a house in the Hollywood Hills, where I met, among others, a naval officer who was due to take command of a new billion-dollar aircraft carrier, the USS *Ronald Reagan*.

It proved too difficult to organise shows for me in New York. As we left, Whoopi gave me a CD of the soundtrack album from *O Brother, Where Art Thou?*

'Until we hang again,' she wrote on the front.

The next time I saw her was in London, when I met her and Tom for breakfast. I found the address, in Holland Park, and was led to the kitchen, where a handsome chef asked me what I'd like to eat.

When we were alone for a moment, Tom whispered to me, 'Do you know whose house you're in?'

'No.'

He looked at me.

'Elton. John.'

'Really?' I said. 'Is he here?'

'No.'

'Is that his chef?'

'Yes,' he said.

Whoopi was entirely unpretentious; she just lived an enclosed A-list life that perhaps I aspired to, with my expensive penthouse, but whenever we parted it was as if we were aboard a hot-air balloon that drifted down to let me off before rising back up to a height I'd never reach.

After California, Julia and I travelled via Fiji to New Zealand, where, five months after I'd poured my ouzo away, I succumbed to some cocktails, since I was being 'boring'.

That it was a mistake to do so became apparent in Australia. Before visiting my family and friends, we flew to Uluru, where we had an argument in our hotel room; I couldn't tell you what it was about as I was bingeing into an alcohol blackout, slipping back as if my period of abstinence had never happened. I went onto the terrace outside our room to calm down. Julia was inside on the phone.

'I've come on holiday with a cunt!' she said.

When I eventually went to go back in, the patio doors had been locked. I had no key, couldn't find Julia anywhere and there were no other rooms available.

Wandering into the bush in the direction of Uluru, a vast shape just visible against the night sky, I lay down on a bench, just a plank really, and went to sleep.

Waking as the sun rose, I watched the light play across the vast sandstone shape of Uluru, shadows forming and shifting in its crevices, oranges, purples and browns swapping and merging, then separating, as if the rock was breathing, alive, like an octopus changing colour to hide.

After a much needed movement behind a bush, covering my gift to the beetles with a pile of red outback dust, I went back to the hotel. Julia and I flew to Sydney in silence and the next time I heard her voice she was on the phone trying to buy a flight home that day.

'Don't buy a new ticket,' I said, and she looked up at me. 'That'll be about four grand; I'll change your return and you can go home tomorrow for free.'

We said goodbye at the airport, Julia in tears.

*

I went to stay with my best friend from school, Danny, and his family, near Botany Bay. He'd emigrated in 1991 to marry Josie (having met her backpacking with friends from Bancroft's, when I was at university).

Their son Tom was four and I played cricket with him.

'Yesterday I hit two fours and took one wicket,' he said.

His little sister, my god-daughter Claudia, was toddling about, falling over every so often as her toes still turned in. I was sad to leave just before Tom's fifth birthday but was heading to Adelaide to visit my Auntie Hazel, Uncle Geoff and two of my four cousins, Janet and Helen.

'Where's Julia?' said Janet, as soon as I was in the door.

'Yeah, Alan, we wanted to meet her,' said Helen. 'We've met *you* before. We like *AbFab*.'

'What did you do to her?' said Janet.

'Nothing, she wanted to go home,' I said.

'You must have done something.'

'Aw, look, it's disappointing, Alan,' said Helen. 'No Julia and no story.'

After a couple of restorative days, I said goodbye and wished, once again, that my auntie had never emigrated in 1963, not least because my mum would have had someone with her when she died. As it was, Dad didn't tell Hazel about the terminal diagnosis until after her only sister was dead.

In Melbourne I stayed with Marnie Foulis and Colin Lane, who thoughtfully put Lano and Woodley's 1994 Perrier Award on the bedside table in my room. They arranged for a night out with my old friend from the Adelaide Fringe, Judith Lucy.

I flew to Singapore and slumped into my seat, wishing that Danny, Josie, Tom and Claudia, Hazel, Geoff, Janet and Helen, Colin, Marnie and Judith all lived in North London. But I wasn't going home yet as I'd been invited to spend Christmas in Indonesia with Bill and Kris Bailey.

I first went on holiday with the Baileys to the Lake District in 1990 and we'd shared several New Years together in those windswept coastal cottages with Jo Brand, Jim Miller and the rest. Those days were gone, though. Jo and Jim had split up, and Jo later married Bernie, with whom she'd recently had a baby. Jim eventually left London, losing touch with everyone, as those times at the Comedy Café and the Red Rose faded away.

This new trip was a long way from Wells-next-the-Sea. I met Bill and Kris in Bali, from where we flew to Sulawesi and then on by ferry to spend Christmas in Banda, where they'd married a couple of years before. At first sight of the island, everyone rushed on deck. This tiny paradise appeared to be approaching us and soon we were looking down at the chaos and colour of the quayside.

Our sizeable party disembarked and for some reason I just knew I was going to feel lonely. And I did, even though we snorkelled, watched ceremonial canoe racing, climbed an active volcano and every meal was colourful, spicy and delicious; the nasi goreng at breakfast alone was the nicest thing I'd eaten on my whole trip and the Christmas lunch was extraordinary.

Sadly, in the wake of 9/11, local Christians had temporarily left Banda and the Dutch church had been vandalised. In the market, a stallholder selling Osama bin Laden T-shirts kept saying: 'Osama, he is hero! Hero!'

The only other shirts featured Nirvana, David Beckham or the Teletubbies.

For reasons unknown, the return ferry didn't arrive so Chief Des Alwi of Banda, who owned the hotel, used his contacts to arrange for an Indonesian Navy Nomad Searchmaster to fly us to Ambon.

The plane was to make two trips and Bill told me we'd be on the second. But there was a risk of missing our connecting flight so, like the rich man in *Titanic* who pushes past women and children for a place in a lifeboat, I insisted on going on the first.

A little family had formed during thirteen nights on Banda and with supreme ingratitude I put a fracture in it.

Osama bin Laden was rumoured to be hiding in Ambon and the advice was not to leave the airport. I remembered the US Navy officer I'd met in California and wondered how I'd managed to go from one extreme to the other. But everyone made their connections and I couldn't make eye contact with anyone, having pushed my way onto the first flight.

Within a few days, I landed in dreary, grey London. It was January 2002. Ahead of me that year was another lengthy *Jonathan Creek* shoot, supposedly co-starring Julia Sawalha. Adrian Edmondson was to play her screen husband, the third of my comic heroes from *The Young Ones* to appear on the show, after Nigel Planer and Rik Mayall. Would that happen now, or had I blown it? What would David and Verity say?

I ambled out, head down to avoid recognition in the arrivals hall. To my right I felt someone was staring at me and I glanced across to see a familiar figure at the barrier, curly hair framing a hopeful smile.

It was Julia.

J

He asked for forty quid, which surprised me and might have explained why he'd spent so long talking to the man in the suit before he came up the road.

I don't suppose the suit could believe it either. Probably asked him, as I did, what on earth he wanted the money for, looking, as he did, about ten years old.

He was twelve, he explained.

The suit hadn't given him anything but I felt well-disposed to him for some reason. So I gave him two twenties. He was grateful; they had no electricity in their flat and his little sister was sitting in the dark, with their mum.

I hadn't heard of anyone having no electricity since the meter ran out when we were students and you had to shove a big old fifty-pence piece in, with a metallic clunk, to get the portable TV and the two-bar fire back on.

One bar only, though, if *The Singing Detective* was on, or else you'd burn through the fifty pence before it finished, with no chance of seeing it again. It seemed outdated to have a coin meter in the eighties. It *was* outdated, in fact. We had one in shabby old Whitstable, though. Our landlady was ancient and possibly considered electricity a luxury, unheard of in her childhood.

Why hadn't the boy's mum gone out asking for money? Silly question. Of course, this Dickensian child was going to elicit greater sympathy. Shameful that there should be street urchins in London in the twenty-first century. But there were. Quite a few.

'She's agoraphobic,' he said.

Louise Rennison had said she was agoraphobic. She wouldn't use lifts or go on the tube, but that's claustrophobia so maybe I misheard. She'd become a good confidante. I'd be phoning her about this.

'Agoraphobic?' I said. 'That must be very difficult.'

I'd read about an agoraphobe in an Alice Hoffman novel. It came and went (the phobia, not the novel); sometimes it was as if a force field kept you indoors. On other occasions you could brave a trip to the shops if you kept to the edge of the pavement up close to the buildings.

'And epileptic,' he said.

I couldn't manage a response so he looked up at me in case I was losing interest. He was small, with cheap, dark sportswear hanging over his bones. Shiny tracky bottoms, unbranded trainers, some sort of showerproof jacket with two stripes on the sleeve. Not enough layers on. Not enough protection. It had been raining earlier; the streetlamps showed the moisture on the surface of the road, amber light reflecting on to the window of the deli a few doors down from me, where I'd buy olives and sundried tomatoes.

'Where do you live?' I said.

'Balfour Road.'

Two streets away, up the top of Corsica Street, turn right and then left and then left again, that was Balfour. Houses on there were one and a half million quid at that time. Ordinary terraced houses with three bedrooms. Some of them were divided into flats. A few were obviously council; you could often tell by the front door.

'Oh, you're near, in a flat?'

'Yeah, ground floor.'

Epilepsy, from the Greek to seize or possess . . . Horrifying. I couldn't let it slide. I had to say something.

'Epilepsy must be terrible.'

He downplayed it.

'She hasn't had a fit for ages. Do you live here?'

I looked behind me to where his eyes had gone, the entrance to my flat, concealed by a high steel gate, not dissimilar to those erected by the RUC in Belfast during the troubles, to fortify police stations.

'Yes, Flat 5,' I said.

'Is it nice?'

I thought about my converted match factory with swimming pool, roof terrace and sleeping platform.

'It's OK.'

'How long have you lived here?' he said.

'Couple of years.'

'I grew up round here.'

I didn't want him to think I was a gentrifying interloper. I'd lived in the area for about twelve years. I wasn't going to say, 'Since I graduated,' though. I was twisting myself into a shape he could approve of.

'I used to live off St Paul's Road,' I said.

That was good. St Paul's Road was less desirable than Balfour Road; it took you towards dirty old Dalston, so I'd been below him at some point. He was looking at me, holding the forty quid in his hand. Did he want to go? Didn't everyone I spoke to? His face was narrow and pale, with dark eyes and black hair. Perhaps he was thinking about his sister, in the cold with their phobic mum.

'What does "Off St Paul's Road" mean?' he said.

'St Mary's Grove.'

'Nice.'

My smile dropped. No nicer than Balfour Road, I thought, but, of course, I'd had a *choice* of street. I was an *owner*. I'd subtly detached from him, though, in that beat, so . . .

'Thanks for the money,' he said, and turned to go.

'OK, bye.'

He set off in the wrong direction.

'Balfour is up that way,' I said, beginning to think I'd been duped.

'I've got to charge up the lecky key,' he said.

'Oh, OK. Where do you go to do that?'

'New North Road.'

'What? Isn't there somewhere on Highbury Corner that does it?'

'No.'

'That's a couple of miles, isn't it?'

'It's not that far. I can get the 271.'

It had started to rain.

'Do you want a lift?'

'No.'

'You sure?'

'I don't get in cars.'

'Really? How come?'

'My dad was killed in a car crash.'

I stared at him.

'Haven't been in a car since.'

'No,' I said. 'Right.'

'It's nice to meet you; you're on TV, aren't you?'

'Not at the moment,' I said, with a practised grin.

Being recognised can bring anxiety or, as in this case, a flush of pleasure but then a tsunami of self-loathing followed as I wondered how I could even have that feeling at this moment. What a mess my subconscious must be in to trigger that warm wave, of dopamine or whatever it is, after I've just heard about this fatal accident, a dead parent. I profoundly resented myself in the face of this boy's life. I couldn't then find a shape for my face to settle into. I needed to show shame, contrition and sympathy. I'd bowed my head to hide my expression and when I thought it was ready I revealed it slowly by lifting it up while exhaling.

He was already walking down the hill towards the bus stop.

I watched him go. He wasn't a smiler but he was without hostility, resentment, or impatience. Lucky sod.

I went in through the steel gate at the side of the giant roller shutters, round to my triple-locked front door with its reinforced glass and up the oiled stairs to the empty apartment, now echoing to the sounds of the door closing and my phone and keys being put down.

The cavernous living space one more floor up was faintly illuminated by moonlight coming through the expanse of glazing along the west-facing wall, twenty feet high all the way along. The only noise was the fan for the pool whirring away.

Maybe I'd go upstairs and open the roof-terrace door to ventilate the pool room. I could switch off the fan then. Save a few quid.

The landline rang loudly. Any sound leaped into this space and expanded unnaturally. I let it go to machine. The caller hung up. Then my mobile buzzed so vigorously it skittered across the atrium table and hit the floor.

Had to be Julia, I could tell.

Things hadn't been great between us since she'd chased me in her campervan through the streets of South London the week before. We'd had an argument in my car on her drive; I'd waited for her to disappear through the front door and then reversed onto the road. I hadn't considered she would actually chase me down. My mobile started ringing on the passenger seat as she loomed up in my rear-view mirror, her phone to her ear.

I should have pulled over, let her shout at me for a bit and then gone home. I was afraid of shouting back and having a public row, so I kept going through a red light and lost her.

At home there'd been a rant on my machine, which she'd obviously delivered while in pursuit. I was both afraid and impressed. We'd talked about buying a house together. I'd met all her family. Her dad was a nice, twinkly man who adored her.

Now, the buzzing continued on the floor. I quite wanted to tell Julia about the urchin, but I left the phone there and went to bed.

Two or three days later, the doorbell rang. I was standing in the pool as if in a trance again. I hadn't been outside the flat or spoken to anyone since I saw the boy in the street.

The bell rang again. Not really a bell, more of an insistent buzzing. I always assumed it would be someone from *The Daily Mail* being all nice before printing horrible lies about me, so I never answered the door. Ever.

The bell rang for longer than even those bastards normally tried and it crossed my mind that the building might be on fire, so I climbed out of the pool, walked through the glass door and down the stone steps to the kitchen, still naked and dripping water, to pick up the intercom.

'*Yeah?*' I said, as if I'd been interrupted. Whenever my dad answered the phone he'd say, '*Yes?*' as if an idiot was bothering him. I hated this or indeed any resemblance. At least Dad had the excuse that he was trying to put my stepmum's friends off ringing the house.

'It's Justin,' said a faraway voice.

'Who?'

'I met you the other night, you gave me forty pounds.'

'Oh yes, sorry. Are you OK?

'We've got no heating. The gas has gone off.'

'Do you want some money? Hang on, I'll come down.'

'We need a heater.'

'Oh, OK. Hang on. Push the gate when it buzzes, OK?'

I pressed the key on the intercom and heard the clanging from outside as he came through the security gate.

In my bedroom, in the walnut-panelled dressing area, there was a pair of Adidas jogging bottoms and a sweatshirt I'd been given by a costume designer after a shoot. Then I went to my office and grabbed an old fan heater that belonged to an ex I'd met working on *Jonathan Creek* who now hated me and everyone I knew, or so she said. The heater still worked and I'd be glad to be shot of it.

Looking down the long stairs to the front door, I could see saw the boy's tracky bottoms through the glass so I picked up the intercom at the top and buzzed so he could come up. He didn't move.

'Push the door!' I said.

He just stood there, damp trainers fidgeting, so, grabbing my wallet off the table, I went down with the heater and smiled at him through the glass. His expression changed to one notch off neutral as I opened the door.

'Come in.'

He was looking between the heater and my mane of dripping hair, which swung about over my face and wet the shoulders of my sweatshirt.

'No,' he said. 'Thanks.'

Could he tell I hadn't spoken to anyone for three days, or that I'd had two bottles of wine on my own the night before?

'Come in, it's cold,' I said, not wanting to send him away abruptly.

I padded barefoot up the stairs so he'd follow.

At the top, he looked around as if he didn't belong here. No one belonged in this place. It was weird, all white walls, light wooden floors, steel balustrades, electric blinds.

'How long has your gas been off?' I said.

'Since last night.'

'Is there an immersion heater?' I said.

He obviously didn't know.

'Is there a big cylinder, for hot water, like in an airing cupboard or something?'

'No.'

'So you have a combi boiler?'

I imagined him in school, never answering anything, unsure what he ought to know.

'Is it really cold in the flat? Is your sister OK?' I said.

'She's got my top on.'

I noticed he wasn't wearing it. His arms were bare and white with a graze on one elbow.

'What's that?'

'I fell over. There's an old bike at the top of my road, it's been chained to the railings for ages. It's got one wheel and no seat now. I tripped over it.'

'Look where you're going.'

He smiled a bit.

'A spoke went through my leg.'

'What?'

He pulled up his trouser leg to show an open wound that had partially scabbed over but was already going yellow at the sides.

'Shitty death, does that hurt?'

'A bit.'

'Have you put anything on it? That'll go septic.'

'No.'

'Has your mum seen it?'

'She put the plaster on.'

I noticed a narrow child's plaster, with a picture on it, that had become caked in blood. Hopelessly inadequate, when this was removed it would open up the part of the wound it covered.

'You need Steri-Strips or stitches, probably, and a tetanus shot. Have they seen that at school?'

He looked down.

'Have you been to school today?'

'My attendance is good, 85 per cent.'

'Why didn't you go?'

'I have to walk my sister to her school first.'

'How old is she?'

'Nine. So I'm always late. I was running and some other kids chased me.'

'Why aren't they in school?'

'They just don't go. I fell over the bike and the spoke went through.'

'What happened with the kids?'

'They took a photo on a camera phone. They said it was disgusting, one of them said he was going to be sick.'

'Where would they get a phone like that?'

No answer, another silly question. They didn't buy it, obviously.

'How long were you lying there for?'

'My neighbour came out. He's a judge or something. He looks down on me. So I got up.'

'He sounds nice.'

He looked at me to check that had been a joke. Now we both hated Judge Bad Deed.

'Have you eaten anything today?'

'No. I'm not hungry.'

'You must be. Is your cooker gas?'

'Yeah, we light the rings and the grill with matches. We did have some biscuits. My sister had them; she was hungry when I went to get her.'

'Don't they feed you at school?'

'We have packed lunches. But my mum couldn't do them. She had a fit in the night.'

'Shouldn't you be on free school meals?'

'My mum can't go down there to get the form.'

'Don't the school just give you that?'

He didn't know. I didn't know.

'Do you want some beans on toast?'

'No thanks.'

'Yes you do.'

I pushed the door to one of my bathrooms.

'Go in there and wash your leg in that shower. There's soap there and a towel. Then come upstairs.'

He went in reluctantly and I heated a can of beans and put some toast on. Then I went to find a roll of Elastoplast I had somewhere and some antiseptic cream. He came up after a few minutes. I put the food down in front of him and he looked at the glass wall that dissected the room as he chewed and swallowed simultaneously.

'What's in there?' he said.

'Swimming pool,' I said.

'Really?'

'Yeah.'

'Do you go in it?'

'Sometimes. Here, show me that leg.'

He held it up.

'Put your hand out.'

He put his hand out and I squirted plenty of cream on to his fingers.

'Rub that in to the whole area, especially those yellowy bits.'

It looked infected.

'You need to see a nurse, OK? Go to Laycock Street surgery, is that your doctor's?'

No reply. He was busy with the cream.

'Go there anyway.'

I held the strip of plaster up and saw that I'd need about twelve inches so I cut off that much and covered the wound without sticking it down on any broken skin. Then I gave him another piece of buttered toast. He put it in his pocket.

'Is that for your sister?'

'Yeah.'

'Here.'

I gave him the rest of the loaf.

'The grill doesn't work. It's gas.'

I unplugged my toaster and put it in a bin bag along with the heater. Then I took my wallet out of my pocket and gave him another forty quid.

'Thanks,' he said, and put his plate in the sink on his way out.

I did twenty lengths the next morning (of actual swimming, with tumble turns) but there was no buzz at the door, no matter how hard I waited. I rang Louise.

'Oh, you're *alive*,' she said, as if I'd neglected our friendship for decades.

'What are you doing?' I said.

'Hiding from my publisher. They won't leave me *alone*; no one's on your side when you get a bit of success, you know. I know you know.'

By this time, Louise had sold mountains of hilarious books to teenagers. We'd been friends for ten years. When we first met she wore big hair, loads of eyeliner and short skirts, like a white reject from the Marvelettes. She was forty-two then and I wondered whether Douglas Adams, in *The Hitchhikers Guide to the Galaxy*, was referring to some equivalent of Louise when he declared '42' to be the meaning of life. Now, at fifty-three, the world had *finally* woken up to her *unique genius* and it had both *improved* and *spoiled* her life in equal measure.

'Just say you don't want to do it,' I said. 'What can they do?'

'My fucking *agent* is in cahoots with them. Now I've got a deadline! A *deadline*. She's supposed to be on my side. She's *my* agent! *They* go out for lunch and talk about *me*. Where's *my* lunch?'

'I'll take you for lunch.'

'What's your agent like?'

'A Tasmanian devil.'

I'd recently agreed to be represented by Michael Foster, who was prone to shouting on the phone but who was nice to me and who'd just set up a new agency. He'd never seen me do stand-up but, at the time, I wasn't bothered about that.

'They've discussed putting me in a room at one of their offices and *checking up* on me,' she said. 'It's like Cuba. I've done *five* of these books now.'

'People love them, Lou.'

'Oh *God*. Have they made you ring me? What are *you* doing? Ruining your girlfriend's life, I suppose.'

'She chased me in her van, for about two miles.'

'Oh, I *love* her, I love that, it's like a film. It's lucky I can't drive; I'd always be chasing people.'

'Imagine you and a breathalyser.'

'Oh, don't be boring. I'd feign madness or something, give them my mum's name.'

'Some kid came up to me in my road and asked me for forty quid.'

'I hope you told him to go away.'

'He says his mum is agoraphobic.'

'I'm agoraphobic, where's *my* forty quid? Have you met her?'

'And epileptic.'

'Have you met her?'

'I don't want to. He was just here yesterday; he's suffering from malnutrition and gangrene, by the look of him.'

'Do you know what agoraphobia means?'

'I thought you had it.'

'No, you know I'm claustrophobic, stop trying to diagnose me, why does everyone want something to be wrong with them these days? They're just looking for an excuse for their terrible behaviour. What was I saying?'

'About agoraphobia,' I said.

'Yes, it comes from the Greek words *agora* and *phobia* and it means "fear of a public square".'

She laughed. 'Square' remained her favourite insult from the sixties.

'If you don't find that funny then you are an *actual square*,' she said.

'We've long established that I'm a square.'

'Don't sulk. You should meet the mum.'

'He's been round to the flat. I gave him some more cash, and my toaster.'

'What if he goes to the *Mail* and says you've been giving him money for sexual favours?'

I hadn't thought of that.

'He doesn't want . . . I'm not groom—'

'Your word against his.'

'He's like a stinky spectral skeleton, this kid.'

'He sounds nice. Well done you: you are a Good Person. Is that what you rang to tell me?'

'No.'

'Are you going now? Are you upset?'

'No, of course not. I'm going for dinner at Bill and Kris's.'

'Seriously, though,' she said, 'maybe stop giving money away? You can do a lot of harm with money.'

Kris had been cooking all day. There were three different curries, coconut and jasmine rice, daal, nasi goreng, sambal dips, salads with blood orange and chillies, plus bottles of icy New Zealand Sauvignon blanc, elderflower water, lights in the garden illuminating the koi carp, joints going round, cool music playing through an invisible sound system. The downstairs loo had a humidifier, head-high rubber plants, a chameleon and a view of an outside shower, which was optimistic for Hammersmith but aesthetically faultless. In the garden there were twenty-four exotic stone pots, each three feet high and individually lit. Bill had everyone laughing as he explained they'd only wanted two, to be shipped from Lombok, but ended up with two dozen as the exporter was overconfident in his use of English when taking the order. A truck arrived three months later, and the pots kept coming.

I coughed my gratitude as another spliff was handed to me. I could feel my phone buzzing in my pocket and answered it, without looking to see who it was; ironically the weed had cleared my usual paranoia.

'Hello,' said a little voice.

'Justin?' I remembered giving him my number, when he left with my appliances, so he could call when he'd had his leg looked at.

'The gas hasn't come back on.'

'Did your mum pay the bill? I gave you forty quid.'

'It's not on yet.'

'Have you eaten anything?'

'My sister's really hungry, she's crying.'

There was a rustle and a pause at his end. I couldn't hear anything over the noise of the laughter, as a story about having the shits in a monsoon reached its uproarious climax.

'My mum's had a fit.'

'Another one? Is she all right?'

'She's asleep.'

'Wait there. What number flat are you?'

I told everyone I had to go, explaining about Justin and his sister. They were all lefty creative types, prone to middle-class guilt. I said I'd buy some food and take it round there. They asked if I was all right to drive. I said I was (I knew there was no risk, must have been really stoned to think that). A couple of people embraced me, like I was a lifeboat volunteer.

At the Sri Lankan corner shop on Highbury Corner, I filled blue plastic bags with bread, milk, cheese, cans of beans and vegetables, Marmite, jam, Doritos, biscuits for the sister. I went up to Balfour Road to put it on their doorstep, keeping an eye out for the judge, and drove away. I rang Justin to say it was there.

The following evening, he was outside the gate when I came home with Julia. He said he'd knocked for me six times that day – his phone had no credit – and his mum wanted to invite me for dinner. I told him that wasn't necessary. He was quite insistent on her behalf but I didn't want to go.

Julia stepped forward and hugged him. I realised that I'd wanted to do that before but couldn't manage it. She held him for ages, her eyes closed, stroking his hair and kissing the top of his head. He had his eyes open. When she'd finished, I asked him to bring their gas bill round the next day.

Typically, the privatised gas company had me on hold for twenty-five minutes, and then I paid the bill. Plus a sixty-pound reconnection charge.

'You know the mum is epileptic, right?' I'd said. 'She can't go out, the dad's dead.'

'Will you be wanting to reconnect today?' he said.

I said I would be wanting to.

The following week, Julia saw Justin on the opposite side of Essex Road, walking with two women with dyed-blonde hair. She'd called out and he waved, but the women had hurried away.

I didn't see the boy for a couple of weeks but didn't feel able to knock for him, as if I wanted to see if he could come out to play. Then he rang me, worried about school; he had a test coming up and he'd be late for it because he had to take his sister in first.

I rang the school for him. Justin said ask for Mr Forrest.

'He's worried about this Year 8 test coming up,' I said, 'because he has to take his sister to her schoo—'

'He's in Year 9,' said Mr Forrest.

'Is he?'

'Year 9 do not have any tests this week.'

His manner was withering. No one had taken such a scornful tone with me since my father scoffed when I received an honorary doctorate from my old university.

'While I've got you,' I said, 'can you at least ensure he comes home with a form so he can register for free school meals?'

Good one, I thought. *You're not even feeding the kids, Mr Forr—*

'He's on free meals, always has been.'

Justin had a way of not reacting when these things were explained to him. I called Islington Council to ensure his family had at least partial exemption from Council Tax, and the Housing Benefit office to find out when their money was due.

'It's fortnightly, on a Monday,' I said, 'two hundred and fifty-six quid. OK?'

He nodded and the next Monday he proudly brought the cheque round to show me. He'd already told me about his social worker, a man, separate from his mum's.

'Speak to him,' I said. 'Say all the things you're telling me.'

Then one day he came round needing money. I told him on the doorstep that I was going to give him a twenty-pound note and I wanted him to pay me back. I knew a housing cheque was due.

'Don't worry about the other money,' I said, 'just this twenty.'

He seemed pleased about this new footing for our friendship. He wanted to pay me back. I watched him go and shut the door.

THERAPIST: And you haven't seen him for how long?

ALAN: A few weeks.

T: Do you miss him?

A: Maybe I do. I mean, I must do if I'm paying you to talk about him.

T: [smiles] What was it about this boy that made you so sympathetic?

A: I think it was his top.

T: What about it? It was a tracksuit, is that right?

A: Sort of, but not Adidas or Nike or whatever, just something cheap, that seemed to mark him out straightaway, it made me think he'd be spotted by other kids in the area.

T: As poor?

A: Just vulnerable somehow. When I was a kid I had a red tracksuit top that I used to wear all the time, aged about twelve, never wore anything else, I didn't have anything else, my dad wore the same clothes for years and we just didn't think about them. We weren't poor – private school, house in suburbia, holidays – but somehow we didn't spend anything. The only restaurant we ever went to was the Wimpy, which I loved, I should say. Then one day friends from school started to make comments about my top, so much so that I couldn't ignore them and eventually had to ask what they were saying.

T: You confronted them?

A: I suppose so, but it was more that they were muttering at me. Anyway, they said why did I always wear the same top, that I always had it on and so on. What can you say?

T: Did you not feel able to ask your father for money to spend on clothes?

A: He gave me an Action Man for Christmas once and said, 'You have to play with this a lot, it was very expensive.' Then I went to a friend's house and he had about six Action Men lying about.

T: Did you play with it a lot?

A: [laughs] Hell yes! I accumulated three in the end, over several years, and my cousin Richard gave me a fourth. I actually took them to university and was still playing imaginary football matches with them when I was twenty-one. I remember being in my third year and I was at my girlfriend Jill's house, everyone else was out, I was watching the FA Cup final when Coventry beat Tottenham and I played with my Action Men on her bedroom floor at half time.

T: Did anyone know you played with them?

A: No, it's funny what men get up to when their girlfriends are out. And this was a house of feminists, very politically aware, God knows what they'd have made of me continuing my childhood at twenty-one.

T: Do you think that's unusual?

A: Maybe all men have a boy inside? We're always told to 'grow up' when we're young. 'Grow up, grow up,' or even, 'Act your age,' which comes from the same place, but it's hard to know how to grow up. I suppose I could have started Action Man Society to see if I could flush out other secret enthusiasts on campus, but I wouldn't have wanted to talk to them. I always played with them on my own.

T: As an escape?

A: It was something I loved to do, when my dad partitioned our bedroom so my brother and me had a shoebox each, I played in that tiny space for hours with those figures. I'd keep score, it was always reds vs yellows after a soccer-skills series on TV with Kevin Keegan, when the teams wore those colours. I gave the players personalities and different skills. It was quite theatrical, perhaps I should have given a performance for my degree.

T: Do you still have the red tracksuit top?

A: No, but I must have got something else. By the time I was sixteen I had a denim jacket with a CND badge on the back saying: TOGETHER WE CAN STOP THE BOMB.

T: It's not easy to grow up if your emotional development is impaired in some way, trauma can hinder the maturing process. And of course you were severely traumatised at six and then, could there be something in the withdrawal to your room, the solitude and yet still playing the games you had as a child, that is connected to your father's interest in you? He might have preferred you to remain small and vulnerable, not growing older. Perhaps, without being aware of it, you were holding back your own development, at least until you became open to influences outside the home, and perhaps that badge on your back is a symbol of that. Was your father a CND supporter?

A: [laughs] No.

T: So it was you marking yourself as independent, but those toys, that link to peaceful solitude, have stayed with you. Do you spend more on clothes now?

A: Not much, though when I was sixteen, now you mention it, the first time I got a pay packet from the greengrocer's I went straight to a shop in Loughton and bought two shirts.

T: Interesting, isn't it?

A: Yes.

T: You know where Justin lives, why don't you go and see how he is?

A: Something's stopping me, I sort of think he'll find a way to survive, maybe other people are giving him money, like a cat being fed in lots of different kitchens.

Years later, Katie was talking to a friend who'd been running drama workshops in prisons. One of the inmates had claimed he knew me. He was in his early twenties, and had been jailed over some motoring offence, but was a promising actor and had already landed a small film role. He was often in trouble when he was young but the one thing he felt bad about was lying to me. It was the boy, of course (his name's not Justin). His mum hadn't been agoraphobic or epileptic; she'd been a crack addict. All the money had gone on drugs. He was very sorry.

I'm Not Saying My Dad Made Me Ill

21st October 2024.

There is evidence now, from lengthy studies of groups of young people known to have been sexually abused or to have had some other Adverse Childhood Experience (ACE), compared with control groups without similar episodes or involvement, that people experience differing life outcomes according to their childhood trauma.

For people who've suffered any ACE there is increased likelihood of drug use, from cigarettes and alcohol through cannabis and into more serious addictions. There is greater likelihood of obesity and self-harm, and greater utilisation of health provision – in other words, in these groups there is more heart disease, more cancers, more strokes, more early deaths, including suicides, than in any control group without ACEs.

If some of the language I'm using seems out of character or lifted from elsewhere, it's because I am indebted, when writing about this, to Bessel van der Kolk's book *The Body Keeps the Score*.

Van der Kolk is a Dutch psychiatrist who has worked for decades in the field of post-traumatic stress disorder (PTSD), a diagnosis only properly classified in 1980, largely as a consequence of treating Vietnam veterans. Van der Kolk has also worked extensively with victims of childhood trauma and his observations, research and studies, alongside those of many likeminded leaders in the field, have culminated in the publication of an accessible book of serious research and discovery that became a compelling *New York Times* bestseller, as well as an excellent audiobook.

So much of what van der Kolk writes about – especially the consequences of sexual abuse, from small things like sensitivity to touch or loud noises, through to the development of addictions due to self-medication and, later in life, the health consequences of a life of smoking, drinking, drug use and so on – ring true for me, as someone who endures PTSD as a consequence of my father's abuse of me as a child.

My PTSD is relatively mild, in that I have managed, albeit not until my late fifties, to talk onstage, in stand-up, about my earliest sexual experience being naked in the arms of my father. I suffer from shortness of breath when I broach the subject. Issues with intimacy have plagued me for years, stemming from a deeply ingrained eagerness to please that meant I couldn't helpfully give directions to my own pleasure. These characteristics make for frequent disappointments in sex because most untroubled folk hope for their partner to enjoy themselves too, and don't want a martyr in the bedroom.

The stress disorder appears most often if I'm in a room by myself, particularly when in bed, and I hear someone outside the door. I'm visited by a chest-tightening fear, which is surely related to the many unwanted visits by my father over the years but also the always-present fear of him coming in.

I first tried to smoke aged eleven, and the idea of it being illicit or rebellious was part of the appeal. Once addicted, which happened almost immediately, I then saw so much positive reinforcement around cigarettes culturally, in films especially, that I was happy to continue. And I knew my father hated it, which was another reason to smoke. Dad telling me not to do it made it more likely to happen.

On one occasion, at sixteen, I took a cigarette from a packet of Marlboro and, seeing it was the last one, threw the box into the gutter. I was outside our family home in Loughton; there was no litter in that street and I wasn't prone to dropping rubbish anyway. It was petulant and shameful and made worse when my father opened an upstairs window and yelled: 'Pick that up!' which I did, scowling.

Had I not had the relationship I did with my primary childhood caregiver between the ages of six and thirteen – when I was at last able to resist the molestation – then maybe I wouldn't have been attracted to cigarettes, or felt the need to force myself to smoke them to impress my peer group at school; maybe I wouldn't have subsequently developed bladder cancer, for which smoking is the main cause.

Who can really say?

Are You Married?

The Brief was an ITV drama conceived by veteran producers Ted Childs and Chris Burt, who persuaded me to take on writer Dusty Hughes's creation Henry Farmer: a brilliant barrister on a bicycle with an estranged wife, a gambling habit and a ten-year-old son on the other side of the world.

To help viewers forget Jonathan Creek, my hair was vigorously becalmed each morning while make-up was literally sprayed onto my face. The other difference was my fee, which was more than I was paid for a year of Abbey National ads, though this would be fourteen weeks' work, not fourteen days.

All the cast were strong, particularly in the fictional chambers with Linda Basset, Cherie Lunghi, Chris Fulford, Steven Alvey and Robert Whitelock, and the stories were interesting, but things weren't helped by anxiety in my 'private life'.

At our unit base in Russell Square one lunchtime, a van pulled up and two photographers jumped out to snap me. I hid behind Rob Whitelock, who nearly dropped his biscuit.

Something was up.

This sort of harassment had gone on for a while.

On one occasion the year before, Julia and I were going to *Creek* rehearsals together on my motorbike. Filtering past traffic at walking pace, we were knocked over by the car alongside us pulling out to its right. I wanted us to get up and go – no one knew who we were inside our helmets – but Julia said her back hurt and an ambulance was called. Thankfully, she was uninjured but one outcome was a tabloid wanting to run a story that she was pregnant. She wasn't. Presumably that was another misinterpreted phone hack, though at the time our paranoia led us to assume that all paramedics and A&E staff were in the pay of the gutter press.

The Mail on Sunday later ran a front-page story that Julia and I had married in secret.

They'd rung my father at home and said: 'Aren't you even going to wish them well?'

'If it's true, of course I wish them well,' he'd said.

They then wrote: 'Alan's father let it slip when he said, "I wish them well."'

After that, my dad apologised to me, the only time he ever did, for not just hanging up on them.

People from Australia and New Zealand sent me their best wishes. I had to keep repeating that the story was untrue. Even my friends were fooled. Keith Dover approached me as if I'd only reveal the truth in a mumbled one-to-one.

'Are you married?' he said.

'No!' I said.

'No, no, that's what I thought . . .'

Julia and I had already split up before all this happened. We'd bought a house together but she never moved in and it was sold. She stayed for a while in my old place on St Mary's Grove. I went to see her but found it empty. She'd gone.

One night I was asleep alone in the huge flat on Corsica Street and imagined I heard her voice. I jumped down from my sleeping platform and out into the cavernous atrium, calling her name, but it was a dream. Other than momentarily at an awards do, I never saw her again.

I found a lawyer and, after several weeks, the fake wedding news was corrected, on page eleven, hardly the equal prominence they were obligated to offer.

Years later, I received a hefty five-figure sum as compensation for phone hacking at that time. I imagine Julia's phone was hacked too. We always felt like the photographers knew where we were. It seemed like there must be a mole in every bar or restaurant tipping people off.

My lawyer said all victims of phone hacking – and she was representing seventy-five of us – report the same thing.

I rented out the swimming-pool flat and moved back into the empty house on St Mary's Grove, just as I'd done in the middle of the first series of *Jonathan Creek* in 1996, when I'd also just broken up with someone. But I was pleased to be there. In the conservatory (that *The Sun* didn't pay for) there were nice new blinds, installed by Bill and Kris because they'd lived happily in that house for eighteen months while they were renovating in Hammersmith, and their cockatoo trashed the place like a crested Keith Moon. There was history within the walls and I wanted somewhere quiet and familiar.

It was during the second series of *The Brief* that it stopped being enjoyable, despite the introduction of Camilla Power to the cast. A script that I liked, about a man convinced his wife is a spy, was dropped in favour of a rape story where the victim was beautiful (Kirsty Mitchell) and the rapist handsome (Alastair Mackenzie) and no comment was made about sexual violence or the justice system. There were so many disagreements, not least because they wanted to kill off Henry Farmer's dad, played by Edward Petherbridge, and I loved doing scenes with him. It became chaotic. Different-coloured pages denote rewrites and my script had all the colours of a set of children's felt-tip pens.

Wandering around Russell Square, I went into a newsagent and bought a Lonely Planet guide to Asia. Looking at the climates of the various countries I could visit after we'd wrapped, I discovered that best choice for April was Vietnam.

So, I flew to Hanoi, by myself, with a backpack and no plans.

At Ha Long Bay I booked two nights on a boat. None of the other handful of passengers were British but they all spoke English.

No one there knew who I was, and no one at home knew where I was. Perfect.

I had so much fun on that boat and for the rest of the trip, visiting Sapa, Hoi An, Hue and Nha Trang. I wasn't drinking and I was up for making new friends. I was bothered for being famous only once, on my last night in Saigon, by a young British woman.

'It is you, isn't it?'

'No.'

I'd befriended a couple of lads and we were going about together, all three of us on one scooter, not unusual for Vietnam.

'You can have the helmet,' the rider had said.

The girl came back one more time.

'I'll go back to England and tell everyone that Jonathan Creek's a fucking wanker, shall I?' she said.

'If you like,' I said.

It was good preparation for my return home.

A couple of weeks later I was on *Friday Night with Jonathan Ross*. They showed a picture I'd given them of me next to a water buffalo in a Vietnamese rice paddy.

'You went to Vietnam for three weeks by yourself,' said Jonathan.

'Yes, it was amazing.'

'That's quite a strange thing to do,' he said.

But I felt somehow realigned, rebooted and positive.

A few weeks later, on 9th June 2005, I spotted a young woman in the audience at a *QI* recording, slim and pretty with bleached-blonde hair.

She was at the bar in the green room afterwards; her name was Katie and she was sitting side by side with her friend Suzanne Milligan. They were there because the literary agency they worked for represented one of the panellists, Andy Hamilton. I hovered around chatting to them and when they eventually made to leave I asked Katie for her number.

On the 18th, we went on a date to Walthamstow Dogs, where the central locking on my car failed in a remote car park. Katie was trapped inside looking at me. Was this a ploy? Thankfully the doors opened after a couple of minutes spent trying, and we had a lot of fun that evening.

A second date followed in a restaurant on Essex Road and it was after that she told me, by email, that she had a boyfriend. I replied, possibly emboldened by the new spirit I'd acquired in Vietnam, that I'd be a much better option. Katie had told me there was a cat hanging around the backyard at the house she shared and when they opened the kitchen window it came in, so I said I too was prepared to wait in the yard.

Later, one of Katie's housemates told her: 'You know he's married, to Julia Sawalha?'

I was thirty-nine and Katie was twenty-six. She told her mum I was thirty-four.

'I googled that man,' her mum said a few days later, to let it be known she was both online and on to me.

There remained a contractual obligation for me to shoot a third series of *The Brief*. Michael Foster and I went to a meeting with the new head of drama at Carlton TV. I complained about the rape story and she said: 'As a woman, I didn't have a problem with the rape.'

She was planning to sack everyone – producers, writers, the entire cast – and start again with just me.

'Why would I stay if you've fired all my friends?' I said.

She mentioned my fee.

'You could double my money and I wouldn't do it,' I said.

'Yes, you would,' she said.

Maybe in the past, but not any more.

It was the only time in ten years as my agent that Michael was speechless. After the meeting, we stood on the pavement outside and, even though it would cost him fifty grand in commission, he said: 'I'll get you out of it.'

Katie and I went to Thailand and Laos for a month.

I gave more consideration to my work-life balance, mainly by dropping the work part. This led to some realignment of existing relationships. *QI* had scheduled a recording on the day of the 2006 Champions League final. I'd asked months beforehand if they'd change it, as Arsenal had a chance of qualifying.

'I can do any other day in May and any day in June,' I'd said.

They didn't change the date. John Lloyd rang me when I was on another holiday with Katie, skiing in Italy. He was cross on the phone, when I wouldn't budge over the possible Cup final, and I hung up.

Addison Cresswell used to say: 'If you want something, you have to be prepared to walk.'

QI 's co-creator John Mitchinson later told me: 'I'll never forget that day. Lloydy rang and said, "I've ruined *QI*. Alan's just called me a cunt." '

The angry boy was still around, it seemed, only this time we were in agreement. Perhaps it was meeting Katie, or years of therapy, but I had more of an idea of which choices I might subsequently regret.

'I told him it would all be fine and you'd make up,' Mitch said, laughing. 'He doesn't understand football, you see.'

When Arsenal won their semi-final, Stephen Fry sent me a congratulatory text.

Now I had a decision to make: should I go to Paris to watch Arsenal play their first ever Champions League final against Barcelona, thereby missing a recording of *QI*, having never done so before? Or be a professional, who knows his responsibilities and the value of loyalty, and watch the highlights on TV?

After ten of us had enjoyed a sumptuous lunch in the shady courtyard of our Parisian hotel, we took an afternoon constitutional in the sunshine before heading to the Stade de France. At the far end, the Barcelona fans held huge banners spelling out *Mes que en club* (more than a club). We watched their heroes lift the trophy. Afterwards, even more people we knew gathered in a restaurant.

Among them was an old friend from the comedy circuit, Ainsley Harriott, once of the Calypso Twins but now a highly recognisable TV chef. We had a long catchup standing in the centre of the restaurant near the bar.

Later, our group were round a table in a corner and I was sitting next to my friend Sean, who, like Ainsley, is of Afro-Caribbean heritage. Other than infectious laughter, there's no similarity between them; Sean's darker-skinned, shorter, with a mischievous, round face under a red LA Dodgers cap.

Eventually a sour-faced stranger came over – it really does seem there's always one – and said: 'I hate *Jonathan Creek*.' Before I could reply, he provided his own punchline when he turned to Sean and said: 'And your cooking's shit.'

And then he left, perhaps not understanding why we were all laughing so much and leaving us with a story we never tire of repeating. Ainsley was two seats away.

That summer, Katie and I rode a Suzuki V-Strom through Spain, chatting away on our helmet intercom.

We'd started on a ferry from Portsmouth to Bilbao, in the middle of which was a cage housing the Duty Frees. I heard one passenger ask for 'a thousand Lambert and Butler, please'. Judging by his breathing, this was an optimistic purchase; he seemed unlikely to make it back to his seat alive, never mind have time left to smoke all those.

In the cafeteria people looked at us as if I'd walked in with a flamingo, on account of Katie being unusually slim and pretty, not because she was standing on one leg and filter feeding through her bill.

Soon, though, we had ridden to Salamanca and were at a table in the beautiful Plaza Mayor. Another highlight was the mosque in Córdoba, made up of scores of pillars that seem to go on forever. It's cool and silent and so captivated the Catholic soldiers sent to tear it down, as they drove the Moors from Spain, that they preserved it. Eventually, a gaudy cathedral was erected in the centre.

We also went to Germany that summer, for the 2006 World Cup, flying first to Munich. We got caught in an electrical storm during a boat trip on Lake Starnberg, so disembarked at Tutzing, thinking we'd take a train back.

While sheltering under the awning of a kiosk on the jetty, and emboldened by the proprietor persuading me to try snuff, I proposed to Katie. We then travelled by train to Berlin, where we found an engagement ring.

Taking Katie to the World Cup final was perhaps a stress test for our fledgling engagement. If you asked her today who won, she'd tell you she can't remember who was playing, only that Shakira gyrated down a huge flight of steps at the Olympic Stadium, telling seventy-five thousand of us that her hips don't lie.

When I look back at 2006 – Katie moving in with me at St Mary's Grove, skiing in Italy, my fortieth birthday party in March, travelling around Southeast Asia, our motorcycle trip, the man in the Berlin jewellers crying out 'Bingo!' in his German accent with his thumb up as my card was accepted to purchase the ring – it was a happy time.

Soon, on 13th January 2007, all my friends came together at our winter wedding in an Essex stately home.

Everyone I'd been to Paris with turned up, having laughed when they realised that Arsenal were playing away to Blackburn that day so we wouldn't have to miss a home game.

John Hegley wrote and performed a funny and touching poem at the ceremony and later, Bill, in his best man's speech, told how our grand and ornate surroundings had been built 'as the base for Puff Daddy's 1996 European tour'.

Part Three

Tired and Emotional

'I can't let you go in, Alan, I'm so sorry. I wouldn't want you to see her as she is now, and so many people have come; she's tired.'

The door behind Anna was closed. Verity Lambert was out of view, weak, diminished, fading. She'd survived breast cancer before but it reinvented itself and returned when she was seventy-one.

David Renwick had rung to say that if I wanted to say goodbye I needed to go straightaway.

Anna was holding my hand.

'Would you like to leave her a note?' she said.

'Yes, thank you.'

'I'm sorry,' she said again. 'I'm not sure she would really know who was there, and it's such an effort.'

I wrote something brief on a little piece of paper.

And then I was back out on the street, having emerged from the building with no idea which way to turn. Nothing seemed to matter; maybe I could cross the road without looking and be knocked down and then see Verity again, elsewhere.

Anna told me later that she'd gone back in and read my note aloud and that Verity knew I'd been.

Maybe my sadness was not just for Verity but was connected to my mother's death. How could it not be? I was denied the chance to even write a note for Mum.

There was always someone to turn to when Verity was alive, even though I hadn't seen her for a couple of years by the end. Shortly after she died, when

Anna was arranging the funeral, I was one of the people she asked to give a eulogy.

When it was my turn, I stood up in the church and went to the front. Verity was next to me, in her eco-coffin, which seemed so flimsy, almost like a wicker basket. She was right there, now silent, which she rarely was in life, and I found it shocking.

I recalled her taking me for lunch at the Wolsey and introducing me to Dickie Attenborough and Lord Puttnam, who were both delighted to see her; I told a story about her enormous dog, named after Arthur Daley, and another about us going to see Arsenal win at Chelsea and then walking back to her flat in Holland Park, when she counselled me on all matters, professional and personal; I expressed regret at not taking her to the newly opened Emirates Stadium, as she'd asked me to; and finally, how I'd had no idea at my wedding that she'd worn a wig to conceal hair loss brought on by chemotherapy.

Louise Rennison had sat next to Verity at the wedding.

'Isn't Verity Lambert brilliant?' she'd said. 'I *love* her!'

The wake was held upstairs at the Groucho Club in Soho, a haven for media people. There was a large turnout and plenty of wine, but little food.

After a few hours, some of the mourners, including Katie and me, went down into the club's main bar. The drinking continued and new people would join us every so often. Jackie Clune came in, after appearing in *Billy Elliot* nearby. At one point the ex-boyfriend of a gay colleague at *QI* sat down next to me, reached across to put his hand in my crotch and squeezed, hard, for what seemed like ages. I didn't know what to do about it and eventually he went away. There was a chaotic feel to the place now, everyone either talking or laughing, the funeral long gone.

By the time I left, terribly drunk, with Katie and Jackie, it was past two o'clock in the morning. I'd been drinking for ten hours.

Some homeless men were demanding money from anyone who came out of the Groucho's front door. I'd been to the club only a couple of times before and never that late so was unprepared for this.

One of them saw me and shouted: 'Jonathan! Jonathan!'

I looked at the ground and headed down Greek Street with Katie and Jackie. In a few seconds, we'd turn left onto Old Compton Street and be gone.

'Jonathan!'

Don't respond.

'Jonathan!'

Keep walking.

'Why are you being such a cunt, Jonathan?'

As I returned to the group of men, an angry boy once again, a surge of feeling was boiling up inside me like a geyser about to blow. I struggled to contain myself and for some reason focused on the fact they couldn't get my name right, even though that had happened dozens of times with strangers. I went up to the one who looked sheepish enough to be the culprit. Resolving not to hit him, so as not to make a scene, I leaned into his ear, murmuring something like: 'My name's not Jonathan, it's Alan.'

That told him.

Weirdly, it felt like we were the only two people there. Other than a specialist conducting an examination, no one would ever look so closely at a stranger's ear. Never mind bite one.

A week or two later, I was cycling round to the garages at the back of my house on St Mary's Grove. I'd been playing seven-a-side football with some other actors and writers and looked ridiculous, still in my kit, with a cycling helmet perched on top.

As I lifted my garage door, a young man in a suit came running up and introduced himself as (name forgotten) from *The Daily Mirror*. He showed me a grainy black-and-white image on a piece of A4 paper, which he said was a freeze-frame from CCTV footage captured outside the Groucho. He pointed at one of the figures in the picture, all seen from above with no faces visible.

'Is that you?' he said.

I peered at the image.

'I'm afraid I can't comment on that,' I said. 'You can't tell who anyone is.'

He told me a homeless man had claimed that I'd bitten him on the ear;

they'd watched the footage, and I'd held on for thirteen seconds. He was keeping a straight face but obviously felt this was a good day to be working for a red top.

'Are you going to run this?' I said.

'Yes,' he said.

'What are you going to say?'

'Jonathan Creek bites tramp's ear.'

I laughed and then said: 'You're not allowed to put that I laughed when you said that; you told me it in a deliberately funny way.'

'OK, I won't,' he said.

They ran the story, mentioning that I'd 'laughed uproariously' when I was told about the headline.

A gaggle of hacks hung around outside the house for a while after that. Katie and I were living with the curtains pulled closed, planning an escape to Spain until it died down. Imagine you've been married less than a year and this is the sort of mess your husband can land in?

At least Verity was never mentioned. I couldn't stand the idea that her name might be dragged into reports about my drunken behavior after her funeral. The irony is, she would doubtless have counselled me about grim Soho drinking dens and resisting provocation.

The CCTV footage was by now with ITN, who wanted to show it on the news. Michael Foster's lawyer prevented that, citing something to do with the ownership of the camera and someone trying to profit from the images. I forget the details. I remember only the shame, the painful embarrassment and the amendments to my Wikipedia page.

Coming out of an Arsenal match with Keith Dover, he said, 'Let's all bite a vagrant,' as we headed to the pub.

In 2021, *QI* regular Cariad Lloyd asked me to guest on her show *Griefcast*. I had spoken about the incident outside the Groucho in a live chat show about ten years previously, at the Royal Vauxhall Tavern with Scott Capurro. The audience there found it hilarious, particularly my insistence that I hadn't wanted to cause a scene and just wanted to clarify my real name on a one-to-one basis, *entre nous*, that need go no further. Scott teased out the details with sympathy but plenty of savage wit. It was unexpectedly cathartic.

Cariad's podcast takes a different tone; there's no audience, and her invitation was prompted by the publication of *Just Ignore Him*. We discussed Verity's funeral and the terrible aftermath. And she put it down to a manifestation of grief, about which she's conducted scores of interviews and published a book.

People might behave irrationally in grief if they're unbalanced by strong emotion, the effect of which is amplified when further deep feelings, perhaps a lifelong buried sadness, are unknowingly brought into play. Throw in five bottles of wine and some disaster is probable.

And, despite my appalling reaction, I took Cariad's point, finally experiencing sorrow for the angry boy I became that night when I was, as *The Standard* put it, using the now traditional journalistic phrase, 'tired and emotional'.

Greek Tragedy

'Right, let's shoot this, Alan's shitting himself!'

So said Gurinder Chadha, the charming director of *Angus, Thongs and Perfect Snogging*, the film based on Louise Rennison's book (the title having been changed from *Full-Frontal Snogging*).

I was supposed to perform a moonwalk across the dance floor in a big party scene with about two hundred people watching.

'You can do a moonwalk, right?' Gurinder had said.

'It would be nice to have a practice,' I'd said.

It didn't matter; it would have been odd if Georgia Nicholson, the teenage lead character, had a dad who could moonwalk like Michael Jackson.

Louise had based Georgia on herself, and her real schoolfriends all appeared in the bestselling series, their names unchanged.

'I'm glad you're going to be my dad,' she said, before bursting out laughing as usual. I was nothing like her Yorkshireman father, who I'd met when we'd all gone to see Leeds play Arsenal a few years before.

At this time, in late 2007, I was going back and forth to Athens to see my own dad in hospital, where he was on intravenous antibiotics for a severe infection in his leg. The septic limb was under a small tent on the bed to keep the sheets off it. Swollen and black for its entire length, it glistened from the constant oozing discharge. I looked once. The prognosis was amputation or death.

Katie was of the view that my brother and sister's refusal to visit their father, despite my offer to buy plane tickets, was more understandable than my waggy-tailed journeying across the continent. I was still trying to please Dad, just as I had been by staying silent when he'd molested me.

Katie accompanied me to Athens twice. When we arrived the first time, my dad dispatched us to find him some new underpants at Marks and Spencer, made some bizarre comments about Katie being there to go sightseeing and was rude to and about the nurses. I took him a portable DVD player and the only British paper I could find, a *Daily Mail*. Then he told us how incredibly caring my sister was because she'd phoned him. Katie left the room rather than tell him the truth about the situation.

A few years previously, my dad had asked me to lend him a hundred thousand pounds. He said his pension fund with Equitable Life had collapsed and he needed twelve thousand a year to live on. I thought this suggested a change in our relationship, and I was in a position to help, so I agreed.

'Couldn't make it a hundred and twenty, could you?' he said.

I met him and my stepmother in a Harvester restaurant by the North Circular with a cheque for £120,000.

Within a month he had a new BMW 5 Series and a widescreen TV.

Years later, when my dad had Alzheimer's, my stepmother and brother took power of attorney over his affairs and when I asked for the loan to be returned she said she had no memory of it and neither did her daughter.

'And she has a very good memory,' she said.

'She wasn't in the Harvester with us, though, was she?' I said.

I had prior experience of people in my family denying actual events and in any case the loan arrangement was in my dad's handwriting, so I retrieved my money. He evidently hadn't needed it.

I'd imagined at the time that I was establishing a new relationship with him but in hindsight can see I was being manipulated again. The same applied to my going back and forth to Greece.

During that first visit, Katie and I stayed out late into the warm evening drinking cocktails at a busy pavement bar. We were actually enjoying ourselves until I descended into stressed-out drunkenness, during which I fell over in the street and then became unforgivably abusive and aggressive towards her even as she tried to help me up.

There was no one else for me to speak to and yet I risked driving her away. It became an example of the harm that an angry boy can do, especially when alcohol abuse is exacerbating his inability to understand or even identify the feelings that are distressing him.

This is one way abuse can be passed on and why it's such a serious crime. It never ends with the act itself, now lost in childhood; once inflicted, it stays for life and affects everything, not least those who care about you. Katie is my witness, because for me that night is lost in alcohol blackout.

Still, she travelled with me to Athens again and helped me bring my father home, his leg saved, on an EasyJet flight to Gatwick.

The insurance company had provided a nurse as a travelling companion.

'Hello,' I said.

'Your father is a very difficult man,' she said.

On our return, I was drained from the experience and regretful of the strain on Katie, unable to properly recognise the depths of love and loyalty she'd shown me by helping with this man.

Somehow, I took pleasure from assisting my father. He expressed gratitude (a rare thing, for him), and the power of my need to please him, at the expense of my wife's feelings and my own, shocks me even now – not just because it was how I was reacting at the time but because it's taken me so many years to understand it.

After Athens, I had to return to the *Angus, Thongs* set to shoot the moonwalk, my last scene.

The film premiere was at the Empire in Leicester Square. I met Louise beforehand and we sat together in the vast cinema as the lights dimmed. How different it was from 1992 and our earliest meeting in Edinburgh, when I was *The Love Child of Alan Ladd* and she was telling how *Bob Marley's Gardener Sold My Friend*.

Teenage Revolution

Near where I grew up there is a statue of Winston Churchill, who was MP for a neighbouring constituency. Every time we passed it in the car, Dad would say: 'Good old Winnie!'

Now I was sitting beneath that statue, cold, tired and alone.

We'd been filming a sequence for the 2010 Channel 4 series *Teenage Revolution*, based on my first book, and the director, Rob Coldstream, had been asking me for some reflections about my relationship with my father. I shut down and turned him away.

We'd interviewed many prominent figures for the series, and Rob had curated an excellent soundtrack from the eighties, but he was curious to know more about me, as the events of the time were being seen through my eyes and I was supposed to be the conduit for the audience.

They interviewed my dad, spending time with him, looking at his old cinefilms. I could have given a truthful interview there and then, under the shadow of his hero, Winston Churchill, but I wasn't ready to tell my story. It was inside me, like a growth that I couldn't access. It felt inexplicably dangerous to say anything.

I was left with documentaries, well-made though they were, that I don't want to watch, based on a book I've never reread, and a new, lasting memory of my father, sitting in his armchair on Channel 4.

Writing that book and presenting those films was an untapped opportunity to talk openly about my experiences, while my father was still a year away from the Alzheimer's diagnosis that saved him from ever being pushed to say sorry. No one else was going to even try to make him acknowledge his wrongdoing.

As someone who took decades to speak up, my sympathies are with those who are carrying secrets. The life they know can continue; it's familiar, and the risk of upturning everything by outing their abuser, often a family member, is scary. Many frightening outcomes seem possible and entire lives are lived in fear of something that hasn't happened.

I hope, if you are one of those people, that you find someone to tell your story to before much more of your life passes. Surviving the telling will be easier than secretly enduring memories of the abuse.

Pinky and Perky

22nd October 2024.

On the day of my operation, Katie and I walked down to the Royal Free for 7.30am. It was a mild autumn morning and all the kids were at home as it was half term. Susie was in charge but the boys were in bed when we left.

On the Sunday before, I'd said to Katie: 'Today I have cancer; in two days I won't have it any more.'

'Yes,' she said, 'that's a good way to look at it.'

The hospital has a cruciform construction with a brutalist concrete exterior built in the early seventies. You can see it for miles around. The seventh floor has signs for North, East and West wards but we were looking for 7 South, where we were shown into a room with four beds. There were signs of occupation on two of them, a few possessions; presumably other day patients like me.

After a while a nurse came in and said: 'We're going to move Alan to Room 19, more privacy.' So I had the good fortune of a room to myself. The Royal Free sits on top of a hill in Belsize Park, and from the seventh floor the view across London was clear. We spent some time trying to work out where we were in relation to a few landmarks but could only really establish the Premier Inn up the road.

A doctor came in, introduced herself as Pinky and went through all the checks to make sure I was the right person.

'You had a cystoscopy?'

'Yes, I also had a CT scan but I haven't heard back from that yet.'

289

'Oh yes,' she said, 'I have that here,' and she checked her phone.

For eight days I'd been waiting to hear whether I had any other tumours, cysts or suspect areas in my kidneys and surrounding organs, and now Pinky casually checked her phone.

'Yes, that was all good; nothing came up in the kidneys or anywhere else so that's good news. Just the small tumour to be removed today.'

Katie and I made eye contact across the room. There was no other cancer, just the one bit that the jackal was going to assassinate.

'And that will be sent off,' I said, 'to the lab?'

'Yes, they'll check what sort of tumour it is, how aggressive and so on,' said Pinky. 'OK?'

'Yes, thank you,' I said.

'Someone from the anaesthetist's team will be in shortly to have a chat with you.'

A few minutes later, a second tall, young doctor appeared, hair cropped short and a big smile on her face.

'Hi, I'm Jaz,' she said. 'I'm part of the anaesthetic team today.' There were a few routine questions about allergies and past experiences of anaesthetic, and she said I was hopefully going to be seen quite early as the first patient had already gone down to theatre.

Another doctor came in. He was tall, too, perhaps early thirties, with short red hair.

'Hi,' he said, 'I'm Ed.'

Ed? Of course, like his namesake Redmayne in *The Day of the Jackal*. Could it be him in disguise?

Ed was going to be wielding the assassin's rigid cystoscope. As far as I understood it, a cutting loop would go over the tumour and slice it off. Then an electric current would be used to cauterize the area, to stop the bleeding. A sample of tissue would be taken from the base of the tumour. Everything would be flushed out and we were done.

Pinky came in a bit later.

'We'd like your consent to perform a chemotherapy wash with mitomycin, is that OK?'

'Sorry, I've not heard of that.'

I'd started searching the side effects of mitomycin on my phone when Ed joined us.

'I was expecting a BCG treatment to stimulate my immune system,' I said.

'Is that what you've been told will happen?' he said.

'No, it was just something my GP mentioned as a possibility.'

'Mitomycin does a similar thing; it attacks any cancer cells. While we have you there under anaesthetic, we can fill the bladder with the solution. It stays inside for an hour or so and then drains out via a catheter. Save you having to come in for additional treatment, hopefully.'

'What's bone-marrow toxicity?' I said, looking up from my phone.

'Ah,' he said, as if I was displaying typical patient behaviour, 'side effects. In your case, the mitomycin will be contained within the bladder; it won't reach other parts of the body and so the chance of side effects is greatly reduced.'

'Can we have your consent?' said Pinky.

'Yes,' I said. 'While I'm here; it's a good chance to do it.'

After a while, a nurse came in looking for my notes. They couldn't find them. There was a delay. Pinky came back up from theatre to sort it out. Everything was pushed back a bit but soon I was being wheeled in my bed to a large lift and then into a small room, where a team of anaesthetists began to work quickly around me. Sticky pads were attached to my chest.

'How are you feeling?' said the senior anaesthetist. 'Or is that a silly question?'

'A bit anxious,' I said.

'Don't worry,' she said. 'We'll be with you every step of the way, when you're in with the surgeon; we won't leave you.'

'Thank you,' I said.

'Now I'm just going to put this over your nose and mouth.'

A clear plastic mask appeared over me.

'This is just oxygen,' she said, 'to help you feel more relaxed, nothing to put you out at this stage.'

'Are you all right? It's all over, you're all done.'

The voice came from my left, gentle, with a soft Asian accent. I looked round and there was a kind face I hadn't seen before.

'You are in the recovery room,' she said. 'Everything is OK. You have a catheter in because you had some mitomycin, so that has to stay in there for a little longer.'

'OK,' I said. There was a clock on the wall opposite. Half an hour ticked by.

'Now, we can take this off.' She was reaching under the sheet. 'The doctor said half past and it could come out.'

I stared at the clock on the wall, with its big hand on the six, while a small hand removed the catheter and attached a clear bag that was hooked onto the side of the bed. Now I could see dark-pink fluid draining out of me.

'This has to be the colour of rosé wine,' said the nurse.

A second nurse then took over. She had the same accent and gentle bedside manner as her predecessor.

A few minutes later, Ed was at my side. *Shouldn't he be travelling to Munich on a false passport? The job's done. They'll be looking for him. (Must stop thinking about* Day of the Jackal.*)*

'All went pretty well,' he said. 'We took it out; it was small, only one centimetre, so we think we got it all. The mitomycin will help in case there was anything microscopic we couldn't see.'

'Thank you, doctor,' I said.

'OK, nice to meet you, good luck.'

And he was gone, to the dark web to negotiate payment for his next hit. (Last *Jackal* reference.)

If tumours only knew how dangerous Ed is to them. He's their sworn enemy and he'll never stop taking their lives.

After an hour or so, the fluid draining out was sufficiently rosé-like for me to be wheeled back to Room 19. There was a bit of changing of lifts as the orderly's pass didn't work, but I was soon back in 7 South. Katie was sitting in the same chair I'd last seen her in that morning.

'Are you OK?' she said.

'Yes, yes, I am.'

'Pinky said it went well; they were pleased.'

'Oh, has she been in?'

'Yes.'

'Have you been waiting ages?' I said.

'It's fine,' she said. 'It's nice to see you.'

A nurse asked whether I wanted something to eat but I declined.

'You need to pass water,' she said. I had a cardboard tube and receptacle under the sheet.

'I can drink more,' I said.

The nurse came back with a jug of water. I drank the lot and after a while felt nature painfully take its course.

Katie found the nurse.

'I've passed water, can I go?' I said.

'You need to eat something.'

'Oh, I didn't realise that. What have you got?'

A cheese sandwich with the words 'vegan' and 'ham' written on the packet was brought to me. But there was no meat inside so I ate it and then we were allowed to leave.

Broken Bones

My last trip to hospital had been to the Whittington in Islington. Katie and I had been living in the little house on St Mary's Grove for three and a half years, and married for last two of those. It was 11th March 2009 and she'd just found out she was pregnant with Susie.

I'd learned I knew little about what happens each month in a woman's body, particularly how narrow the window of opportunity actually is. Ovulation-testing kits arrived and shed light on the proceedings. Katie was delighted to be expecting; she'd been on the verge of stealing a baby in a pub one Sunday lunchtime.

On that night in March, I'd gone round the corner and met some friends, Tayo Popoola, Chris Blacklay and his brother Ollie, to watch Arsenal play away to Roma in the Champion's League. It was the same pub we went to after every Arsenal home game. After this night, we never went back.

At the bar, a man of about five seven with a green bomber jacket and black hair cut like a Mod had recognised me and was nagging me to buy him and his friends drinks. I was rudely dismissive and hoped to never see him again.

The game went to penalties. There was euphoria when Arsenal won, not least from me, as I'd been there for three hours and drunk two bottles of Sauvignon blanc. And then the man from earlier came back.

'Who do you think we'll get in the next round?' he said.

'I don't know,' I said.

'But who do you think we'll get?'

'Come on, mate, that's enough,' said one of my friends.

'I've no idea, have I?' I said.

'But who do you think, though?'

'Oh, mate, do fuck off,' I said.

And someone pushed me over a table. My friends were trying to persuade these people to leave me alone, but then I found my feet, lunged forward and took a drunken swing at the man.

Next thing I knew, Chris and his girlfriend were squatting next to me as I lay face down on the ground outside.

'Are you OK, Alan?'

This brought me round.

'Yes, I'm fine.'

'Are you sure?'

'I'm going to go home,' I said.

'Do you want us to come with you?'

'No, no, it's not far.'

I wandered back to St Mary's Grove. The back of my hand was scraped as if it had been trodden on. I had other bruises but it was the swelling on the side of my face that hurt.

As soon as I came through the front door into our kitchen, Katie's usual smile dropped.

'What's happened?'

'I don't know.'

And she drove me to the Whittington. Although she did ask me to park the car, as the space we found was tight and I'm better at those manoeuvres than her, even after two litres of wine and a concussion.

An X-ray showed that my zygomatic arch was snapped. That's the bone on the side of your head above your cheek. You can feel a thick hard line, the zygomatic process, which leads back towards the ear and forms the arch. My mandible (jaw) on the right side had dropped, my teeth no longer aligned properly and my bite was off. I was told the maxillofacial team would be in touch.

I had to ask Tayo to describe the incident to me. He said they'd all ushered me out of the pub, urging me to go home while trying to prevent three men from pursuing me, but then a staff member opened a door. I was knocked over from behind and kicked in the head, and the Blacklay boys had possibly saved my life by tackling my assailants. The bloke from the bar, once he'd been grabbed, had been saying: 'I'm sorry, I'm sorry.'

This wasn't the first incident of its kind.

I'd been to watch Arsenal lose away at Liverpool the previous year, also in the Champion's League. Katie had travelled to Liverpool too, as her schoolfriend and maid of honour Holly now lived there. We'd arranged to meet in a bar after the game. But they were a long time coming and the angry boy was drinking alone, hanging around a group of Arsenal fans he didn't know.

When Katie, Holly and her friends arrived, I needed to join them or go back to our hotel; but I was involved in some mindless goading outside with one of the Arsenal fans, a twenty-something investment banker in a Brazil shirt who unexpectedly ran forward and smashed his head into my face.

'Sorry, Alan,' said one of his friends, as they all ran off while blood splashed onto the ground outside the entrance to the bar.

I went to the toilets to stop the bleeding and then joined Katie at their table, clutching some tissue and hoping no one could properly see me. A few days later, there was a big lump on top of my nose that changed my appearance noticeably. There was swelling too; it was a mess.

I decided the lump had to go and pushed down on it as hard as I could with the fingers of both hands. This was agonising but it slowly disappeared and my nose looked normal again.

I went to a doctor and after examining me he said, 'Who reset this?'

'I did,' I said.

'That's unusual,' he said. 'I imagine that hurt quite a lot, did it?'

A couple of weeks later, Katie and I were at an immersive, interactive theatre experience across two floors and multiple rooms at Battersea Arts Centre. Everyone was required to wear papier-mâché masks. Mine pushed painfully into my injured nose.

Actors would move among us, sayings things like: 'The pestilence, the pestilence.'

It was incomprehensible, apparently by design. Then one of the cast lightly pushed me on the shoulder and I did the same back, thinking this was part of the action, but she was already on her way somewhere and didn't respond.

A couple of minutes later, a skinny man, also in a mask, beckoned to us to follow him, which we did, imagining we were being taken to another room we hadn't yet discovered. We went through some double doors and into a bit of starkly lit ex-council corridor. We'd gone off-piste. The man removed his mask.

'If you push one of the actresses like that again, you'll be asked to leave,' he said.

'She pushed me first!' I said.

'We want to leave,' said Katie. 'We can't find the way out.'

'I only did what she did,' I said. 'I thought that was in the show.'

'Would you like me to show you how to get out?' he said.

'Yes,' said Katie.

We passed through the main hall, where actors were dancing to Saint-Saëns's *Danse Macabre*, known to many as the theme from *Jonathan Creek*. I was glad of my disguise but once we were outside I took it off and felt my sore nose.

'Why did you push her?' said Katie.

'She started it,' I said.

My tiresome capacity for conflict could find an opening in the most unlikely of spaces.

Now, several weeks after the incident in Islington, I was still waiting for the Whittington's maxillofacial team to contact me. I rang the hospital and was told they had no record of my attendance.

A private specialist described the techniques they might have deployed to repair my face had I come to them earlier, but now the bone had set in the wrong position and there was nothing they could do.

The jaw has gradually realigned, although I did have to wear a bespoke mouthguard for two years to stop my teeth grinding at night. I can feel the lump in my zygomatic arch now, much as I can the knuckle that I broke on Jim Miller's frontal bone.

To be charged with grievous bodily harm you must have caused injuries such as broken bones, lacerations or concussion. A Section 20 GBH carries a maximum sentence of five years. According to the Crown Prosecution Service website, to be charged 'the suspect must intend, or foresee, that the act might cause some harm'.

But I didn't go to the police, dreading the inevitable press coverage.

My fear, shared by Katie, was where the angry boy inside me would surface next. Could I ever control him? We were about to start a family.

You're Going to Have to Leave the Theatre

Katie had an elective caesarean, claiming to be 'too chicken' for a natural birth, and Susie appeared at ten to four in the afternoon of 7th December 2009.

Then there was some consternation. The obstetrician thought perhaps he'd cut through Katie's urethra (he hadn't) and they were 'just going to get a urologist to take a look'.

The epidural was wearing off, so Katie was put under general anaesthetic. The doctor turned to me.

'You're going to have to leave the theatre.'

In the recovery room I was handed a tiny baby, swaddled so she looked like a cone with a head where the ice cream should be. I'd only held my nephew once before and didn't feel qualified to be in sole charge. Katie was long since in love with the tiny child she'd grown, but it all started for me when I had Susanna May in my hands.

I didn't think I'd wear a wedding ring, but I do; I didn't think I'd cut the umbilical cord, but the nurse took me over and handed me the scissors; and I didn't think I'd change nappies, but I've changed hundreds.

As I held Susie, I hoped that no disaster unfolded in the operating theatre that would leave just the two of us. I spoke to her but she seemed to be ignoring me. Babies are ungenerous listeners. After an hour or so, Katie was returned to us and I'd never experienced such relief.

We moved into the newly renovated swimming-pool flat on Corsica Street in late 2009, so Susie had eighteen months there, taking her first steps – a moment I caught on my phone – in the vast living room almost nine years to the day since the New Year's Eve party I'd thrown. But there were too many hazards in that place (not least drowning) so we sold it and moved to a house on Furlong Road in Holloway, with a beautiful garden backing on to a churchyard.

Though Katie and I had no recollection of his being conceived, Bobby was born on 18th June 2011, the sixth anniversary of our first date. He was granted most of his mum's attention so I happily took Susie, perched on a seat attached to a wide elasticated belt – since she could not tolerate perambulation of any kind – to Gymboree, Little Kickers, swimming lessons, parent and baby screenings and the Ten O'Clock Club in Highbury Fields. She was my new best friend.

Would It Be Any Other Way?

ALAN: On the way here, my train went past the station.

THERAPIST: Really, it didn't stop at Denmark Hill?

A: No, and it was meant to. It slowed down a bit after it had passed the platform and then just carried on to the next station. All of us who wanted the previous stop got off. Four or five passengers were furious, they ran up the platform to shout at the driver. Some people were asking each other what to do or looking for staff to help.

T: It's fascinating how something like that can bring different reactions from people. What did you do?

A: I went to the opposite platform and waited for a train back.

T: You didn't want to remonstrate with the driver?

A: No, it was too late anyway, and I wanted to get here.

T: Do you think you might have reacted differently at other times in your life?

A: I remember as a student trying to listen to the football results on my radio one evening, after the news – I had a small transistor – but I missed the scores and I banged the flat of my hand on the radio as hard as I could. My girlfriend at the time was there and she was quite shocked.

T: Maybe you can manage those moments better now?

A: Mostly, but I don't feel like I'm better. After years of therapy – and I know it's doing me good, I advocate it – I can spot feelings, identify them, express them, they don't bubble up so much now, unless I'm drunk. But when will I be better?

T: Have you considered reducing your drinking?

A: I have had extended periods of abstinence.

T: That's good.

A: But controlling alcohol is hard when I resume. I tend to binge, but it's helpful to numb things. When people say, 'I need a drink,' they rarely notice that it's a craving best ignored, but my desire to drink isn't just alcoholism, there's still all this stuff in my head, memories, that and the feeling that no one in my family really wants to believe me.

T: They want you to—

A: Just shut up.

T: Just shut up, yes.

A: Which I possibly could do if they would dare to challenge our father, or if I could forget. But I can't.

T: Do you understand scapegoating, in families, have you heard that term?

A: Not in relation to families.

T: There are so many issues in bereavement, and with you, your father and siblings all processing things separately, there must have been such an uneven mix of feelings, all unspoken, so the focus is unclear and when everyday life throws up problems they can seem insurmountable because of the unstable environment. So then ordinary things become inexplicably difficult and that can be uncomfortable or even embarrassing, so a person might look for a reason outside of themselves for their mistakes or upset.

A: They need a target.

T: It's inevitable, particularly when the pattern of scapegoating is established by the authority figure. Scapegoating is common for victims of abuse.

A: Seems unfair.

T: It is.

A: I understand all that, I get it, but despite all this insight, I can't seem to get happy, to be better.

T: Would it be any other way, Alan? Given all that's happened to you, would it be any other way?

The Rise and Fall
of Roland White

Richardson was a sitcom about a frustrated fantasist and daydreamer, out of step with his co-workers in the call centre he managed. The name came from my school woodwork teacher who sat in his office smoking all day. He was the only member of staff who'd pick you up from the bus stop, if he was passing in his Talbot Horizon. He never spoke, his ashtray was overflowing and his gear lever squeaked with every shift.

Objective Productions had paid me development money in 2008 but the reason given for the rejection of my script, even after a good rehearsed reading, was the BBC's pointless reboot of *The Fall and Rise of Reginald Perrin*, which was being made by . . . Objective.

The upside for me was being around the BBC Comedy department when they were casting a much better sitcom: *Whites*. The writers, Matt King and Oli Lansley, had written a brilliant first episode set in a kitchen and restaurant and I agreed to play chef Roland White.

After I was cast, unflattering descriptions of Roland began to appear in the scripts. His face looked like it had 'been inflated' and he had 'a woman's hair'.

It turned out that the writers had hoped to play the main characters themselves and I'd been imposed on them. Much later, when we'd all become good friends, Matt hinted as much when he said: 'We didn't want you to do it.'

But I did well in a wonderful role and the rest of the cast – Darren Boyd, Isy Suttie, Katherine Parkinson, Steven Wight, Maggie Steed and Amit Shah – were flawless. The camaraderie, mutual respect and new friendships remain a highlight of my life. And we knew the show was funny. I had to do one scene with Steve that was difficult to get through because the look on Darren's face made us laugh so much.

We filmed in a studio near Bridgend with a friendly, almost entirely Welsh crew. When they started speaking their native language we laughed because it meant someone had made a cock-up. At lunchtime we ate in an inflatable dining room, set up in a gravel car park, that Matt compared to the facilities provided for the British Army in Helmand Province.

I was also happy because on three weekends when I was away and couldn't get back home Katie flew down from Northumberland (where she was staying with her mum) and arrived in Cardiff with eight-month-old Susie in her hand luggage.

The six episodes went out on BBC Two, with the fourth watched by 1.5 million viewers, the fifth by 1.6 million and the last by 1.7 million.

We were all keen to make *Whites* for years. Matt and Oli were commissioned to write scripts for a second series.

And then we were canned.

No reason was given. It upset me more than anything else in my career, and I say that as someone who was fired from his own sitcom, spent four hours a day having a prosthetic face put on for *The Midnight Gang* and had to make profiteroles with Simon Rimmer on *Sunday Brunch*.

David Renwick himself had said you can't properly judge a show until series three. It was suggested to me by the BBC that Matt and Oli might create something else for me, which sounded like actual madness – it had taken four years to develop *Whites* and Matt was a former chef; every kitchen worker I heard from said how accurate and hilarious the show was. Matt and Oli have never written together again.

The final Kafkaesque word came when the heads of Comedy and BBC Two told Michael Foster that they'd meet with me but not to discuss *Whites*, only to reiterate their 'faith in my talent'. I declined.

I'll Never Be Funny Again

A weekly podcast about Arsenal came at the invitation of Mike Leigh, who had a stable of football shows that recorded in his office at Playback Media. Andy Linden was involved with *The Spurs Show* and my old friend from *One for the Road*, Iain Coyle, was making one about Liverpool FC.

I called Keith Dover, who seemed baffled by the concept. Neither of us had heard the word 'podcast' before. So, Ian Stone and Tayo Popoola were my first two contributors, on what became *It's Up for Grabs Now* in November 2009.

We effectively recorded a pub conversation among friends. I'd write down five or six things that had made me laugh that week – in my obsessive watching of football and monitoring of Arsenal Football Club – in the same way as I noted ideas for stand-up, and then go through them on the show. There was no script. I loved radio but there was always some restriction – of time, usually, but also editorial control. Now the only rules were self-imposed. I wanted no serious opinions, since none of us had been anywhere near professional football other than paying to watch it, and no swearing, which wasn't easy when emotions ran high.

As soon as we sat down to record, our rapport from twenty years of going to games together, travelling up and down the country and abroad, made the task easy. And with a microphone in front of me, I pushed the show along like a stand-up doing a gig, a feeling I hadn't had for some time.

We made ourselves laugh, expressing our frustration at Arsenal who were, helpfully, in the middle of a barren period without success for a decade, making us much funnier.

After about a year, a producer friend, Chris Blacklay (who'd helped me up when I'd had my cheekbone broken), said we could record our podcast in his front room, any time it suited us.

After sending Mike Leigh a thank-you note and a case of wine, we set up independently as *The Tuesday Club*, going on to make dozens of shows over more than a decade, with tens of millions of downloads.

Keith, Tayo and Ian were joined by occasional contributors Damian Harris and Oliver Scott and we all enjoyed it so much it didn't matter that we were unable to monetise our new maverick brand. I decided never to charge for the podcast, via Patreon or any of the new emerging platforms. It was better that way, as I'd frequently refer to the listeners as freeloading scum and be incredibly rude about their emails. There was no marketing, just word of mouth among fans.

Keith became a cult hero. He'd been a stand-up for over twenty years but was in a rut with Jongleurs gigs around the country each weekend. Our audience loved his surreal references to his role at the club in the thirties and conspiracy theories about football's deep state holding Arsenal back.

Before long there was interest from producer Simon Crosse and soon we were on Radio 5 Live making shows called *Armchair World Cup* in 2010 and *Armchair Euros* two years later, following England through tournaments. We'd have real footballers on as guests but tried to maintain our approach, which led Arsenal defender and Ivorian international Emmanuel Eboué to say, 'Is this really the BBC?' during his interview.

My favourite exchange came with the arboreal ex-England centre half Terry Butcher.

'What was the worst injury you ever had?' I said.

'Broken neck,' he said.

'Did you come off?' I said.

'No,' he said.

*

But, despite all the fun I was having with podcasting and being back on radio, I still hadn't picked up a microphone in a comedy club. Other than a few gigs at the Old Red Lion in Islington in early 2002, I hadn't done any stand-up for ten years.

That changed in 2011, when it was arranged for *QI* to tour Australia as a live show.

Months before we set off, Marnie Foulis contacted me from Melbourne offering to promote me on a stand-up tour.

'I don't have an act,' I said.

'Doesn't matter,' she said. 'Do old stuff. You've never toured Australia and that's ridiculous, Davies, ridiculous, you've done what over here?'

'Adelaide Fringe and the Melbourne Comedy Festival,' I said.

'Yeah once, about a hundred years ago. You are a great stand-up, Alan Davies, and you should be on that stage, making people laugh; audiences want to see you. You were the funniest thing going and you just stopped. Come on, get your act together, I'll introduce you to Bec Sutherland, she is the *best* promoter you'll ever meet. You're over here anyway for *QI*, stay on and do some shows.'

I remembered an exchange I'd had with Jonathan Ross on his BBC One chat show a year or two after I'd stopped performing live.

'I think,' he said, 'that you're afraid to go back to stand-up.'

'Do you?' I said.

'Yes,' he said.

'I do *QI*, that has a live audience'

'It's not the same.'

And he told me to get back up there and do it again.

Now Marnie had put tears in my eyes with her pep talk.

And I said yes.

Katie had begun writing, and a couple of months after Susie was born won the Waterstones Children's Book of the Year for *The Great Hamster Massacre*.

She had a four-book deal and then published *The Great Rabbit Rescue*, which was equally funny but also included a moving divorce plotline that I can't deny caught my attention.

Nonetheless we were happy at Furlong Road, even if Katie was finding writing the third book, *The Great Cat Conspiracy*, something of a challenge with two adorable little children to spend her time with.

From our new front door, it was no distance at all to the Pleasance Theatre, where a studio space is available to comedians for work in progress gigs.

With Australia in mind, I'd been making notes in my phone, just as I had when I was starting out in the eighties, except back then I'd often scribble them on beer mats.

Write it down or forget it.

I took pages of notes to the Pleasance and read them to an audience. Later that evening I was in our kitchen, head in hands, telling Katie: 'I'll never be funny again.'

Katie had never seen me do stand-up and was convinced I was right, based on the laugh count around the house.

But I did ten more of those gigs, re-ordering the notes, dropping bits, linking other things together, and the strange internal alchemy that is creating new material was reawakened, after a dormant decade.

There was a weekly show in town run by Phil Nichol and Tiff Stevenson called *Old Rope*, where a noose hung next to the microphone. If the comedian held the rope they were doing old material; if they let go they were trying something new. I booked myself a slot.

As I waited to go on, the Canadian comic Mike Wilmot, a veteran of thousands of gigs, sidled up to me. He must have noticed some trepidation in my demeanour.

'Hey,' he said, 'enjoy yourself up there.'

It was the single best piece of advice I've heard since Bill Bailey told a young comedian to 'keep saying lots of funny things'.

And I did not hold the rope. I really had something.

Marnie and Bec asked for a title for my show and I took a line I'd heard used by an Eastern European nanny to a crying toddler.

'Life is pain,' she'd said, before adding, 'everyone you love in life will betray you', which possibly made the parents' job harder when the child was returned.

In Australia, Marnie organised some club gigs in Melbourne to warm me up. I was almost as nervous as I'd been starting out. The last of them was at a good-sized venue that held around two hundred and fifty. It was packed, with people standing at the back and sitting on the floor at the front.

The previous year, as a judge on an ITV comedian's talent show called *Show Me the Funny*, I'd exhorted the comics to 'get on the front foot' and show a confidence they didn't necessarily feel. I followed my own advice; this wasn't to be a whimsical hour but a cathartic release for a man whose sex life had been curtailed by children who wee in his face when he's changing their nappies. I stormed it, a chicken korma that Jo would have been proud of.

Marnie and Bec put me in for single gigs in five cities but I did extra shows everywhere, six in Melbourne, four in Perth. It was a revelation to me. The audiences were fantastically responsive and loud; that tour of Australia remains the most enjoyable I've ever done.

Katie and our two tiny children came with me to Australia, as did her mum and dad, who shared the childcare for six weeks in a hot Melbourne summer without complaint, living together in a rented house while I criss-crossed the country doing thirty-three shows for *QI Live* and *Life Is Pain*.

It was only later that Katie told me how hard it had been. She'd had to push her book deadline back to after our return and remembers breastfeeding Bobby in the dead of night while typing with one hand. Susie was ill with a bad chest infection and was used to falling asleep in my arms at night, but most evenings I wasn't there.

But for me, ten years had passed without the confidence boost each night of hearing laughter, sparking the creativity that comes alive only onstage. I soon parted company with my agent Michael Foster and approached Eddie Izzard's promoter about touring the UK in 2012, after which I was described as:

'Wildly funny' – *Time Out*

Marnie and Bec took me to New Zealand in early 2013 for my first tour there in fifteen years, fitting in a couple of memorable shows at the Sydney Opera House on the way.

The Kiwi audiences were as gratifying to play to as their Aussie counterparts. I absolutely will not be drawn on which was the better crowd, as setting up any point of difference between those two great countries is an act of madness unless you want to get some laughs in Australia by being rude about Kiwis and vice versa.

When I returned to the UK, *Life Is Pain* was recorded live at Hammersmith Apollo for release as a DVD.

In December 2013, with the DVD out for Christmas, I went on the panel show *Eight Out of Ten Cats*, hosted by Jimmy Carr with Sean Lock and Jon Richardson as team captains.

Since it was Christmas, Jimmy had a present for each of the guests. Mine was a life-size gelatin head, like a huge jelly baby, bright red and sticky with two big ears sticking up. Jimmy encouraged me to try it.

'Just take a bite,' he said.

I lifted it up and bit the end off the nose, which tasted horrible, so I heaved the whole head off the front of the desk. It landed on the studio floor with a thud. Only then did I realize it was a setup: I was meant to bite it on the ear, to play along with a vague reconstruction of my never-to-be-forgotten shame outside the Groucho Club six years before.

I haven't been invited back to that show and was left with the understanding that someone there harboured a low opinion of me.

On top of that, it was broadcast on 29th December – so outside the PGP (primary gifting period) and useless as a sales plug for my DVD. I'd been commercially thwarted and publicly shamed but smiled through it.

Iain Coyle was by now working for the Dave channel and had received a proposal for a round-table chat show. We'd reconnected through podcasting and he asked me to host what became *Alan Davies: As Yet Untitled*.

Each guest was asked to bring along a couple of anecdotes they were happy to tell, and that I never heard in advance, around which conversation flowed off the cuff. I'd never make a guest uncomfortable by revisiting their worst mistakes, although they sometimes brought those up themselves, and the recordings were often hilarious.

We made seven series, with appearances from old friends like Jo Brand, Bill Bailey, Isy Suttie, Colin Lane from Melbourne, Wes Borg from Three Dead Trolls in a Baggie and Stephen Fry, from Norfolk.

As Yet Untitled was later released online. I was also hired by ITV to podcast during the World Cup in Brazil, though we recorded in London and Leeds, not Rio, alongside two Bradford City fans, Tom Fletcher and Dom Newton, who I'd met through their show, *Bantams Banter*.

In our house, 2014 became known as the Dry Year: from 1st January, after a small New Year's Eve party at home, I abstained from alcohol for twelve months. I also played the Edinburgh Fringe for the third year in a row and at one point the UK podcast charts showed that the top three shows were:

1 *Alan Davies' Brazilian Banter*
2 *Alan Davies: As Yet Untitled*
3 *The Tuesday Club*

It's true to say there were nowhere near as many podcasts around as there are now, but it was still an achievement I took pride in.

Also in 2014, Jo Brand asked me to be in her excellent social-worker sitcom *Damned* on Channel 4, where I found Kevin Eldon and Isy Suttie among the cast. For two series, that became another happy family alongside *The Tuesday Club*.

I went back to Australia in 2014 with my next show, *Little Victories*, which also toured in the UK. I was supposed to go to New Zealand late in 2015 but everything changed when Katie fell pregnant.

Marnie and Bec pulled the whole tour forward and over two weeks we did thirteen gigs in ten different cities, culminating in a recording at the Wellington Opera House in August.

*

So, from the ashes of more sitcom frustration in *Whites* had come the motivation to do something funny as myself.

As a screen actor, pretending (as I had done) to be a policeman in *Marple*, a quiz host in *Lewis*, or another chef in *Hotel Babylon*, the real me was confined to sitting on foldout chairs, eating on dining buses and being driven home in the back of a car. You can become a largely passive animal, waiting for, receiving and following instructions, trying to recall someone else's lines and counting the hours until the day ends, always hoping for some good company in the cast – which is often the best part, hanging around with the other actors.

But the self-esteem you can build in stand-up, the sense of your own creativity, the knowledge that without you there is no show, gives you a different sense of achievement. Creating something new can unblock many thoughts in your mind and that in itself is valuable.

Writing, playing music, drawing, sculpting, making something – any of these seem to me to be essential activities, all of which are lost to so many people.

If you try to be creative you will likely surprise yourself, which is why I prefer to see my children (if they're not playing outside, or halfway up a tree) with a pen and a blank piece of paper, or picking up an instrument, rather than staring passively at their phone screens.

And it's why, while I enjoy acting, I really love stand-up: because it's good for me. For ten years, whenever I was asked to state my profession, perhaps when filling in a form, I'd say something like 'writer/performer'. Now I would happily put:

STAND-UP (race and gender not relevant)

Down Under

In early 2012, a few months after returning from the Australian *QI* tour, Stephen Fry attempted suicide.

During an interview for Richard Herring's podcast the following year, Stephen said that after swallowing many pills and a great deal of vodka he'd suffered such bodily convulsions he broke four ribs. He was found and saved.

There were moments in Australia when Stephen had seemed anxious, or when some darker cousin of that emotion was perhaps visiting him. I never saw him between shows, though, apart from at one enjoyable lunch in Fremantle with Ben Elton and his wife, Sophie Gare, her sister Anna and former NBA star Luc Longley. I went along with John Lloyd, *QI* producer Piers Fletcher and Stephen, who I noticed was speaking a lot while somehow out of sync with the busy conversation around us.

Something wasn't right but I'd just drunk more of Ben's wine and made no real effort to see how Stephen was feeling.

A few years before, Stephen had snapped at me during the final recording of a *QI* series and I'd been quiet for the rest of the show. I tried his patience often in the thirteen years we worked together but this was one of only a couple of occasions when he showed real irritation.

I was in my dressing room afterwards with my old friend Sue MacLaine when there was a knock at the door. It was Stephen.

'Are you all right?' he said. 'Was that a bit much?'

'It was a bit,' I said. 'I'm not really all right, no; I was upset.'

'Oh dear, I'm *so* sorry,' he said. 'And on the last show as well.'

'Don't give it another thought,' I said. 'The fact you've come to see me means a lot, thank you. It's been a pleasure to sit next to you again – you make it look easy, and I know it isn't always.'

'Thank you,' he said. 'You've been terrific, the audience love you.'

'They love you, Stephen,' I said. 'Everyone does.'

He smiled as if I was talking absolute tosh and wandered off.

'That was very gallantly done by two nice men,' said Sue.

'Everyone does love him, but he doesn't believe it,' I said.

'Lots of us find it hard to believe we're loved,' she said.

The Metaphor

So, I'm lying in Times Square on a bed of nails, with tourists milling around. People don't immediately come in for a closer look, just another New York scene, perhaps. It's getting dark and I've been on the bed for a few minutes. Passersby are stopping now to see if they recognise the person on the floor.

'Who is it?'

'Is he on the actual ground?'

'He can't be – that's dirty, man.'

'Git up, sucker.'

Other remarks can be heard in Spanish and Chinese (simplified).

'¿En qué está mintiendo?'

'他为什么不动?'

I'm experiencing pain in my back. I've been told the nails won't hurt but there's an uncomfortable patch just below my shoulder blades.

'Let's go, he ain't gonna do nothing.'

'Wait a second, he's on nails.'

'What?'

I want to lift my weight off the painful spot but that would mean pressing down on the nails with other parts of my body.

'Motherfucker is a fakir!'

'A motherfucking fakir!'

'A motherfakir!'

A familiar face appears above me. It's James Baylan, who used to be the costume designer on *Jonathan Creek*. Why's he turned up? He looks pleased to see me. We enjoyed working together. But he's concerned he might be bothering me.

'All right, Al?' he says. 'It's me, James.'

'Yeah, I know, good to see you. What are you doing here?'

'I'm just on holiday.'

'Right, of course.'

'You?'

'I'm lying on a bed of nails.'

And then he leaves, presumably not wanting to interrupt; he always did look restless, like he had somewhere to go.

James used to sell off all the costumes after a shoot, like a barrow boy. One year he found a home for a full-sized frog costume. He knocked around with Darren and Rob, the prop boys. I hadn't seen him for ten years, since we finished the episodes with Julia in 2003. They all loved her.

Filming drifted along like a canal boat. Then someone'd be on a walkie-talkie, hurrying you from the other side of a toilet door. On set Julia knew her lines and hit her marks but the precision of everything was too much for her, like she was a trained parrot.

Why am I thinking about Julia? Because we went to New York together when I was making a documentary about John Lennon. She kept me company.

I had to lie on an ambulance gurney once, on Jonathan Creek. *A paramedic threw two straps over me and pulled them tight. I smiled, thinking he'd slacken them off since I wasn't going to be moved. But he left me alone, with no one in sight, trapped there in my duffel coat.*

When I get to Vegas, I'd better have this back pain looked at.

'Alan, are you OK?'

It's Louise Hooper, the producer/director.

'My back hurts.'

There is a bit of laughter.

'No, it does, not from the nails, I don't think.'

'You can get up now; we have everything we need.'

'OK, give me a minute.'

I am filming something, not dreaming.

Sean Lock once cornered me, at a party, about QI.

'I hope they pay you a fuck of a lot of money, the way they treat you on that show,'
he said.

'It's OK,' I said.

'OK? I hope you get paid a fuck of a lot of money, the way they treat you,' he said
again. 'A fuck of a lot.'

I'm up off the bed of nails now, going back to our van. There were five of us
plus the driver, who left the engine running so he could have the heater on.
It was December 2013, and we were making *The Magic of Houdini with Alan
Davies*. One evening we were shooting on Brooklyn Bridge. We set up on
the pedestrian path with the cycle lane next to it. There's a thick white line
between the two and at one point I strayed across it. A cyclist announced his
presence assertively: 'Get out of the fucking way, you fucking asshole! Move
your fucking ass!'

He didn't touch his brakes and then, over his shoulder: 'You can't see the
fucking line? You're fucking blind?'

There is a building close to the bridge with a red digital clock on the roof
that alternates between time and temperature. It was showing –5 degrees. I
did a piece to camera and fled back to the van before Louise had a chance to
ask me to do it again.

It was a friendly crew with two Americans (including the sound man,
Sean, who was very alert when we held a séance to contact Houdini) and
two Brits, another little temporary family. The driver was an older African-
American man who wore a thick hat pulled down, a coat, a shacket and
gloves. I asked him what he'd done before this job and soon he was talking
about his time serving in Vietnam. I said I'd been there and we talked about
Hue and then he told me that the locals used to sell the young American
soldiers weed to smoke, and that they would put it into the barrels of their
guns and turn the weapon into a pipe.

'If you looked along the line at night, when we were dug in, you could see
the orange glows from all the different rifles right the way down, like fireflies.'

*

317

In Las Vegas we were picked up in another van, only with blacked-out windows and a long banquette around the interior so we sat facing each other. In the middle was a pole. I reached down into the gap behind me and found a seatbelt. I was the only passenger who wore one, probably ever.

The MGM Grand Hotel can be seen from the airport. On its side, six storeys high, was the face of the magician and illusionist David Copperfield, who we were to interview about his collection of Houdini's props.

Later we had front-row seats for Copperfield's show (he did three a day). It was both impressive and ridiculous. He made a car appear, which was amazing, but it evidently wasn't real, just some hastily assembled lightweight panelling, a smoke machine for an exhaust pipe and an engine sound effect. Nonetheless, we enjoyed the elaborate setups and tricks, moving large numbers of audience members from one place to another so quickly they looked as amazed as the rest of us. The theatre must have been purpose built with tunnels, as if designed by the Viet Cong.

Before recording the interview, I went to the Sunrise Hospital and Medical Center and two nurses looked at my back.

'Ooh, has this thing been there long?' said one.

'I don't know, I haven't really noticed it,' I said.

'Oh god, does it hurt?' said the second nurse.

'Only when I lie on a bed of nails.'

'Oh yeah,' she said, 'that'll do it.'

'I was told the nails wouldn't hurt,' I said.

'Who said that to you?'

'My boss,' I said.

'Figures.'

'You must really trust your superior?'

'I suppose I do,' I said, thinking of Louise, who had also strung me up by the ankles in a disorienting recreation of one Houdini trick, as well as sitting me in a bath before filling it with ice.

'It hurts in that one spot,' I said. 'We flew in yesterday and I had to keep moving around so I wasn't leaning on it.'

'You've been carrying this thing for a while.'

'Yes, I suppose I have.'

'No, you definitely have,' said the second nurse. 'These things start out small, but if you don't address the problems you carry, they will grow, and really affect your whole life.'

We were all silent for a moment as that sunk in.

'Are you going back to England soon?'

'In a couple of days,' I said.

'Well, this thing needs to be drained, but you could wait till you get home and do it there. Do you have insurance?'

'I'll do it when I get home,' I said.

'OK, well, it was great meeting with you. We'll write you a script for some painkillers, just pick them up from Walmart, that's the cheapest way.'

We were asked to push the interview back a day but I had to go home for Susie's fourth birthday. Having an actual family can simplify some decisions. Copperfield was persuaded to meet early the next morning. He seemed to think I didn't know what I was doing, moving me by the elbow at one point, but he was interesting about Houdini and we thanked him and went to the airport.

After a couple of days at home, the lump ruptured. Katie retched and was sick in her mouth helping with the discharge and says she is still haunted by it.

A few years later, during lockdown, the lump returned and became tender. A dermatologist said it was a sebaceous cyst that had to be removed under a local anaesthetic at a cost of (she appeared to be reaching for the highest number she could think of without laughing, before doubling it) 'a thousand pounds'.

It's not like removing a snooker ball; there are roots clinging to the host like knotweed. I had six injections of local anaesthetic as the dermatologist hacked it out piece by piece with a nurse swabbing away while trying not to gag. A sizeable scar remains.

It's always a good idea to do some work on yourself sooner rather than later, because bad things can grow, out of sight, and then something really nasty might reveal itself.

Growing Maturity

One crisp winter's morning in December 2014, I rang Katie to tell her I was hiding from the police in the Swiss Cottage Leisure Centre soft-play area.

I was familiar with the layout of the place, having visited many times since we'd moved house to nearby Hampstead, where Susie, five and Bobby, three, were going to primary school and nursery.

While we were renovating the new house in 2013, I'd been back on duty as Jonathan Creek for the last of three specials with Sheridan Smith as my sidekick and the first with Sarah Alexander as my screen wife.

Sheridan's much younger than me and her arrival had given the show an injection of energy, but it was only when I saw her at the Savoy Theatre in *Legally Blonde* that I realised quite how much va-va-voom she'd been keeping under the bonnet as she effortlessly purred along in second gear with us. She was amazing.

David Renwick, having watched me marry and start a family, had decided that Creek too should be married, to reflect the reality of maturing and settling down. Jonathan now worked in advertising and had an unexpectedly attractive wife called Polly (it was noted by some that Jonathan was punching above his weight).

I'm not sure I was maturing, though; if anything, the long days of parenting, a busy work schedule and lack of sleep brought fatigue and with that came the risk of the return of the angry boy.

Sure enough, he'd surfaced at the leisure centre, of all places, when taking my two little ones to their swimming lessons. A man tried to hurry us down a flight of stairs. At the bottom, I'd grabbed him by the collar, he'd yelled assault and the police were called.

Susie had been knocked over and both children were crying. I went to console them and after a couple of minutes their teachers took them to their lessons.

On my way out through the foyer, I saw two police cars, lights flashing, parked at an angle with their noses nearly touching. Uniformed officers in stab vests were taking the steps up from the street two at a time as I ducked into the busy soft-play area. I knew how to behave like a parent in there, so hoped to be inconspicuous, though I didn't typically have my hood up, and I usually had at least one kid with me.

The officers found the man unharmed, looked at CCTV, spoke to witnesses and left, blue lights off. Dissatisfied by this conclusion, the man contacted a tabloid and said I'd attacked him. Fortunately, we were going on holiday to Barbados the next day.

While we there, happily, our third child was, you know, made.

A baby was on the way and I knew I had to control myself better, or the angry boy might damage all of our lives.

Return of the Monarchist

The International Artistes agency were connected to the Variety Club and an invitation to appear at the Royal Command Performance had come soon after I'd agreed to be represented by Bob Voice in 1992.

Bob had seen it as an accolade and a chance to advance your career before millions of viewers, but I hadn't want to do the Royal Variety; it seemed uncool, embarrassing even, and I thought it would be hypocritical for me to appear given my belief that all the inherited titles and associated land that still exist in this country, from the House of Lords down, should be reclaimed. As a student I'd admired the theatre company *7:84*, whose name came from the statistic that 7 per cent of the population own 84 per cent of the land.

By 2016 I was represented by the recently formed United Agents; and, when I was invited to the Royal Variety for the first time in over twenty years, I realised how laughable it was that I should turn down anything for being uncool, let alone a show whose alumni include Laurel and Hardy and the Beatles.

So, this time, I said yes, indulging my weakness for being a spear carrier in a big celeb turnout, standing in line next to Gary Barlow. And there was every chance I might not be invited to appear again, so I forgot about the stench of inherited wealth and another tiny voice of opposition was snuffed out like a candle on a child's birthday cake. I'd long since traded in my gun for a badge.

I went to the Comedy Store for a warmup at a charity gig, wanting to banish the memory of walking off that stage in 1999. A short set can be like a hundred-yard dash and I tore into it. An old friend who was there later sent me a much appreciated text saying I'd been 'almost unbearably funny'. No one could have found a gap to shout, 'It's a perm!' even if they'd wanted to.

The Royal Variety would be at the Hammersmith Apollo. I decided to enjoy the night, and I did, largely because of my fellow occupants in dressing-room number . . . 'Just keep going up the stairs, all the way, past the broom cupboard, up another flight, and another, go behind the water tank, find the last door, and that's you, with the Chuckle Brothers and Bernie Clifton.'

I'd gone so far up I felt I was in showbiz heaven. My veteran roommates were affable and unpretentious with a willingness to chat as if we were cellies on a two-stretch. Somewhere in the building were Sting, Robbie Williams and Lady Gaga, but I was happy to belong where they put me.

We watched the show together on a tiny TV in the corner, placed on a bench under which lay Bernie's famous ostrich suit. On the back of the door were the Chuckle Brothers' two brown coats.

Cirque du Soleil was introduced and a young dancer appeared, waving veils of chiffon. She crossed this way and that as we waited for the rest of them to drop from the lighting grid or swing across like Tarzan. A minute or two went by and it became apparent that this was it.

'Imagine the driver sent to pick them up from the airport?' I said. 'He's got a coach for twenty with room for their gear, and a sign saying "Cirque du Soleil".'

'And one young woman comes out,' said Bernie.

They started laughing.

'Yes, young lady?' said a Chuckle brother.

'I'm Cirque du Soleil,' said the other Chuckle.

'Where're the rest of 'em?' said Bernie.

'I am zee only one,' said a Chuckle.

'Do you want help with your luggage? No, I 'ave only zis,' I said.

'And she's holding up a tiny bag!' said Bernie.

'With a chiffon scarf in,' said a Chuckle brother.

'But I've brought the big bus!' I said, and we laughed in a way that reminded me of being with Sean Lock, Ian Cognito and Steve Murray at Styal Mill in 1989.

It's possible that the Apollo, being a converted cinema, couldn't accommodate the sort of stage gear Cirque du Soleil often use, I've no idea. In any case, it was the highlight of our evening.

'She's a good dancer though, to be fair.'

'Oh yes, she's smashing.'

'Very good, yes. They'll take her back to the airport on a taxi bike.'

Later there was a knock on our door and we opened it to a young woman wearing a headset.

'Are you OK in here?' she said.

'Oh yes, love, we're smashing.'

'Can I get you anything at all?'

'No, no, no, we're just fine.'

'Actually, can I have a black coffee?' I said.

The other three looked at me.

'Yes, of course,' she said. 'I'll get that for you now. Anything else for anyone?'

'Would I be able to have a tea?' said Barry Chuckle.

'Yes, of course you can? Milk and sugar?'

'Ooh, yes please.'

'How many sugars?

'Six.'

'Six?'

'Are they sachets?' said Barry.

'Yes.'

'Yeah, six.'

And when they arrived he put the lot in his tea as we continued to watch the show.

Rob Beckett and Joe Lycett were the comedians on ahead of me. They were both in their twenties and they held their nerve impressively but it's not easy up there, with an audience of tuxedos and evening gowns lit up for television and Charles and Camilla in the front row of the circle in a makeshift 'Royal Box'.

In 2012, soon after I'd returned to stand-up, I'd been invited to the Albert Hall as part of a bill for the Teenage Cancer Trust.

I was the only comedian who'd asked for a dressing room, because I was so nervous I needed my own loo. It was a once-in-a-lifetime chance to play the Albert Hall. I did three number twos.

I was following Jimmy Carr. Five thousand people erupted in laughter at the end of each of his lines. The Canadian comic Stewart Francis came up behind me and said, 'I'd hate to be following this guy,' making us both laugh.

I went out, hands shaking, and took a minute to get going but I went down well and now wanted to repeat that at the Royal Variety.

Down in the wings, waiting for David Walliams to introduce me, Mike Wilmot came to mind: 'Hey, enjoy yourself up there.'

I barrelled on, acting as if it was my gig, asking if anybody there had been born, like me, in the sixties? There was a cheer.

'There they are, my people!' I said, and did an impression of them: 'This seat is so uncomfortable . . . My knee's killing me; how long is it going on for? I can't remember where we parked . . .'

Perhaps some people thought I was doing this in sympathy with Prince Charles, but in any case, when I started my material, everything worked.

I trotted back up to the attic to be greeted by my new comrades, who were beaming.

'Well done, son.'

Bernie put on his Oswald the Ostrich outfit and off they all went to take part in a sketch at the end of the show.

Afterwards I met Prince Charles in the lineup, nearly twenty years on from our last encounter.

'You've still got plenty of ideas, then,' he said.

James Macabre

On Monday 19th November 2018, I met Jo Brand at Euston and we travelled to Manchester for Jim Miller's funeral.

At Rochdale Crematorium we met Jim's friends Pete and Fiona, with a handful other mourners from his extended family as well as a couple of female comics we knew. Simon Munnery was supposedly coming too but we heard he'd gone to Rotherham by mistake, which lightened the mood for a moment.

After the service, we went back to Pete and Fiona's for a wake that was a low-key affair, inevitably, since only a few people knew what had happened to Jim and the story was percolating through the gathering.

'I just assumed he'd drunk too much,' I said. 'So maybe it was liver disease.'

'No,' said Pete. 'He'd been drinking much less lately, not at all he said, and he'd been OK last time we saw him.'

Speaking quietly, his head down in sadness, Pete told us that when Jim was found, in the small flat where he lived alone, he'd been dead for three weeks. He'd sealed up the door and window of his bathroom with damp towels and lit disposable barbecues, the smoke from which rendered him unconscious and then slowly poisoned him to death with carbon monoxide.

Jo and I thanked Pete for telling us what had happened, stayed a little longer and then said our goodbyes to him and Fiona, two kind people who'd found themselves in a most terrible situation.

I called our mutual friends Jez Feeney, Bill Bailey, Mark Lamarr and

Keith Dover, so they'd know what had happened to Jim. Mark said: 'That's hard to hear.'

Something prompted me to look at Jim's Facebook page. On 14th September he'd posted a link to YouTube with the note:

> Joy Division live "In a Lonely Place" a few days
> before Ian Curtis died.
> As dark, perhaps, as pop music's ever got.
> Work of genius.

On the same day, he also posted:

> Got bad asthma and Steam rooms really
> help. Have heard you can make your own in
> your bathroom for not too much outlay.
> Anyone know??

Recently a group of us, including Jo, Bill, Keith and Andy Linden, who went on all those New Year breaks in the nineties with Jim, met for a reunion lunch. After one or two in the company had struggled to contribute to a conversation about hearing aids, due to deafness, we looked at some old pictures. There was Jim, paisley scarf round his neck.

Still photos couldn't capture his knee bouncing anxiously up and down whenever he sat at a table, or the cigarette going back and forth to his lips, but his expression was unmistakeable

'Look at him,' said Keith, 'he's bored, just looking around to see who he can wind up.'

And we laughed, as we so often did in Jim's company.

Writing to Learn

Our third child, Francis, was born on 4th September 2015. He was a most welcome addition, not least because Katie had miscarried the year before, an extremely distressing experience that began with the absence of a heartbeat at the first routine scan. We'd just begun to talk about names.

So, we felt lucky to have three healthy children. In no time it became unthinkable not to be a family of five.

Soon, though, I found things difficult, going back to square one with nappies and baby seats and the cot reassembled. Katie, perhaps necessarily, as part of a mother's innate coping mechanism, saw only upsides to our new circumstances.

At the end of 2016, I made a New Year's resolution not to argue with Katie any more, which was in itself a sign that I was struggling.

I wasn't conscious of it at the time, but with hindsight I understand that my decision to enrol on a part-time creative-writing master's at Goldsmiths College, when Fran had just turned one, was a clue that I knew I had to wrestle the truth out of myself.

I'd talked about my father in my stand-up but still, despite having turned fifty and writing comedy material for more than half my life, I hadn't approached the subject of my abuse. Towards the end of my first year at Goldsmiths, in May 2017, I wrote a non-fiction piece for assessment, called 'Hands', in which I described my father's molestation of me. This was to be submitted anonymously, with only a student number identifying the author. If it were poorly received, no one would know it was mine. My secret would be safe.

Two anonymous assessments came back and the response was encouraging. I'd finally been able to tell my story; this was the first step.

Days later, my sister rang to say that our stepmother had revealed our dad's addiction to teen-boy gay porn and my understanding of his abuse of me shifted forever.

Dad was a predatory child molester and I was the nearest boy.

By now I'd agreed to try couples counselling. I was drinking too often and Katie and I were arguing. Three small children needed both parents and, irrespective of my obvious love for them, things had to improve.

One night, after a drunken row, Katie called the police. It's hard for me to recall the sequence of events. I was in alcohol blackout after drinking too much in the cinema, believe it or not. At one point I locked Katie out of the house. I gave our babysitter a lift to the tube station, endangering both of us and everyone else on the road.

I'd become enraged when Katie told me that one of my friends had said I was probably mentally ill. I was by now not just the angry boy but a drunken adult incarnation of him, demanding to know the identity of this so-called friend.

Did I really need evidence? Was it not apparent that my mental health was fractured? Why was I so incensed at the suggestion? Katie obviously saw there was a problem and the fact that someone I'd known for twenty-five years had said something to her was significant.

When two police officers were in our house I panicked, and locked myself in the loo, just as I used to do as a child.

They were outside the toilet door while I tried to recall whether I'd done something unthinkable. Had I hurt Katie? Was I going to lose her, and everything else, marriage, family, home, career, the lot? All of it was on the verge of shattering irreparably, like my childhood family had decades before.

What had I done? I couldn't remember. What had I *done*? Minutes were missing, spaces in memory appearing instantly as if walking along a street and looking behind to see only blackness, no pavement, houses, nothing, like an approaching eclipse washing over everything. Memories seemed to dissolve. Where had we been to, what had been said?

Eventually, after the officers had asked whether I was all right several times, they told me they couldn't leave without ensuring I was unharmed and they began to twist the lock while I held it tight. I opened the door.

'You can go now,' I said.

They could see I was fine. I didn't know where Katie was but they said she was unhurt. I was shaking as I escorted them out of my house.

'Go now, please,' I said putting my fingers into the back of the female constable on the way up the stairs.

'Don't push me, please,' she said.

Then the male constable told me that they didn't include the names of well-known people when reporting 'this sort of situation' and I needn't worry about this 'getting out'.

'Thanks,' I said.

Katie and I began therapy sessions together. I didn't recognise several of her descriptions of me, which tells you what a cavalcade of self-deception she'd endured over the years. She was 'walking on eggshells' around an angry man, not a boy, and things had to change or we'd split up.

Our therapist, who was steadfast in her expressionless self-control, let slip a flicker of shock on hearing that my father had molested me. We began to work through how we could better understand what had happened in the past, which was not behind us but in the room, inhaled and exhaled daily.

We also talked about reporting my father to the police for historical sexual abuse, which I did after a few months, though there was little hope for prosecution, since my stepmother had waited until he was rendered helpless with Alzheimer's before telling us what she knew about both his homosexuality and, more importantly, his obsession with boys.

Katie and I moved on to a second therapist, and we had sessions for three years in all. I spent a year back in individual therapy too, with someone new who was local to me.

When things were most difficult, whenever I left the house I imagined – exactly as I had as a boy – that the people there would be happier if I never came back.

With my new therapist, I recalled a time in 2010, when I'd been filming *Whites* in South Wales and had been able to travel up to Northumberland to see Katie and Susie, who was a baby. The three of us were in our car, Susie strapped into her seat in the back, and we'd parked so I could pick something up from the chemist in Corbridge.

Katie told me that as soon as I left to go into the shop, Susie, watching me with wide eyes through the car window, burst into tears and didn't recover until I returned. It was amazing to me that she so clearly didn't want me to leave, having no way of understanding whether, this time, I was going to be gone for five minutes or five days.

Only in that moment did I understand that I was loved, that I was needed. Susie's emotion was real. If a person says they love you they can be disbelieved; sometimes it feels less dangerous not to accept it.

Sitting in the car, soothing Susie, I had tears in my eyes, feeling I'd never experienced love like that before.

Now, I'm beginning to understand that perhaps my mother loved me in that way, though I don't remember it. The affection must have been so deep that I've unconsciously searched for it all my life, hoping to replicate it with the love of the audience.

Writing my story in *Just Ignore Him* improved my self-perception, and shifted how I felt about my place in the world. The truth is out there, as they used to say in *The X-Files*, a phrase that always resonated somewhere with me. The book helped Katie to understand me, too, and we stayed together, as I'd always hoped we would.

Writing this new book has opened my eyes to my search for a surrogate family in almost every situation I've encountered in my working life, and has helped me spot the work of the angry boy on so many occasions. It may seem absurd to talk about carrying him inside as I head towards my sixties. Should I not, by now, have learned to control him?

In truth, while I was harbouring painful secrets, nothing could change. The traumatic times of my childhood were locked away and continued to exert a powerful influence. Nowadays, the potency of the angry boy is greatly diminished, though my children have seen him many times and I'm sorry for that.

I can now see my search is over. I have a family, and the five of us being together has brought a huge quantity of new, precious memories. Having said that, it can be challenging finding something on television we can all watch together. The only thing we agree on is that it should not have me in it, unless it's *Taskmaster*, where I made a fool of myself every week, which is pleasing for those who love me.

Histology

30th October 2024.

A consultant and a urologist joined me on a call to discuss my histology report eight days after the operation.

'All good news,' said the consultant. 'No cancer cells found from the site beneath the tumour, suggesting, as hoped, that they got it all. It was a low-grade cancer, not particularly aggressive. There is a chance of recurrence; with bladder cancer this is quite common. We will keep you under observation for five years, with regular cystoscopies. The first of these will be in three months. Would you prefer that to be at the Royal Free?'

'Yes, please.'

'Do you have any more questions?'

'Will I have further mitomycin treatment, or a BCG treatment or no treatment?' I said.

'With no cancer cells present there is no need for any more mitomycin-C treatment at this time, or BCG treatments; you are considered a low-risk patient, as opposed to medium or high risk. The policy is to observe you for five years and hopefully you will then be discharged back to your GP.'

'Thank you, doctor,' I said.

My old therapist might have been interested to hear that, on the day I was put on a cancer pathway and was about to have my first blood tests, I sat in an empty coffee shop, making some notes for this book, and recalled the session when I'd said to him that although therapy was to be recommended, I was frustrated that difficult thoughts and emotions still visited me, causing upset and distress despite my being able to accept the truth behind the question: 'Would it be any other way?'

He'd smiled softly, and I realise now that helping me to identify those emotions, before they surface, often in the form of the angry boy, had always been his aim. In recent years, by abandoning the secrecy around my abuse, which was always such a burden, I have made a little progress.

Three months after surgery, I had a cystoscopy. No cancer was found.

The Day That Didn't Exist

In 2023, I was on holiday with my family. We were going to Melbourne and Sydney so the children could see their Australian relatives in their natural habitat.

Our flight, direct from Los Angeles to Melbourne, departed on 2nd August and I told the kids that we would land in Melbourne on 4th August, so in that year, we would not have 3rd August.

This was confusing for them and because I couldn't clearly explain the International Date Line it was a bit disconcerting for me too.

We took off, heading for the date line, and somewhere over it my dad died, on 3rd August, the day that didn't exist. So that was weird.

I hadn't seen him for six years, and didn't want to go his funeral. He was absent from my life and that was why it was odd that he finally left when I wasn't technically on the planet.

A year later, I learned that our father had left each of his three children a significant and identical sum in his will. I accepted the money, even though it felt like one last act of denial. In leaving equal amounts, he appeared to be saying he bore no hard feelings towards the son who went public about his childhood sexual abuse, perhaps because he was spiteful, perhaps because he was mad. Either way, Dad chose to just ignore him.

My sister sent me a box of some of Mum's belongings, including her school reports, in which was she was chastised several times for being 'argumentative', probably not a criticism that would have come up if she was a boy. It made me proud of her.

I began this book recalling my unsuccessful search for my mum's grave and it occurs to me now that I don't know where my dad's grave is either.

One Christmas, Katie was talking about what her parents and siblings were up to, using the phrase 'my family' several times. Francis, then aged about five, was perplexed.

'But *we're* your family,' he said.

Under questioning, Katie acknowledged she has two families that she loves, and they're connected, but eventually satisfied us by confirming that ours was the most important one. It certainly is to me.

By far.

Acknowledgements

Thank you to Katie for reading everything many times, offering encouragement through periods of doubt and alerting me, often with a judicious use of silence, to moments when things were heading in the wrong direction. Your help was invaluable.

Many thanks also to Mandy Martinez and Oliver Scott for support, friendship and so many helpful notes.

And thank you to my agent, Zoe Ross, for helping me find a publisher who understood what I was trying to do even before I did.

About the Author

Alan Davies is a comedian, writer and actor, best known for starring in the hit BBC series *Jonathan Creek* and for his regular appearances as a panellist on *QI*. In 2016 he took a Creative Writing MA at Goldsmiths College, University of London, which led to the publication of his childhood memoir, *Just Ignore Him* (Little, Brown, 2020). The book was widely praised for its honesty and humour while sensitively dealing with issues such as bereavement and child abuse.

This monoray book was crafted by Jake Lingwood, Alex Stetter, Mel Four, Megan Brown, Matthew Grindon, Emily Campbell, Monica Hope and Sarah Parry.